C0-AKQ-804

WITHDRAWN

WITHDRAWN

THE CHALLENGE
OF CULTURAL PLURALISM

Edited by Stephen Brooks

Westport, Connecticut
London

Library of Congress Cataloging-in-Publication Data

The challenge of cultural pluralism / edited by Stephen Brooks.
    p.   cm.
    Includes bibliographical references and index.
    ISBN 0–275–97001–9 (alk. paper)
    1. Multiculturalism.   2. Pluralism (Social sciences).   I. Brooks, Stephen, 1956–
HM1271.C47   2002
305.8—dc21   2002022473

British Library Cataloguing in Publication Data is available.

Copyright © 2002 by Stephen Brooks

All rights reserved. No portion of this book may be
reproduced, by any process or technique, without the
express written consent of the publisher.

Library of Congress Catalog Card Number: 2002022473
ISBN: 0–275–97001–9

First published in 2002

Praeger Publishers, 88 Post Road West, Westport, CT 06881
An imprint of Greenwood Publishing Group, Inc.
www.praeger.com

Printed in the United States of America

The paper used in this book complies with the
Permanent Paper Standard issued by the National
Information Standards Organization (Z39.48–1984).

10 9 8 7 6 5 4 3 2 1

To Kenneth D. McRae
a scholar's scholar

Contents

Acknowledgments

The chief inspiration for this book comes from the writings and teaching of Kenneth D. McRae. Students of comparative politics, in particular the politics of linguistically divided democracies, know him to be one of the foremost authorities on issues of cultural pluralism. His series *Conflict and Compromise in Multilingual Societies*—Switzerland, Belgium, and Finland, with a projected fourth volume on Canada—represents a seminal contribution to the literature on cultural pluralism.

I wish to thank Dr. James Sabin of Greenwood Publishing for his support of this book and Deborah Whitford for her invaluable assistance in the editing and preparation of the manuscript. I would also like to thank Lucia A. Brown, Lorraine Cantin and Ashima James of the WordPro Centre at the University of Windsor for work above and beyond the call of duty in preparing the camera-ready copy of the book. My team of student assistants, Kelly Anne Smith and Stephanie Plante, helped in proofreading, checking citations, and preparing the index. I am grateful for their excellent work.

Introduction: The Challenge of Cultural Pluralism

Stephen Brooks

> [I]n the political tradition of the West, and in its transmission through the centuries as an intellectual heritage, there has been a recurring element of selectivity, not to mention systemic bias, that has worked to the detriment of cultural pluralism and diversity in Western societies.
>
> McRae, 1979: 676

When Kenneth McRae spoke these words in his 1979 presidential address to the Canadian Political Science Association, the idea of constitutionally entrenched recognition of communities within nation-states was chiefly restricted to some of the small plurilingual democracies of Western Europe—notably Belgium and Switzerland—and to those countries whose history and religious divisions had given rise to consociational institutions and practices between elites representing separate "pillars" in divided societies, such as the Netherlands and Austria. The dominant tendency in political thought and practice, among those opposed to the argument of ethnic nationalists that states ought to be drawn along the lines of ethnolinguistic communities, was, in McRae's words, "universalist, fusionist, integrationist, or assimilatory" (676) Citizenship tended to be understood in the universalist terms made familiar by the French and American Revolutions. In constitutional and legal terms, the only community to which citizens belonged was *la république française* or the United States, respectively. Communal identities and loyalties based on language, ethnicity, religion, or culture could, of course, exist within the framework of this citizenship, but they were not expected to challenge it and certainly were not expected to be embedded in the constitution, in ways that would recognize different communal categories of citizens.

It would be a gross overstatement to say that the political tradition of the West has undergone a dramatic refashioning over the last generation. Moreover, it is probably fair to say that, in general, Western political thought and practice remain unreceptive to community-based notions of rights and citizenship that somehow challenge the idea of citizens, *tout court*, having a uniform status under the constitution. At the same time, however, it is obvious to any observer that this tradition has come under increasing challenge from a number of quarters. The idea that formal recognition of societal pluralism is fundamentally hostile to respect for individual freedom is rejected by many of today's most prominent political thinkers. Indeed, communitarian thinkers like Amy Gutman and Charles Taylor argue precisely the opposite, that the formal recognition of communities within states is necessary to ensure the dignity of individuals and permit them to experience freedom in a way that affirms their sense of who they are, a sense that is shaped by their communal identity.

Taylor has proposed what he calls recognition of "deep diversity" as an alternative model of citizenship to that which is rooted in universalist notions of equality. Deep diversity achieves a sense of communal solidarity through permitting "a plurality of ways of belonging [to] be acknowledged and accepted" (Taylor, 1997: 183). To put it more concretely, one's attachment to a country like Canada would be experienced at one remove, through the fact that Canada represents a common identity pole for, say, québécois, Cree, Déné, and communities in English Canada, each of which can belong to Canada in a different way.

The intellectual challenge to universalist liberalism comes from other directions as well. In Canada and Australia the aboriginal populations have made demands ranging from greater autonomy to forms of self-government that resemble the status of sovereign states. These demands are based on a rejection of universal liberalism and its allied notion of equality as being, inevitably, assimilationist and a continuation of the colonial relationship imposed on aboriginal communities from the time of Europeans' arrival in the New World. The idea that Natives should have the status of "citizens plus," an idea that has been explicitly proposed by some in Canada and is implicit in many proposals for aboriginal self-government, represents a frontal challenge to conventional liberal notions of citizenship.

Multiculturalism also poses a strong intellectual challenge to the dominant liberal tradition. The multiculturalism movement is premised on the belief that cultural pluralism and equal respect for different cultural communities cannot be achieved if culture is considered to be merely a private affair. State intervention to protect and promote cultural communities is seen as necessary to guarantee the viability of those cultural communities which, for historical or other reasons, do not have the economic, social, or political clout to place themselves on an equal footing with the dominant cultural group(s). Laws and constitutional guarantees of multiculturalism, language protections, school curricula reflecting the history and culture of nondominant groups, and affirmative action programmes are among the sorts of measures seen as necessary to ensure equal respect and opportunity for the members of different communities, without requiring that they integrate culturally into the dominant group.

As important as these intellectual challenges are, particularly in academe, there is no doubt that the most serious challenge to universal liberalism and the idea of civic nationalism in Western democracies comes from another corner of the Western political tradition, that of ethnic nationalism. Nationalist movements in Québec, Scotland, Wales, the Catalon region of Spain, Flanders and, most spectacularly in recent years, in Eastern Europe, have rejected the idea that the rights and demands of national communities can be adequately protected and represented within state structures in which these communities have minority status (or, in the case of Flemish nationalism, a status not proportionate to its population and economic importance). This sort of nationalism, which leads to demands for self-determination and independence, is not only opposed to the way that the dominant liberal tradition views groups and their relationship to the state but also hostile to the idea of constitutionally entrenched recognition of communities within pluralistic states, which contemporary communitarian thinking supports.

Cultural coexistence under the roof of a single state does not require that the communities love one another—no one who has spent any time in Switzerland would suggest that the ethnolinguistic communities there feel warmly toward one another; nevertheless, the Swiss model has proven to be remarkably durable—but rather that they be willing to accord each other equal respect. This, requires that communities be recognized *as communities* (the precise form of this recognition will depend on the particular historical and social circumstances of intercommunity relations within a state), a requirement that cannot be satisfied if the relationship between individuals and the state is not seen to be mediated by communal identities.

The critics of legal and constitution recognition for communities regularly argue that such recognition is by its very nature exclusive—one is either a member of a particular community or not—and so ends by undermining the equality of individuals under the law and reinforcing divisions between segments of the population based on the linguistic, ethnic, or other communal characteristic that is recognized. But those who argue for the recognition of communities within states suggest that the dominant political tradition of the West tends to undervalue the importance of intermediary groups that exist between citizens and the state, failing to treat them as "something more than mechanical groupings of individuals, something more than mere legal fictions defined and permitted to exist by the state, something with a meaningful existence and personality independent of state or citizen" (Taylor, 1997: 684). Nationalists, of course, agree with these sentiments. But it is possible to believe that communal identities are both durable and profoundly important without accepting the nationalist demand that is drawn to coincide with ethnic and linguistic boundaries. This is impractical and potentially intolerant. "In a world of steadily increasing urbanization and intercultural contact," McRae writes, "one could not redraw political boundaries so as to eliminate minorities without imposing severe costs upon the global economy and perhaps most heavily upon the more peripheral cultures themselves" (1974: 687).

In the more than two decades since McRae delivered his presidential address to the Canadian Political Science Association the notion of cultural pluralism—what it means and how and why it should be recognized—has gained ground in Western democracies. Many believe that we are passing through a period during which, due largely to globalization's challenge to the idea and sovereignty of nation-states, there is intellectual and political space for the construction of new models of citizenship, new relations between individuals and their governments that may be mediated through recognized communities within states. It would be unwise, however, to underestimate either the durability of traditional ideas of the ethnic and civic nationalism and the nation-state, or the strength of the forces ranged against the future imagined by communitarians and the intellectual architects of cultural pluralism.

All of the so-called New World societies have histories characterized by cultural pluralism, if only because in no case did European immigrants arrive in a place that was unoccupied. But on top of this original layer of pluralism—a layer whose importance in such countries as the United States, Australia, and Canada has increased in recent decades—were added additional layers of diversity as the pattern of immigration to New World societies changed over time. Different New World societies have responded to the challenge of immigration-generated pluralism in different ways. The American model, as is well known, has involved a sort of civic nationalism that is expected to override ethnic, linguistic, and other loyalties. Canada, it is usually argued, has been less demanding of immigrants and their identities and has long embedded important recognition of cultural pluralism, at least in regard to the French- and English-speaking communities, in its laws, constitution, and political practices.

The debate on the ideological character of New World societies and, in particular, on how best to explain the dynamic evolution of their political cultures is associated with the work of Harvard historian Louis Hartz, who developed the notion of New World societies as ideological *fragments* of Old World societies. According to the Hartzian fragment thesis, societies like Australia, the United States, English Canada, French Canada, and other European settler societies experienced a different ideological development than their parent societies for complex reasons having to do mainly with the absence, or relative weakness of challenges in the New World society to the dominant ideology implanted by its founding immigrants.

Gordon T. Stewart engages this long standing debate on the nature of New World societies, and in particular their ideological relationship to European parent societies, in his chapter "Is Canada De-Europeanized—Or Does Anyone Remember?" He takes issue with John Ralston Saul's controversial claim that "Canada is profoundly un-European," a claim that Stewart argues relies on a recasting of Canadian history that is too ready to ignore evidence in favour of a revisionist historiography whose conclusion is that "Canada is above all an idea of what a country could be, a place of the imagination . . . it is very much its own invention." In this way Saul can argue that contemporary political demands for aboriginal self government, special status for Québec, and a regime of cultural pluralism flow naturally from Canada's history. Stewart has no argument with the particular vision of Canada that Saul advocates and agrees with the premise that historical perspectives that have not been adequately expressed in the past deserve to be taken seriously. He worries, however, that in their eagerness to provide a historical justification for contemporary ideas of cultural pluralism, Saul and others may be engaged in a postmodernist historiography that sees all historical narratives as inevitably cultural and so has no difficulty imagining a new history to support a new Canadian identity.

Jill Vickers comes at the problem of interpreting the history of New World or settler societies from an angle that has something in common with Stewart's. In "No Place for 'Race'?: Why Pluralist Theory Fails to Explain the Politics of 'Race' in 'New Societies,'" she picks up on Stewart's admission that non-conventional historical narratives can help enrich our understanding of a society and its history. In particular, she argues that the explanations used to understand the political cultures of settler societies, including Hartzian fragment theory, ignore the important role that ideas about race played in the formation and subsequent histories of these societies and their states.

The problem, Vickers argues, is that the mainstream of Western political theory is, in fundamental ways, blind to the real meaning of cultural diversity and hostile to its recognition through constitutional and other structures of governance. This blindness is especially incapacitating, Vickers maintains, when it comes to race. There is, she says, no place for "race"—which Vickers insists needs to be treated as a socially constructed, changeable, and highly problematic concept—in the framework of mainstream Western pluralist theory. Her chapter challenges the reader to rethink pluralism in Western democracies from a standpoint that places race, as well as other forms of social-cultural diversity, at the center of any attempt to interpret their histories.

In "The Narcissism of Minor Differences: Reflections on the Nature of English Canadian Nationalism," Brooks addresses a rather different issue that flows from the Hartzian interpretation of New World societies, that of the cultural relationship between English Canada and the United States. The conventional wisdom among English Canadian intellectuals and opinion leaders is that there are significant differences between the political values and beliefs of these two societies. English Canadian nationalism, which has long been reflected in protectionist cultural policies of various sorts and a rejection of American policies, institutions, and values as being un-Canadian, is generally understood as being rooted in these value differences and a reaction to the real and persistent threat of American cultural imperialism.

Brooks does not argue that there are no significant differences between the political cultures of English Canada and the United States—although he clearly thinks that they tend to be trumped up by nationalist intellectuals and opinion-leaders who have a vested interest in promoting popular belief in these putative differences—but he suggests that these differences tend to be invested with disproportionate significance by English Canadian nationalists for reasons that can be found in Freud's writings about hostility in relations of intimacy. His argument has broader implications for understanding inter-communal relations. Instead of trying to explain national rivalries and animosities purely in terms of respective material self-interest, cultural distinctiveness, strategic concerns, and other rational considerations, Brooks suggests that these relations and images of oneself and the other should be understood in the context of the intimate emotional and psychological sentiments that develop between peoples connected by history and culture.

Part II of this book includes four chapters that examine various aspects of consociational theory and its contemporary application. In "Accommodating Multinationality: Is the European Commission a Case of Consociational or Weberian Administration?," Liesbet Hooghe offers a careful, empirical test of two hypotheses that seek to explain the behaviour of officials in the European Commission. One is that these officials will behave according to the Weber ideal-type of the administrator, whereby rational considerations of merit rather than their national background shapes the way they approach their job and the issues before them, so that their attitudes and conception of their role reflect a general European interest. The other hypothesis is that officials of the European Commission will reflect in their attitudes and behaviour a consociational model, seeing themselves as representatives of their respective national interests and thus reproducing the diversity of the European polity within the commission and its deliberations. She finds that the evidence tends to support the consociational model hypthesis, although there is considerable variation between national groups of officials in their orientations to nationality. Hooghe's findings run against the grain of the widely held view that the European Commission is, in her words, "intent on substituting diverse national concerns with a uniform European interest." Instead, she finds that the commission is an important venue for consociational accommodation.

The chapter by André Bächtiger, Markus Spörndli, and Jürg Steiner begins with an examination of deliberative democracy, which, following Joshua Cohen, they say is characterized by "a commitment to the resolution of problems of collective choice through public reasoning" and where political institutions are seen to be legitimate "insofar as they establish the framework for free public deliberation." They argue that the deliberative conception of democracy, strongly influenced by communitarian political theory, is less elitist than representative democracy and more adaptive than the majoritarian model of democracy, grounded as the deliberative model is on the concept of mutual respect for all positions brought to the table and an expectation that positions and preferences may be transformed through the process of deliberative decision making. The authors argue that consociationalism "encompasses a set of institutional devices (proportionality, grand coalition, mutual veto) as well as cooperative and respectful attitudes of political elites in segmented societies, leading them to transcend the borders of their own groups, to be receptive to the claims of others, and to accommodate the divergent interests and claims of the segments." In other words, consociationalism is characterized by the chief elements of the deliberative model of democracy and thus holds the promise of achieving intergroup accommodation and acceptance of these results where majoritarianism and representative models might fail.

To test their hypothesis, Bächtiger, Spörndli, and Steiner develop what they call a "Discourse Quality Index," which, in future work, they intend to apply to ten selected countries that range from national cases with clear histories of consociational governance, including Belgium, Switzerland, Austria, and the Netherlands, to the United States and the United Kingdom at the majoritarian end of the continuum. Canada, France, Germany, and Italy are intermediate cases that they examine. Their Discourse Quality Index is constructed of seven indicators that are built around four concepts: participation, justification, respect, and constructive politics. Through the application of this framework to selected political debates in their national cases, the authors plan to explore the linkages between institutional settings and modes of decision-making.

The applicability of the consociational model to Canada has been a matter of controversy. Some have argued that majoritarian decision-making structures and the universalist notions of rights and citizenship that tend to accompany such structures have aggravated Canada's centuries-old conflict between French- and English-speaking communities. In "From Jean Bodin to Consociational Democracy and Back," Can Erk and Alain-G. Gagnon continue this exploration, arguing that consociationalism provides, at present, no way out of the longstanding impasse in Québec-Canada relations.

For consociational accommodation to succeed in Canada, Erk and Gagnon argue, it was necessary that the French-English duality of the country—involving full recognition of the French and English ethnolinguistic communities as equal founding partners of Canada with equality of rights and status throughout the country—be realized in practice. This has not happened. "Once dualism is out of the picture and all historical opportunities for a consociational accommodation have been squandered," they maintain, "the remaining option is to support Québec's demands to opt out from this union when it is clear that a partnership is not on the table." Erk and Gagnon argue that between the inapplicability of consociationalism to Canada and what they argue to be the inevitable recognition of a sovereign Québec state as a way out of the Canada-Québec impasse, there is the intermediate ground of "constitutional ambiguity." Such ambiguity over constitutional relationships between territorial components of a state, where territory and ethnicity/language coincide to a large degree, and over the jurisdictional competences of these components may, Erk and Gagnon argue, help to maintain the workability of a federal state. This requires, however, that there be "a feeling of solidarity among the constituent nations" or, less demanding, mutual trust on the part of the constituent communities. In these circumstances, constitutional ambiguity within a federal state may provide a not-so-neat substitute for other accommodative structures.

From reflections on the inapplicability of consociationalism in Canada, Thomas O. Hueglin's chapter takes us to broader philosophical questions regarding the nature of sovereignty in a world very different from that which gave rise to nation-states. In "Althusian Federalism for a Post-Westphalian World," Hueglin makes two related arguments. One is that the conventional idea of sovereignty as something possessed legally and exclusively by internationally recognized nation states has been left behind by events, notably, the processes of globalization and the particular case of integration in the European Union. The other argument is that, in light of these developments, it is high time that we paid less attention to such thinkers as Hobbes and more to those such as Johannes Althusius, whose thinking about governance allows for the possibility of shared sovereignty and partially autonomous communities linked under a consociational or supranational umbrella of governance.

Hueglin argues that our times call for forms of pluralized governance that go beyond and break the traditional mold of nation-states and other territorial units. Althusius, he says, provides the intellectual framework for a challenge to the dominant nation-state model. "The general principle of social organization was for [Althusius]," he writes, "that all communities share in the desire for a prosperous and just life. But in order to achieve this end each community—or consociation—would require specific laws and political arrangements. " Hueglin points to the Belgian constitution's recognition of linguistic communities qua communities as an example of how the consociational principles of Althusius can be incorporated into contemporary governance.

The case of Belgium is the subject of Kris Deschouwer's chapter, "Causes and Effects of Constitutional Changes in Multilingual Belgium." Deschouwer examines the history of ethnolinguistic conflict and constitutional reform in Belgium up to the present day. His chapter documents and analyzes the important developments that have taken place in Belgium over the last generation, including the major constitutional reforms of 1993, the regional-ization of the Belgian party system, and the fairly dramatic decentralization of power that has occurred in the Belgian federation.

The experiment in evolving consociationalism that Belgium represents is subject to a number of stresses that led Deschouwer to conclude that it is too soon to declare the rather fluid Belgian model a success. These stresses include the economic disparity between the comparatively prosperous Flemish region and economically stagnant, French-speaking Walloon Region; a greater desire in Flanders, particularly among elites, for more autonomy for their region; recurring conflicts in the linguistically mixed region of Brussels, which is chiefly Francophone, and its mainly Flemish-speaking periphery; and the absence of federal political parties. This last factor is, Deschouwer argues, of crucial importance. "There is," he says, "no central forum for political debates. There are two unilingual debates." To the degree that successful consociational accommodation requires forums and institutions for deliberation and collaborative decision making between constituent communities, the failure of parties to play this role does not augur well for the future of the Belgian federation.

Deschouwer's analysis of the Belgian experience in managing intercommunity conflict is followed by two chapters that examine the Canadian case. In "Revisiting Bilingualism and Biculturalism, in Canada" Milton J. Esman examines the legacy of Canada's Royal Commission on Bilingualism and Biculturalism and the 1969 adoption of The Official Languages Act. Esman brings to this task the dispassionate eye of a non-Canadian, with no political or emotional stake in Canada's centuries-old ethnolinguistic conflict, and the keen historical perspective of a longtime student of politics in ethnically segmented societies.

Esman acknowledges that Canadian politics continues to be characterized by practices and institutions that reflect the collaborative and community-oriented logic of consociationalism. These include such features as official bilingualism at the federal level, linguistic balance in the federal public service, and

Francophone representation on the Supreme Court, and others. He concludes, however, that the bilingualism and biculturalism's vision of, in his words, "a robustly bicultural country" has failed to materialize. The reasons for this failure, Esman argues, involve the intensity and persistence of Québec nationalism, notwithstanding the regime of official bilingualism put in place since the 1960s, and a lack of support for the linguistic partnership vision of Canada among nonfounding peoples—those of neither French nor British ethnic origins—in English-speaking Canada. He concludes that the partnership concept of Canada has become increasingly irrelevant as a two-tiered pattern has developed in Canada: official bilingualism at the national level but, for practical purposes, the atrophy of viable minority official language communities in all of Canada outside the so-called bilingual belt from New Brunswick in the east to Sault Sainte-Marie in Ontario. The departure of Québec from the Canadian federation would, he suggests—and most students of Canadian politics would agree—sound the death knell for official bilingualism in a Canada without Québec.

From linguistic developments and tensions in Canada, the focus shifts to the Québec scene in A. Brian Tanguay's chapter. In "The Politics of Language in Québec: Keeping the Conflict Alive," Tanguay attempts to solve what appears to be a paradox. The paradox is, in his words, "that in spite of the improved status of French in Québec today, which is the direct result of the passage of Bill 101, linguistic tensions in the province have not declined appreciably."

Tanguay first surveys the history of linguistic relations in Québec, isolating the factors that were responsible for language conflicts that burst onto the scene during the 1960s. He then turns to the contemporary situation in order to determine whether linguistic conflict is kept alive or defused by the relationship between language and social structure in Québec. Finally, he examines the factors that continue to fuel the politics of language in present-day Québec and speculates on the future of North America's only predominantly Francophone jurisdiction.

The paradox of a Québec society in which the predominance of the French language appears to be secure but where the separatist drums continue to beat— sometimes loudly, other times more softly—is explained, Tanguay says, by three main factors. These include the persistence of linguistic extremism at both the Anglophone-rights and *Québec français* ends of the spectrum, the fact that many Québec separatists believe that they must fan the flames of linguistic conflict for tactical purposes, and the very thorny issue of immigration. This last factor is very important and, as Tanguay rightly observes, gets at the question of what sort of society Québec will become. Most of Québec's non-Francophone, non-Anglophone immigrants have sent their children to French schools, and thus the ability to speak French is now widespread among new Québecers, especially among younger age cohorts. But they often do not adopt French as their home language or their preferred language of public discourse, leading some Québec nationalists to suggest that many new Québecers do not really integrate into French-speaking Québec and that, on the contrary, they may eventually contribute to the erosion of the distinctive culture and character of Québec. This, of course, just begs the question: What will be the form and future of cultural pluralism in Québec? The answer to this question resonates far beyond the borders of Québec and Canada.

PART I

POLITICAL CULTURE IN NEW WORLD SOCIETIES

Is Canada De-Europeanized—Or Does Anyone Remember?

Gordon T. Stewart

In his wide-ranging and provocative assessment of Canada at the end of the twentieth century John Ralston Saul made the startling claim that "Canada is profoundly un-European" (1997: 102). If this characterization of Canada is true, then much of the history writing about Canada is dead wrong. A sustained theme in that historical writing has been that Canada retained affinities and connections with Europe that had disappeared, or been severely attenuated, in the case of the United States. The United States is conventionally pictured as having taken some European ideas and institutions that were re-interpreted at the time of the Revolution and Constitution-making era (1776–1787) and forged a political culture and institutions of law and government that were distinctively American. There has always been a debate about the intensity of American exceptionalism compared to Europe, but broad agreement that the United States created its own new political space in the world. By contrast, Canada is portrayed as having retained many principles, attitudes, and institutions that were shared by European polities—monarchy, Parliament, respect for the state, acceptance of social hierarchy, and deference. These are the classic distinctions between Canada and the United States. Seymour Martin Lipset has highlighted these in his recent book, which sums up a life time of scholarship comparing these two North American states and societies. The Revolutionary origins of the United States meant that the ultimate source of legitimacy and authority was "the people." In Canada, the new government saw itself as,

> a continuation of the ancient English monarchy and sent its constitution [in 1867] to London to be enacted by the British Parliament and proclaimed by the Queen. The revolutionary republic was suspicious of state authority and adopted a power-constraining bill of rights which produced a strong emphasis on due process, judicial power, and litigiousness. The counter-revolutionary dominion followed the Westminster model, with power centered in a cabinet based on a parliamentary majority and with no limits on the authority of the state other than those derived from a division of jurisdictions between national and provincial governments. (Lipset, 1990:xiii)

Lipset is not alone. Much conventional scholarship explores that line of distinction between Canada and the United States, including that of Kenneth McRae. He and other similarly oriented researchers have elucidated the impacts of the persistence of some Old World values brought to Canada by the French colonists of the seventeenth century and the loyalists of the eighteenth century and examined the ways in which the post-1867 Canadian polity exhibited similarities to the workings of states and societies in linguistically segmented European countries. The question of the moment is whether Saul's startling proposition undermines the edifice erected by generations of political scientists and historians who have written about a Canada still influenced by European outlooks and assumptions about the state, civil society, and the purpose of politics.

It is essential to recognize that scholars who looked at Canada in comparative terms never for a moment proposed that Canada was a copy of Europe or merely partially derivative of some European precedents. On the contrary, their main point was that Canada had developed its own distinctive political culture. Nevertheless, this Canadian culture retained closer connections to European models than did its American counterpart. The ways in which Anglophone and Francophone elites accommodated tensions and rivalries in the interests of maintaining a state with bilingual features were viewed as similar to the elite accommodation practices that held together countries like Belgium, Finland, and Switzerland (McRae, 1974). Such European-derived features have had multiple consequences throughout the entire sweep of Canadian history. The allegedly more socially and politically conservative Canadian political culture that gave more trust to the state than in the United States was explained in terms of the retention of values brought over during the French colonial period, when the Crown and its officials played such a key role and there was the impact of the loyalists with their self-aware respect for monarchy (McRae, 1964).

The starting point for this approach to understanding Canada was Louis Hartz's *The Founding of New Societies: Studies in the History of the United States, Latin America, South Africa, Canada and Australia* (1964), with the section on Canada written by McRae. Hartz viewed all the new societies in the United States, Canada, Australia, and all the South American states, which emerged from colonial experiences, as being formed by some of the key European forces that were at play during critical formative periods for these polities. None of them were full replicas of the European societies from which they derived—each was a fragment or a range of fragments of the more extended 'European spectrum. Figuring out the nature of those fragments would enable scholars to sketch out the defining characteristics of the states and societies that developed in the new overseas settings. The United States was born of a liberal (in the Lockean sense) fragment that emphasized individualism and property as guarantors of freedom against governments always tending toward tyranny. Australian political culture reflected the radical myths brought over by the first waves of nonconvict emigration from Britain in the 1830s and 1840s. The conservatism of Québec (Hartz and his followers developed their theses in the 1950s) could be explained in terms of the feudal, statist fragment that had been New France from 1608 to 1760 and the persistence over the next 200 years of a traditionalist Catholic Church cultural influence.

The approach did allow for dynamic transformations that had not been part of the original fragment theory. In the case of Canada, for example, it was ingeniously and persuasively argued that the statist view associated with New France and then the Loyalists did, on the one hand, put in place a conservative foundation (respect for government) in Canadian political culture but, on the other hand, made possible acceptance of substantial government interventions in the late nineteenth and twentieth centuries (Horowitz, 1978). When socialist ideas about the role of the state emerged in the modern era, Canada's statist tradition gave socialism room to breathe, whereas the antistatist United States was much more hostile ground. Socialist parties not only were tolerated in Canada but flourished compared to in the United States, where socialist parties were always deeply distrusted. The approach was flexible and open, to be sure, and in the hands of Horowitz and McRae it gave full attention to Canada's special circumstances. However, the entire approach rested on taking for granted that there were certain residual European features deeply at work in making Canada what it is today.

Saul makes a direct challenge to this way of thinking about Canada. Although he is a novelist and now a public intellectual with a primary interest in literature, his case hinges on a rereading of Canadian history—especially those episodes, such as the loyalist migration, that were so central to the Hartzian-McRae vision of Canada's origins and Canada's fate. According to Saul, the American Revolution and the actions of the new state created by that Revolution continued European ways on the continent. The United States acted as a nation-state dominating internally and projecting power externally as it moved across the continent conquering or absorbing the land of the native peoples. The loyalists "had a radically different view of life on this continent from that proclaimed by the European-style revolutionaries." Whereas the new Americans thought in terms of subjugation and domination of land and native peoples, the thin Canadian population faced with a more intractable northern frontier thought about sharing, compromising, and recognizing the shaping forces of the landscape itself. So, argues Saul, there are two models in Euro-North America: "one a conquering European model; the other a more complex accommodation with place and circumstance." The key to this difference is that the frontier could never be conquered in Canada, and so notions of a single, dominant nation-state imposing its will never took root (Saul, 1997: 104, 106).

This version of the Loyalists who settled in Nova Scotia and Québec is at odds with much of the scholarship on the subject—and not just American scholars. Canadian specialists in this topic such as Janice Potter, Neil Mackinnon, and J. M. Bumsted have sketched out loyalist ideology and attitudes that suggest that they were still thinking in colonial terms—as British subjects in North America rather than as deracinated new men and women coming to terms with wilderness and inventing a new, non-European culture in the process

(MacKinnon, 1986; Potter, 1983; Bumstead, 1986). Saul's case depends on riding roughshod over the work of other scholars, but his case retains a fascination because of its sheer power—it is like a waterfall that wins out over doubt simply because it keeps coming in volume, and in this age of uncertainty when postmodernism seems to validate any viewing point, cases can be accepted even when specialist historians dissent. Saul wishes to invent a new Canadian past, and who are historians to stand in his way?

Much of Saul's case, which is argued con brio, runs counter to received historical wisdom—not to mention historical evidence. In order to portray Canada as unlike European-style states that are preoccupied with domination and growth (at the expense of others), Saul asserts, for example, that confederation in 1867 was not an "economic scenario" and suggests that it was simply another example of Canadians trying out interesting new social experiments (1997: 66, 125, 182). The assertion that confederation in 1867 had nothing to do with economics would certainly have surprised its leading participants like Macdonald and Cartier, who not only talked at great length about economic growth, including such mundane things as tariffs, but actually went so far as to include a clause about the intercolonial railroad in the constitution itself, the British North America Act. The political leaders who brought about confederation were all too aware of the consequence on the British North American colonies of the British shift to free trade in the 1840s and 1850s and the American termination of reciprocity in 1866. They needed to attend to creating their own markets and their own possibilities for economic expansion—which included preparing for expansion into the western territories then occupied by indigenous and Métis peoples. No one thought of consulting the Métis or the Amerindians in the northwest.

The Canadian politicians in 1867 are not usually portrayed in the league table of world constitutionmakers as revolutionaries, but Saul insists that the decision of the Canadian leaders to go down to Charlottetown and persuade the Maritime colonies to join a larger scheme "was the sort of bold action rarely seen in constitutional negotiators anywhere." He hastens to argue that their goal was not to create a state to rival the United States or imitate European states. It was rather to create "a nation as a mechanism of reform, as opposed to a military or economic or tribal reason." Herein lay the originality of Canada. Saul traces a tradition running from Mackenzie and Papineau in their failed 1837 rebellions, through the reform coalition of Lafontaine and Baldwin in the early 1840s, and on to Cartier and Macdonald by which Canadian political leaders understood that, because of geography and linguistic diversity and small population, they could not and should not try to implement the old European-style state models but rather create a never-ending experiment in intergroup relations (1997: 122, 177).

From this historical base Saul reads large cultural consequences. Canadian literature is often about the powerlessness of men and women when faced with the great northern solitudes but also about the lessons in humanity that can be gleaned from that tension between intractable frontier and human frailty and human hopes. This fragility gives almost an animist cast to Canadian culture as

Canadian authors read spiritual values into landscapes. Canadian painting has always had a rich vein that explores the beauty and mystery and impact of untouched northern rocks, lakes, forests and "icescapes" on the self and on general human perceptions of the world. "The Canadian sensibility," he proposes, "is that of the edge, the unknown, the uncontrolled. In the art this produces there is an assumption—sometimes consciously political, sometimes unconsciously creative, sometimes both--that place and art are the same thing; not place in the common physical sense, but place in the sense of the whole, the animist idea of borderless inclusion" (Saul 1997: 204). He castigates free market elites who turn their backs on this culture and this history and see Canada's future as linking to the global economic forces that bring materialism and consumerism in their wake.

It is easy for historians to undermine Saul's case because he makes so many questionable generalizations. The political leaders who brought about confederation, for example, were not economic innocents. They also had immediate expectations of territorial aggrandizement. They were spurred into action by the economic consequences of changing policies in Britain and the United States. They were convinced that there was a military threat from the United States—the plausibility of which was enhanced by the Fenian incursions. They expected that their new dominion would expand westward to provide for future population and economic growth. They barely gave a second thought to the indigenous and Métis people who lived in those western territories. In spite of these huge holes, Saul's reading of Canadian history deserves to be taken seriously because it does force a reexamination of some of the unspoken assumptions upon which the main corpus of Canadian historical writing rests. The influence of imperialism on Anglophone historians in the 1880s-1920s era, the influence of Québec patriotism on Francophone historians in the same years, and the impact of centennial nationalism in the 1950s-1970s era may well have burdened much of Canadian history writing with problematic frameworks.

The master narratives created between the 1880s and 1970s that have dominated accounts of the Canadian past are under siege. This has led to some anguished debates as historians like J. L. Granatstein, in his 1998 book *Who Killed Canadian History?*, have lambasted what they see as the abandoning of Canadian national history. The reply most recently expressed by A. B. McKillop in the *Canadian Historical Review* is that disaggregating the traditional nationalist history and giving voice to previously ignored sectors in fact produce a much richer, truer account of Canada's pasts. In McKillop's view Granatstein is defending a very narrow and rather old-fashioned version of Canada's history. "It is national history seen, in effect, as the political history of the nation-state and the apparatus of statecraft and state formation.... As such it encompasses the history of political institutions of the nation: political parties, government departments, federal policies." McKillop makes the point that the recent work in social, cultural, and gender history is improving our knowledge of how all Canadians experienced the past. These multiple narratives are necessary to achieve a comprehensive, rounded, inclusive version of Canadian history, and these kind of approaches to writing history have taken root in the discipline of history internationally—they are not signs of Canadian parochialism (McKillop, 1999, pp. 276).

Saul is elusive to pin down in this sharp debate about the meanings of Canada and the writing of its history. In one obvious sense his book on Canada is dramatic confirmation of Granatstein's argument that Canadian history has been abandoned, for here is a major Canadian intellectual figure writing about Canada's past with a cavalier disregard for what has previously been unearthed by scholarly research and writing by historians—to Saul, getting a grasp of extant historical explanations simply does not seem to matter. In another sense he can be seen as yet another sapper undermining any hope of a unifying national narrative because he argues that a conventional nation-state simply cannot evolve in Canada. So, it could be argued, he is an illustration—if an odd one—of Granatstein's case. On the other hand, Saul also castigates the political elites whose members are the favourite subject of study for Granatstein, yet in a third sense he is as fierce a nationalist as Granatstein because he argues that there is something unique about Canadian history, literature, art, and society that has not been reproduced anywhere else and that Canadians should take pride in this distinctiveness. His configuration of Canadian nationalism is not the same as Granatstein's. Granatstein wishes a return to a commonly revered national political narrative; Saul sees Canada as consisting of multiple, even mysterious antirational narratives. He uses the Canadian case to extend the arguments that he made in his *Voltaire's Bastards: The Dictatorship of Reason in the West* (Saul, 1992), about the pernicious effects of using reason and allowing experts to set agendas for humankind. The uncertainty of Canada's narratives about Canada is to be celebrated, not taken as a reason to be disheartened. Canadians have liberated themselves from the confining cultural and political straitjackets that have created the more "successful" nation-states in the United States and Europe. Although he might recoil at the label, Saul in many ways reflects the penetration of postmodernism into contemporary culture. He states bluntly and confidently that "Canada is above all an idea of what a country could be, a place of the imagination ... it is very much its own invention." (Saul, 1997: 171). Such an approach is a classic manifestation of the post-modernist assertion that realities are inventions by culture. Saul believes that various historical, literary, and cultural events and themes can be reinvented and brought into contact to imagine a new Canadian identity. Part of that process is an almost playful reinventing of Canadian history. He argues for a Canadian identity based the triangular interplay of the Anglophone, Francophone, and native peoples who sparsely populate the vast northern landscape of Canada.

> Canada's strength—you might even say what makes it interesting—is its complexity; its refusal of the conforming, monolithic nineteenth century nation state model. That complexity has been constructed upon three deeply rooted pillars, three experiences—the aboriginal, the Francophone and the Anglophone. No matter how each may deny the other at various times, each of their existences is dependent on the other two. That is what I mean by positive solitudes as opposed to a negative state of isolation. Each of their independent

beings has been interwoven with the other two over 450 years of continuous existence on the northern margins of the continent. (Saul, 1997: 81)

This triangular reality is what Canada's history and culture have been all about. Some hard pieces of evidence support Saul's case. The most powerful surely is that the overactive constitutional debates since the 1960s, the perennial uncertainty about how Canada should be organized, have allowed aboriginal voices a much more legitimate and even powerful role in Canada than, let us say, in the contemporary United States—or would have been the case had Canada's identity and federal system been nailed down in 1867. The Meech Lake Accord of 1990, which almost settled some ancient historical issues between Québec and the rest of Canada, was scuppered by an Amerindian voice—that of Elijah Harper, a Cree member of the Manitoba legislature. While careful commentators will point out that the demise of Meech was also caused by other factors such as the failure of Newfoundland to ratify the accord and the unpopularity among ordinary English Canadians of the distinct society cause, the drama of Harper's vote was taken by many to symbolize the power of native voices in the constitutional fluidity that had developed in Canada since the "patriation" of the British North America Act in 1982. This was a remarkable attestation to the presence and impact of native voices. Another sign of the attentiveness paid to indigenous peoples is the creation of Nunavut, a huge experiment in First Nations self-government that has no direct parallel anywhere else in the Americas. This confirms Saul's point that the tenuous, self-doubting Euro-Canadian population on the vast terrain of Canada means that they are inclined to listen and take into account aboriginal voices that remain silenced in the United States. In the same vein it can be argued that the constant questioning of the foundations of power and of the structure of the state in Canada has allowed more room for women's voices and the voices of other hitherto marginalised groups in shaping the Canadian future. Canada itself is marginal and therefore allows marginal voices to flourish.

In spite of its apparent novelty, Saul's vision of Canada does, in fact, have roots in previous scholarship. In the case of the historians there was a period in the 1920s and 1930s and 1940s when Canada's past was seen as dominated by its geography. The great nineteenth-century French historian Jules Michelet once stated that geography comes before history, and Canadian historians like H. A. Innes and the early D. G. Creighton certainly took that maxim to heart. In developing their theses about the northern landscape and how that landscape had shaped the Canadian economy and society, they were proposing that Canada could not be understood if it was seen simply as a replication of European models or as a duplicate of the United States. The notion of Canada's nordicity has long been argued by historians—as well as being part of Canadian popular self-images. But those earlier arguments about the impact of the landscape and the northernness of Canada were used to buttress a version of a single Canadian nationalism. Those fresh insights of the 1920s-1940s were folded into the powerful nationalist narratives (heavily tilted toward Anglophone notables and male-dominated high politics) that surged into fashion with the prestigious Canadian centenary series published between 1963 and 1988.[1] It has been a sometimes bitter struggle in the last twenty years to let in other readings of Canadian history and other voices to that noticeably patriarchal framing of the Canadian past. In that sense Saul is pursuing some earlier historians' threads that had fallen into disuse—he is reviving rather than inventing. These affinities with previous historical scholarship along with his widely accepted characterization of Canada literature and art do lend some credibility to Saul's case.

Saul's propositions, while dramatically presented as cutting against the grain of the establishment historians, are not so iconoclastic as they appear even with respect to contemporary historical scholarship. Desmond Morton, Director of the McGill Institute for the Study of Canada, sums up much conventional wisdom in the discipline when he states:

> More than any other nation the history of Canada is multi-centric. This country is too vast to be seen from one perspective....Our history is dominated by material realties like the land, the weather, and the necessity to earn a living, and not fall behind our powerful neighbors....Space, time, and knowledge conspire against us. Historical knowledge is always a work in progress that follows many distinct and sometimes divergent trajectories. (1999: 17)

To be sure, an easy consensus on this recasting of Canadian history, this developing of a multipolar approach that undermines the certainties of the Canadian Centenary series, has not been developed without a backlash. As we have noted, powerful commentators like Granatstein urge a rededication to a strong version of national history. He argues from almost the same premises as Saul that since Canada is such a fissiparous thing, it is important that some common understanding of a national identity be promulgated. In polities like the United States, where a strong sense of national identity exists, pursuing particularist histories is not as threatening as in Canada, where there is a danger that any sense of a national past or even two or three national pasts will disappear without trace amidst the welter of work on localities, regions, and groups. Granatstein has been taken to task for refusing to recognize that the older version of national history focused on high politics and wars and simply did not begin to take into account the lives and experiences of millions of ordinary Canadian men and women. McKillop's point is that we are only now beginning to get a true national history in the sense that we are bringing in lots of narratives and voices that have simply been ignored. While McKillop scores a palpable hit in making that argument, the publication of Saul's book suggests that Granatstein does have a point. Saul writes alarmingly ignorant things about Canadian political history as though he assumes that most of his Canadian readers do not know or even care anymore about that history.

It is perhaps also worth adding that this debate could be raised to a more sophisticated level if it took into account what is happening outside Canada. Morton's assertion that Canada's history is more multicentric than any other country's history seems a bit dated. Multicentered approaches are all the rage in the United States (and cause the same type of public debates about the loss of national history as in Canada).[2] British history cannot now be done from one national (usually English) perspective, as a legion of historians has taken up J.G.A. Pocock's challenge to write British history that fully takes into account the Welsh, Scottish, and Irish. Surely a history of India or Turkey or Yugoslavia or Russia or the United States or Britain or even modern France needs to be multicentric. What is happening in Canada is in this sense not a sign of special grace, as Saul would have us believe, but simply Canadian scholarship following the multiperspective paths that have taken over much of contemporary historical scholarship everywhere. McKillop makes this cardinal point when he shows how much of the work in Canadian social history is not inward-looking but is, in fact, applying international advances in the discipline to Canadian cases (1999).

Where does that leave the historians and political scientists who have tended to emphasize European-tinged, statist analyses of Canada's past and Canada's current predicament? Like all of us, McRae could not escape his time. He was writing when there were a privileging of politics at the national level and a consuming curiosity about the ways in which Canada had developed compared with the United States and other newer states like Australia and those in South America that had emerged from settler colonies—and how all that compared with the historical processes that had evolved in the old European countries from the same shared origins. The conclusion arrived at by McRae was that Canada represented a mixed development that could not be explained except by utilizing concepts developed by American and European commentators. This was certainly the case with the way in which he imaginatively applied the work of Arend Lijphart on elite accommodation and consociational democracy and the sensitivity of his tracing of the fragments that lay at the root of state formation in what became Canada (Lijphart, 1968).

Because he wrote when he did, certain blinkers were difficult to take off. The first was the sense that colonialism could be understood by looking at metropolitan forces and the ways in which these were applied or adjusted in colonized settings. Much recent work on colonialism has moved beyond this unidirectional view and emphasizes exchange, reciprocal influences, and hybrid outcomes. As Frederick Cooper and Ann Laura Stoler sum up these trends:

> The scholarship of the 1980s and 1990s has witnessed a major shift in orientation: from one that focused primarily on the colonized and assumed that what it meant to be European, Western and capitalist was one and the same to [an orientation] that questioned the very dualism that divided colonizer from the colonized, that sought to identify the processes by which they were mutually shaped in intimate engagement, attraction, and opposition. (1997: viii)

When the Hartzian-McRae approaches and models were developed, there was very little awareness of this multidirectional hybrid world constructed by the tensions between colonizers and colonized. While there was recognition of the divergences from European patterns created by settler societies—indeed, the entire set of theses about new societies hinged on tracing those divergences—the entire analysis remained within the European sphere. Patterns established in Europe came to New World settings and were altered and then took on a new life of their own. The direction was always from Europe. There was no mention in any of these studies of the United States, South Africa, Australia, or Canada of the peoples who lived there before the arrival of Europeans and then interacted with Europeans in a range of ways. The dramatic shift in perspective that occurs if this is done was nicely summed up in the title of a 1990 essay by John Murrin. His survey of recent scholarship on the American colonies, which brings the Native American peoples fully within the framework of analysis, was called *Beneficiaries of Catastrophe: The English Colonies in America* (Murrin, 1990). In short, McRae and others were writing in a period when European-centred perspectives still had a firm hold. That is why Saul's work is so intriguing in spite of all its problems. He is suggesting that Canadian history can be recast as a grand synthesis of Euro-Canadian (with the distinct Anglophone and Francophone versions) and Native American histories and cultures as they have interacted in the geographical setting at the northern edge of North America.

As a consequences of the cultural fields of force at work in the formative years for the Hartzian-McRae concepts, there was a masking of voices other than Euro-Canadian ones. The last twenty years have seen much more attention to native peoples and female voices and other contestations to the dominant Euro-Canadian modes of thinking. Quite a different view of Canadian history comes to light if the fifty percent of the population that is female is brought front and center into the analysis (Strong-Boag and Fellman, 1991). But no era gets history right for all time—even the one we are living through now will be seen to have particular culturally influenced perspectives and agendas fifty years from now (if these have not already been exposed). McRae's view was a dynamic and comparative one. He was reluctant to make statements about Canada's uniqueness without actually examining what was happening in other countries. This dimension is often missing in current scholarship, as, for example, when it is asserted that Canadian history is more multipolar than any other. That may well be true, but it can be shown to be so only if some comparisons are made. It is similar to Daniel Goldhagen's case that the Germans were the most anti-Semitic society in modern Europe before the Nazis came to power. The proposition implies comparison and can be sustained only by assessing the situation outside Germany, too—let us say in Poland and France. All such claims to uniqueness are questionable unless sustained comparisons are made. The older monolithic national histories of the United States and Britain have been under siege for over twenty years now. Multipolar approaches are the order of the day. It may be that Canada's case is indeed exceptional, but that can be gauged only by actual work that brings Canada's circumstances into sustained contact with other polities faced with linguistic, ethnic, and regional diversities where older master narratives are being undermined. One of the reasons that the great Canadian intellectual game that is so engaging for Canadianists in Canada attracts relatively little attention outside Canada is an absence of this dimension that enables outsiders to relate to Canada's conundrums. When the preoccupation with Canada's identity took off in the 1960s and 1970s, it was arguable that this preoccupation was distinctively Canadian. Novelists and historians either seriously or in fun noted this complaint as singularly Canadian, but that is no longer the case. The recovery of other voices, and the deconstructing of traditional national identities have been taking place in many countries.

The paradox here is that in this era of globalization, when many nationalities, communities, and groups fear being homogenized into an American-influenced market system, Canada does have a special role given by history. Apart from the Native Americans, Canada has the longest historical experience of living alongside the American economic and cultural behemoth. Placing Canada in a global context rather than a parochial one will encourage others to pay more attention to the historical lessons learned by Canadians—lessons that have shaped Canadian government, society, and cultural policies. The histories that together make up Canada will always have an attractive edge to them if they operate at this global, comparative level rather than merely internally. To bring out fully Canada's world significance requires sustained comparative approaches to Canada's history and following some of the pioneering paths of those scholars like McRae who have studied Finland, Switzerland, Belgium, Australia, and the United States to better understand Canada. The Euro-Canadian presence on the ground is certainly lighter and more scattered than is the case in the United States. This leaves more room for native voices and influence—and even for tentative re-creations of native states. The Euro-Canadian presence has also never been as consolidated as in the United States in the sense that there have been perennial uncertainty in Canada about the Québec issue, an intense regionalism, and never-ending questions about the nature and purposes of Canadian federalism. From Canadian literature and art it is plausible to argue that the people who inhabit Canada are inclined to be less domineering in their views of nature than mainstream American views. Whether this makes Euro-Canadians animists who therefore have deep affinities with indigenous peoples is a more problematic proposition but certainly interesting to explore. These new approaches and insights developed by Saul and others are therefore welcome as a stimulus to rethinking some big issues. So, too, is the comprehensive rewriting of Canadian history in an effort to include as many voices and perspectives as were actually present in the past.

While allowing full weight to all these new approaches, it still remains true that Canada has been influenced by vestiges of European institutions and modes of thinking more than the United States has. Baldwin and Lafontaine, the un-heroes for Saul, viewed themselves as colonists working out solutions within a context that was less radical than the republican and democratic one in the United States—they knew, and gratefully accepted, that they had not broken away from European values and institutions. They were colonial patriots, not animists. Macdonald saw Canada as taking British institutions and adapting them to North American conditions while resisting absorption into the American culture and economy—and a big part of his solution was to build railways and take over territory across the continent and through Métis and Native American lands. Thousands of English Canadians were attracted to the imperial idea in the 1880–1920s era. Even many Québecois preferred a Canadian Constitution that remained in Britain to one that was patriated and apparently gave too much power to the English- speaking majority. Euro-Canadian peoples may have been unusually formed by indigenous landscapes, but they were also formed by the vestiges of European forces as these were transformed by the Canadian setting. Much of the old history did get it wrong—or at least provided only a partial accounting of Canada's multiple pasts—but it was right in seeing Canada's evolutionary, rather than revolutionary, relationship with Europe as a significant formative influence in the making of Canada.

It is important to rethink and reconceptualize history in order to take into account as many of Canada's complexities and uncertainties as possible. But if the only way of doing this is to rewrite Canadian history as though evidence and historiography did not matter, then the New World is not so brave after all. To airbrush out of the picture features of Canadian history that do not fit current perceptions and preoccupations is to be utterly condescending to all those Canadians—indigenous peoples, men, women, and immigrants--who made Canada what it is today. In that context Granatstein has a point. He is on thin ice when he castigates social and multicultural history, but his case would be stronger if he argued that Canadian history is in danger of becoming a zero-sum game in which all previous accounts of the past are pushed out of the picture by presentist framings. This is what Saul tends to do. He and other scholars also make implicitly comparative statements about Canadian history and political culture without bothering to actually study other countries. Michele Jean, deputy minister, Health Canada, observes that, "I have been in the federal government for ten years [and] I have seen one document that had a section on history. It went back to 1995" (Williams, 1999: 103). Let us hope that Canadian scholars are not going to mimic Canadian bureaucrats and simply rewrite Canadian history as though all people in that history thought and acted as if they were living in the 1990s.

NOTES

1. There was much wonderful scholarship in the series, but, taken as whole, it framed Canadian history in Whiggish terms, as the main theme followed was the rise of national unity against great odds. Representative titles that suggest this theme include Careless, (1967); Morton, (1964); Waite, (1971); Brown and Cook, (1974); Creighton, (1976); Granatstein, (1986); Zaslow, (1988).

2. See, for example, Schlesinger (1998).

No Place for "Race"? Why Pluralist Theory Fails to Explain the Politics of "Race" in "New Societies"

Jill Vickers

Western political thought in general has so compellingly, if not comfortingly, shown little understanding or respect for the cultural diversity of mankind and has made scant allowance for it as a possible concern of government.

K. D. McRae, 1979

[T]he ultimate source of these shortcomings [of the Canadian political system in dealing with diversity] lies...in attitudes rooted deeply in Canadian political culture, attitudes that fail to comprehend the meaning of a plural society. In the traditional political thought of the English-speaking world, minority status is [seen as] a temporary phenomenon....In the politics of segmented pluralism—whether based on religion, language, or race—minority status is far more likely to be a permanent fact of life, an ascribed characteristic, a burden to be carried perpetually by the smaller group or groups. In such a setting, appeals to the majority principle can be highly dangerous, and special accommodatory devices may be needed for resolving inter-group differences. English-Canadians collectively have never grasped this fundamental point.

K.D. McRae, 1979

The basic lesson that I learned from Professor McRae was how to be an intellectual who is engaged in the world. Observing him in the 1960s and 1970s, a major Bodin scholar who was grappling with Canada's French–English conflict, I learned that political theory that remains purely an artefact of academic debate is worth less than if it forms part of projects to achieve greater justice in the world. The greatest compliment that we pay our teachers is to follow their moral example. In this chapter, I pay McRae that compliment by exploring how to insert the politics of "race"[1] into political science paradigms and how basic assumptions of Western political theory limit our ability to understand "race" conflicts. My thesis is that pluralist theory lodged within Western political thought persistently ignores or misperceives diversity, especially diversity involving "race." I argue that this is so because most Western political thought assumes that a homogeneous polity is necessary for the polity to cohere and to achieve democracy and justice, assumptions that shape and limit even pluralist thought. Hence, if we are to understand how people of different "races" and nations can best live together in a political system based on justice and democracy *and* respect for difference, these assumptions must be fully explored and, where necessary, renovated.

In this text, I proceed from a postcolonial perspective, although I do not think that colonialism in Canada is "post" since we have not yet faced up to how our country was formed. Canada was formed as a nation-state when Europeans supplanted and dispossessed the indigenous nations and subsequently oppressed, marginalized, and forcibly assimilated them, first with imperial force and the colonial administration and then through the institutions of the new settler state. These acts and the "race" doctrines used to justify them were integral, not incidental, to this history of state formation and nation-building achieved through "race" regimes[2] that embedded "race" into state institutions, laws, and practices. Hence, "race" is deeply embedded in our political system despite efforts in recent decades to achieve internal decolonization and to remove "race" bias from state institutions. Achieving such changes is very difficult, however, because everything from citizenship and nationalism, to the rule of law and the administration of justice was deformed by their implication in "race" regimes. The history of nation-state formation differs both from that of European nation-states and also from the histories of most postcolonial states. Canada has not gone through a process of decolonization or one of truth and reconciliation. Collectively, we have not yet fully faced or repudiated the "race" doctrines basic to colonialism; and we have barely begun to deconstruct the structures, practices, and "race" doctrines it involved. Nonetheless, our national *amour propre* rests on a belief in our superiority on "race" matters to the United States or South Africa. To understand the role that "race" regimes—state practices and doctrines—played in the formation of state and nation requires first that we overcome the denial that is still our predominant collective and individual response to the "race" conflicts that are increasingly the stuff of contemporary Canadian politics. As V. Seymour Wilson argued (1993), the belief persists even among political scientists that "race" issues need to be examined because Canada is "no place for 'race.'" Many political scientists, like many "ordinary Canadians," believe that "race" problems never really existed in Canada or that they have been resolved by Canada's adoption of multicultural policies. Others still frankly advance theories of cultural superiority arguing that "primitive" peoples were legitimately governed by those at higher levels of "development." Since the 1960s, overt racism has become unfashionable or not politically correct. Nonetheless, many racist ideas and practices exist, although reshaped into the new form of democratic racism (Henry et al., 1995).

McRae argued in the 1970s that Canadian political culture and political science did not "get" diversity, partly because little in Western political thought allowed us to grasp "the meaning of a plural society." Moreover, the pluralist theorizing of McRae and others met with "relative neglect" two decades later. As Wilson demonstrated, even in the 1990s, "race" was still viewed as an "apolitical force" (1993: 645-646). It is my thesis that this reflects the fundamental weakness of applying European-inspired ("Western") political science paradigms and theories to settler societies like Canada, because these theories assume the homogeneous, nation-state form to be normal. Political science remains the captive of categories of analysis that ignore the impact of colonial and imperialist projects in which dispossession, exclusion, marginalization, and oppression legitimated by doctrines of differentiation used by state institutions played a critical role. This fact is self-evident to those who share characteristics with the dispossessed and oppressed and/or who work within the assumptions of postcolonial thought, but the writings of those affected by slavery, apartheid, internal colonialism, segregation, and so on are little known and often marginalized. As the African–American philosopher Cornel West notes: "[T]he idea of taking black people seriously in the life of the mind is a very new notion of white people" (1992: 704). The same is true concerning indigenous scholars and activists and scholars writing from the perspective of the previously colonized "two-thirds" world. These ideas from the margins are rarely integrated into the discipline's canon or paradigms because white ideas and experiences continue to be endowed with epistemic privilege. Europeans and those descended from Europeans remain the "WE" who Western theorists deem to be the makers of history. Those who exist on the margins (indigenous thinkers, black scholars, postcolonial writers) mostly remain othered, as is reflected in reactions to multicultural projects that decentre Western culture even slightly in the educational curriculum. It is also reflected in the persistent teaching within political science of a canon that privileges only Western political theorists, especially those who advance monist premises that homogeneity is universally the proper norm of the polity.

In this chapter I argue that pluralist theories developed within the Western political tradition mainly reflected the experience of western European nation-states and of the United States; that is, of nation-states based on Enlightenment ideas in which states are empowered to assimilate and oppress those who are different, to create a homogeneous national culture in the cause of cohesion, modernity, and, most recently, democracy. I argue that this is an inadequate framework for understanding "race" conflicts because it literally has no place for "race" in its theoretical formulations and is weakly equipped at best to deal with other forms of diversity. While pluralist theory as developed by Lijphart, McRae, and others theorizing the consociational experiences of smaller European democracies did prove useful for understanding diversity involving language and religion within Christianity, it, too, has proved inadequate for understanding "race" conflict and "race" regimes. Analyses of plural societies in a postcolonial framework produced valuable insights, but they were applied mainly to racially segmented "Third-World" societies such as Malaysia and Lebanon and were rarely applied to Canada or other settler societies because Canadians saw themselves as living in a multicultural democracy, not in a racially segmented society. Consequently, state-administered regimes of oppression based on "race" within the nation-state were deemed outside the norm. Hence, even most pluralist thinkers assumed that "race" didn't matter within a democratic nation-state. They also assumed that differences involving "race" were no different from other forms of difference and so could be incorporated into an interest-based pluralist model of the polity.

It is my thesis that "new," "settler," or "supplanting societies"[3] and their state forms cannot be understood in a conceptual framework that assumes homogeneity and devalues difference because such societies were forged through colonial conquest and continuing systems of oppression and privilege based on "race." "Race," in its modern sense based mainly on skin colour linked to the doctrine of primitivism, is not a feature of internal state formation in Europe, although nationalisms assume a homogeneity of "race" used in the earlier sense, which held French, Germans, Jews, and Slavs to be distinct "races" because of different cultural characteristics including language, faith, culture, and history. I focus on how to understand "race" where state institutions were *designed* to supplant pre-existing polities and maintain white dominance as they were in settler societies and where this occurred through actions of political regimes explicitly based on "race." Although we continue to use a European ideal-type of homogeneous people in a cohesive society in a nation-state, I theorize that this history shaped the nature and functioning of settler societies fundamentally and indelibly, especially affecting their states, to justify making them a different type of nation-state.

Instead of viewing the experience of nation-state formation of settler or supplanting societies as similar to those of European nation-states, I assume that they form their own distinctive type, a type shaped by *both* European political concepts and ideas derived from state-administered, "race" regimes and from the indigenous peoples whose polities coexisted with colonial polities, often for long periods of time. This contradicts the assumptions of fragment theory that hold that only influences from Europe shaped the "fragments" that evolved into "new societies." In my framework, South Africa's system of apartheid ceases to be the work of a "rogue nation" and becomes one end of a continuum in how "supplanting states" dealt with legally sanctioned dispossession, state construction of "race," and the use of "race" difference to maintain regimes, including internal colonialism, slavery, apartheid, segregation, white Australia, and democratic racism. Supplanting societies occur along this continuum according to how their states "make race," administer it, and are now trying to extricate themselves from their racial histories.

Euro-American[4] pluralist thought ultimately assumes that all "parties" to social conflict within a nation-state have the same standing vis-à-vis the state, although not necessarily the same amount of power. It does not comprehend people permanently excluded because they are (or were) slaves, "Abos," "Indians," "Asians," "coloureds," "half-breeds," or any one of the other "race"-based terms used in law and politics to exclude those racialized from the nation, deny them its benefits, and justify such acts. Although "race" is constructed socially and politically, the burden that it imposes is not easily avoided through group pressure or elite accommodation. Just as supplanting states "make race" in ways fundamental to their basic nature, for example, by constructing compartments to administer different systems of justice, social service, and education to populations categorized by "race," they also display distinctive modes of mobilization against "race" regimes. Fighting such regimes, moreover, involves battles against legally sanctioned discrimination, exclusion and oppression, but it also includes struggles against the doctrines to justify differential treatment based on "race." Ultimately, science, education, religion, medicine, the justice system, public administration, and the media of supplanting states were warped by their implication in "race" regimes. Hence, Euro-American political theory, even when resisting oppression, is inadequate because it values "racial" or "ethnic" homogeneity and imagines the good polity without difference, literally as with "no place for race." I conclude that we can best begin by inserting "race" and "race regimes" into the political science paradigm. To do so, however, we must first understand how "race" regimes shaped the states that administered settler colonialism.

The remainder of the chapter has three parts. First, I explore briefly some ideas about why there has been no place for "race" within Western political theory and political science and why it matters. I also explore some ideas about racism that emerged within Euro-American discourse and that relate "race" concepts to colonial/imperial ventures. Second, I explore pluralist ideas within Euro-American political theory and political science to illuminate why they fail to theorize adequately the role of states in "making race." I conclude that "race" regimes were invisible even to most pluralist theorists for two main reasons: first, because the experiences of supplanting societies[5] were ignored and explanations of their political systems were based on Euro-American political theory with its norm of a homogeneous "people" or nation; second, because assumptions underlying Western political thought at its deepest level construct "race" as something that WE who make history do not have but that we assign to "others" because of their difference from us, which we also assume makes them inferior. That is, Western thought uses categories and tools of thinking in which the WE who are doing the thinking (and making history) are unmarked by "race" (Day, 2000). The WE at the centre of history-making are also male in the Western tradition, as I have demonstrated elsewhere (Vickers, 1997). In the final section, I suggest how we can begin decolonizing political science by crafting a theoretical "place for race" and by ending the epistemic privilege that WE enjoy through the genuine inclusion of the knowledge of those usually marginalized and excluded. I am influenced here by indigenous scholars, critical race theorists, postcolonial theorists, and by Australian historians and theorists of "race" regimes in supplanting societies.

"THE DOG THAT DIDN'T BARK"

There is no typology classifying political systems according to their "race" relations or according to the presence (or absence) of state-administered "race" regimes. Some states that exterminate or visibly and extremely oppress their inhabitants based on "race," such as Nazi Germany and South Africa, may become lightning rods for international disapproval, but their actions are considered rogue or abnormal, just as racism is often viewed as the product of the abnormal psychology of racists. Their actions are rarely compared to segregation, forcible assimilation, or denial of citizenship and civil rights based on "race" as in the United States of America, Canada, Australia, and other settler societies. Moreover, dominant, Western political science frameworks fail to explain why some, but not all, societies practice state-administered racism.

"Race," then, is like the dog that didn't bark in a Sherlock Holmes mystery. Its absence from the core texts in political theory and from political science paradigms is our clue that they are not sufficient for understanding the politics of "race." This is not to say that political theorists don't deal with "race" in their writings, often in ways that would discredit them in the eyes of modern readers. Such "embarrassing" texts are simply not taught and are excluded as atypical or part of a theorist's embeddedness in his or her times. Despite this silence, theoretical ideas about "race" inform their ideas and are embedded in political science paradigms at a deep level. This deliberate forgetfulness likely stems from the fact that the horrors of fascism in Europe were associated with racism. Despite decades of decolonization and United Nations–sponsored refugee and human rights campaigns, Europe's concerns about having people who are racially different in non-European ways within its borders seems somehow new, whereas it is a very old concern within the settler societies.

Immanuel Wallerstein links contemporary European racism to a paradox in Western thought when he observes that "[t]he major challenge to racism and sexism has been universal beliefs; and the major challenge to universalism has been racist and sexist beliefs" (1991: 29). He links this paradox to capitalism, arguing that racism and sexism limit the application of univeralist principles in order for capitalism to mark portions of the workforce as "others" who can be excluded from the equal treatment and rights dictated by a universalist ideal. Hence, racism is understood as a strategy of capitalists to increase profits. The desirable norm remains universalism or homogeneity in the sense that the difference marked by "race" (and sex) should not matter. Australian Andrew Markus (1994), by contrast, theorizes that Europeans created modern "race" doctrines to explain their easy conquest and near elimination of indigenous peoples whom they supplanted through settler colonialism. Although he believes that the building-blocks for racism e.g., (fear of the stranger) exist in all societies, the modern idea of "race," he believes, contains meditations on how non-European peoples could be supplanted and whole continents appropriated for European settlement and exploitation so easily. He believes that this led to the belief that the peoples supplanted must be profoundly inferior to white Europeans; so the concept of difference (which need not be hierarchical) was joined to a judgment of inferiority embodied in the idea that the people supplanted were "primitive" (at a lower stage of "development") and so were legitimately dispossessed and ruled by Europeans. This myth of the primitive or underdeveloped forms the core of modern "race" doctrines and is also used to justify why Europeans should dominate and benefit in global systems of exploitation. The West or North, which greedily outconsumes the East and South, is seen as "developed" and "modern" and so justified in its affluence by contrast to poorer "underdeveloped"/"traditional" peoples. The belief in the natural superiority of those who are "modern" or "developed" shares much with "race" doctrines as Markus explains them.

The invention of modern "race" doctrines did not disrupt European beliefs that their polities should be homogeneous and this state concept was transferred to the European fragments in settler colonies. Indeed, Cowlishaw (1997) suggests that in Australia, where egalitarian ideas prospered, the pressure to exclude those considered too different to be equal was especially intense. Democracy for "Australians" (including white women) could be built only by excluding the unequal others (Aboriginals, Chinese, non-Anglo-Celtic Europeans). An especially brutal "race" regime to supplant and exclude Aboriginals resulted. A second result was the official "White Australia" policy to exclude and exploit Asians, passed as the first act of the new federated Australian Commonwealth. Official preference for white labour was maintained, moreover, despite capitalists' desire (and constant lobbying) to use cheap Asian labour even at some cost to white taxpayers, as the history of subsidy programs such as for "white sugar" (sugar produced by white labour) reveals. "Race" understood as skin colour and/or "primitiveness" in living style and culture became the main markers for exclusion, exploitation, neglect, attempted genocide, and forced assimilation.[6] The combination of egalitarian democracy, based on universalist values and rights, with systematic exclusion, exploitation and even attempted extermination based on "race", therefore, is a common feature of modern, Western nation-states, although best observed in settler societies.

The combination of universalist, democratic values and values of exclusion based on "race" does not just exist at the level of grand theory. Contemporary empirical evidence suggests that many citizens in Western democracies hold universalist ideas supporting equality and human rights simultaneously with exclusionary racist and nationalist sentiments. Francis Henry et al. (1995) document this in Canada in describing democratic racism. Many Canadians hold values of democracy and racism simultaneously, they conclude, because of a set of bridging ideas used to make democratic and racist values seem to fit together. Some of these bridging ideas are that: "racism cannot exist in a democratic society" (denial); that "discrimination is a problem faced by everyone from time to time" (dilution); that "white European immigrants also faced discrimination" (dilution); that "racism is a result of immigration"; that "racial conflict occurs because races mix" (blame abstract processes); that "minorities are unable to fit in and adapt to Canadian society"; that "minority group change the national identity; people of colour have cultural problems" (blame the victims); that "all we need to do is treat everyone equally" (race is like any other form of difference); that "racism comes from ignorance; education will eradicate it"; and that "anti-racism is racism in reverse" (308). Democratic racism, therefore, is possible because some democratic values—including the normativeness of homogeneity, the majority principle and equality based on individual but not group rights, and equality understood only as same treatment—are easily combined with racist beliefs and values. Democratic racism, in fact, constitutes the contemporary "race" regime in Canada. It also reflects particular experiences of settler societies, moreover, such as the fact that migration is viewed as normal (the myth that "we are all immigrants"), which make it vital to those of the dominant culture that the consequences of migration do not include dilution of their sense of the nation ("no turbans in my legion").

In their study of Belgians' view of "the migrant problem," Blommaert and Verschueren (1996) found value contradictions that, while similar, reflected the difference in the historical experiences of European, colonizing nation-states. They report that migration and migrants both are viewed as aberrations by "ordinary" Belgians, who believe both that a society should be homogeneous and that they are a very tolerant people. Blommaert and Verschueren found that overt racism was "played down to the point of disappearance" (111) in their discussion of their views. Overt racist ideas were not needed to explain people's desire to exclude migrants, since exclusion is considered normal and *consistent with being tolerant*, so not in need of explanation. They conclude: "[H]ow can racism be fought if the premises of a racist discourse are accepted, in particular the idea that homogeneity and resistance against heterogenerity are normal?" (111). Tolerance is extended to those who are different only within a very limited set of characteristics that can be assimilated, which is difficult for those who are not white and of European origins. It is deemed legitimate to exclude most migrants because they will infect the polity even with their difference, even if it can be privatized. This also sets the limits within which Euro-American pluralist thought works.

The differences and similarities in the Canadian and Belgian cases are worth noting. Many "ordinary" (white, Anglophone) Canadians accept migration as normal but also consider expressions in the public sphere of the greater diversity that results from migration to be unacceptable. In both cases, support for cultural tolerance is asserted and universalist, democratic values upheld. But members of the dominant culture also assume that homogeneity is normal and that resistance to heterogeneity and support for assimilation are compatible democratic values. Overt racism and ethnocentrism, therefore, are not needed to justify values hostile to tolerance and universalism.

John Rex (1996) sees this combination of ideas as part of a response to a crisis of identity in multicultural democracies resulting from a backlash to globalization. While the current wave of globalization undoubtedly exacerbates the trend, in settler societies it reflects a long-term conflict between the fundamental values of Western political thought and experiences of extreme diversity under settler colonialism and, in Canada's case, rapid immigration. As such, the response is not new because the idea that nation-states should be homogeneous never fit the historic experiences of supplanting states formed through dispossession and immigration. It is worth considering, therefore, why it persists. The myth of a common origin of nations certainly was often, but not always, used to support equality, but equality among "the people." Ghia Nodia reminds us that: "political nationalism understands the nation in much the same way that liberalism understands the individual...the fight for national independence is only legitimate because it affirms the universal principle of human rights" (1996: 107). Yet there were clearly limits to who could be included in "the people" and featured in "the nation," even as conceptualized by those who espoused a so-called civic nationalism.

This assertion of inclusiveness based on universal moral principles while excluding those who are *too* different (usually because of their "race" or sex) is characteristic of much Western political thought. For example, while Immanuel Kant's understanding of human autonomy, based on a key Enlightenment concept of the inalienable right to individual and national self-determination, seems less open to racism than the Romantic movement's interpretation of nationalism, which stressed the struggle of the collective spirit of a people for self-realization and for liberation if subject to the will of others, a close examination of Kant's thinking on "race" shows otherwise. Mark Larrimore asserts: "Kant's understanding of the *a priori* nature of the moral seems to prevent any account or theory of human difference from leading to prejudice or discrimination....On the other hand, Kant defends race itself as an *a priori concept*, and the specific content of his anthropology seems to justify exclusion from moral concerns in a new and dangerous way" (1999: 99). Larrimore concedes that there is room for disagreement about the implications of Kant's "race" ideas because "[t]he theology of Kant's race theory is discontinuous with that of his philosophy of history and "[a]s...[with his ideas on] women, his anthropology and his ethics seem simply to talk past each other" (100). Nonetheless, Larrimore concludes that Kant's anthropology excludes nonwhites from the work of civilization.[7] His analysis of Kant's ideas about "race" is revealing. In *Reflection #1520*, for example, Kant declares: "All races will be wiped out, except for the white," which suggests that he may exclude the WE who make history (white Europeans) from having "race" at all.[8] He also argues that "Americans ('Indians') and negroes cannot govern themselves...[t]hus are only good as slaves" (Larrimore, 1999: 114), both suggesting "the white man's burden" theme and accepting the myth of the primitive. In fact, Kant subscribed to an understanding of "race" that, like Aristotle's, naturalized inequality and excluded white Europeans from racialization. Those racialized and deemed "primitive" are disqualified from participating in "universal" history.

Australian "race" theorist Roberta James (1997) notes that the image of "natural man" in liberal thought as savage or primitive was used persistently as a discursive device by Rousseau and others to make racism normative and consistent with universalism and democracy. Those *too* different were assumed not part of "the people" to whom democratic ideas and nationalism applied and so were put outside history and democratic citizenship. Neither Enlightenment universalism nor Romanticism's "the people" include "others" who were "too different" because of their "race" (sex or, in the case of Jews and Muslims, a conflation of race and faith). Colonialism assumed that the different peoples whom the colonialists ruled, whether "primitive" (African, American, and other Indigenous) or "Oriental," would always be outside history and the democratic polity. Moreover, they usually were outside the territory of the home states (expelled or ghettoized). In settler societies, however, they were *inside* the territory governed by the supplanting state but were considered too different to be included in the settler polity. This resulted in attempts to exterminate, exclude, and isolate and later to eradicate through forcible assimilation (rape, coercive education in residential schools, etc.). So, state institutions simultaneously ruled those similar enough to be equal (often including white women) and those systematically excluded from citizenship because they were deemed too different because of their "race."

Balibar links "race" and racism to European colonialism and the emergence of the nation-state and nationalism in Europe. Both Balibar and Wallerstein focus mainly on racism as an ideology that facilitates capitalist accumulation. The main business remains firmly focused on the economic base and the ideological superstructure. But neither theorizes the roles of nation-states in constructing and maintaining official state racism in supplanting societies where the role of racialization is more complex. After the initial colonial period in which naked force prevailed, the elites who controlled state institutions operated at least two different legal and political regimes: one to legitimate dispossessing the *supplanted* inhabitants, incarcerating them, executing them for resisting, and denying them civil and political rights and a second regime to legitimate the *supplanting* inhabitants' acquisition of property, civil, and political rights. Subsequent regimes were needed for other racialized groups such as Asians who occupied median positions between the supplanted and the supplanters. Each regime allocated oppression and privilege, inclusion and exclusion on the basis of "race" categories created by the state.

Critical race theory makes it clear that approaches to "race" that focus only on ideology (i.e., racism) and neglect the role of the state are fundamentally flawed. While focusing on racism helps us locate transitions in ideology used to justify new, additional "race" regimes, it leaves unexplored deeper theoretical concepts that do not overtly involve "race" such as the idea basic to liberal thought that modern nation-states practice universalism in administering the rule of law. Critical race theorists challenge this assumption. Their work also points to a deeper level in Western political thought—that of underlying tools of thinking and deeply embedded, but unstated, assumptions such as the assumption that the WE who make history do not have "race" and that the WE who are the dominant culture vis-à-vis a state don't have ethnicity. Critical race theorists challenge the premise that adjudication by impartial judges is actually a central feature and benefit of liberal society. In Locke's theory, the most compelling reason that he offers for "men" to consent to civil society is the substitution of the rule of law and of a common impartial judge for the disadvantage of everyone's acting as his or her own judge. Feminist theorists first challenged this myth, arguing that the historic maleness of those who create, administer, and adjudicate the law meant that women did not enjoy this benefit of civil society at all (or perhaps not until recently and then incompletely). They argue that Western democracies and their justice systems remain patriarchal in the sense that they are still dominated by men in all of their powerful institutions and often still act on behalf of men by administering rules that privilege men.

Critical race theorists challenge the idea that courts act impartially concerning "race." They demonstrate that the rule of law and the courts—indeed the whole justice system, even in liberal nation-states—were and are major tools in the state's constructing and administering of "race" categories and "race" regimes." They also show how liberal values of judicial neutrality, impartiality, and universalism may actually establish the rights and privileges of the dominant "race" as benchmarks for determining the goals of legal equality and justice. The white WE are the norm, the unmarked citizen, the "ordinary Canadian" or "ordinary Belgian." Their thesis is not that legislators, judges, and police discriminate consciously against those who have been assigned "race," although the experience in supplanting societies shows this has been the case for much of their history. Rather, they assert the existence of structural or systemic racism[9] in which *purportedly neutral* universal rules and values privilege the dominant group ,which is not assigned to "race" (or ethnic) categories then used to disadvantage, exclude, or oppress those racialized (or ethnicized).

Constance Backhouse's research (1999) reveals a distinctive Canadian history of how legislators and courts that represented the values and interests of dominant elites as if they were universal and neutral actually constructed and administered "race" categories. She also shows how Jews and French Canadians were "racialized" along with those marked by distinctive physical characteristics. (Note that these assignments change: Catholic Irish, Slavs, and Italians were racialized in the nineteenth and early twentieth centuries but became part of "English Canada" after 1970, when changes in immigration policy meant the admission of a large number of nonwhite immigrants.) Critical race theorists also analyse how systemic racism[10] works through institutions and norms that privilege the dominant majority while disadvantaging racialized minorities. Like European neo-Marxist approaches, however, they fail to identify how and why states act to establish "race" regimes.

Although the questions of why systemic racism came to exist and why states play such central roles in "race" regimes are too complex to answer here in any detail, the literature has signposts that are suggestive. Australian Andrew Markus, for example, believes that the ease with which Europeans dispossessed Indigenous peoples in the Americas led to the idea that Europeans were superior to "primitive" natives and invented "race" doctrines to this effect, which infiltrated legal, philosophic, and political thinking. He concludes that Europeans did not need such doctrines to engage in their imperialist projects but that elites in the new settler states found them invaluable in consolidating states that oppressed some inhabitants while seeking to create national solidarity based on democratic values for the dominant group. As Anthony Marx (1998) demonstrates for the United States, Brazil, and South Africa, "race" doctrines formed the basic character and structures of the nation-states involved. He asserts that "[s]tates made race" (2) through the whiteness of their nationalisms adopted to bind together whites of different origins, classes, and ideological positions and by manipulating citizenship to include, exclude, privilege, and deny on the basis of state-made and state-administered "race" categories. In supplanting societies, therefore, white settlers inherited the "race regimes," which were built into their state institutions and official ideologies by European colonial authorities and settler governments. Their national identities contained "race" scripts in which they conceptualized themselves as white, "Western," and superior and so deserving of dominance. Elite descendants of white settlers[11] and white immigrants continued to dominate the state through internal colonialism over supplanted Indigenous nations. The new nation-states restructured and built on initial "race" regimes still function as agents of white settler descendants despite their commitment to democratic values.[12] The sight of federal Fisheries officers in the summer of 2000 swooping down to deny Indigenous fishers, who control only a tiny fraction of Canada's fishery, greater access to the resources clearly shows that the Canadian state continues to act on behalf of the supplanting society members despite rhetoric of acting for "the common good."[13]

The particular reluctance of Canadians to explore the "race" dimension of our state politics may reflect the fact that English Canadians construct their collective identity mainly in opposition to the United States, especially on "race." Nationalists portray Canada as innocent of state racism on three grounds: first, because they (incorrectly) believe that, unlike the United States, Canada was not implicated in slavery; second, because they believe that Canada treated "our" Indigenous peoples better than the United States through purportedly peaceful settlement with no "war against the Indians" as in the United States, and, third, because they believe that Canada's invention of multiculturalism reflects a greater tolerance for diversity, including greater racial tolerance, than in the United States.[14] This misframing of our history has led to a systematic denial that a "race"-differentiated state and state-administered "race" regimes exist in Canada. The idea that the border between Canada and the United States somehow insulated us from racism has been a convenient fiction. It let us conclude that our intellectual world had no place for "race" because it needed none. No "race" theory of our supplanting state existed because Canada had been virtuous on "race" issues, at least compared to the United States. Moreover, we persistently repress our real history by teaching the European-derived *imaginaire* in western political thought in which the nation-state is homogeneous, and there is "little understanding or respect for . . . diversity." Postcolonial thought and critical "race" theory challenge these practices.

THE FAILURE OF PLURALIST THOUGHT TO EXPLAIN THE POLITICS OF RACE

In this section, I explore why pluralist thought in the Western tradition failed to comprehend diversity in ways that could explain "race." Bhikhu Parekh, in a recent exploration of the "limits of pluralist imagination," asserts that "[f]rom Plato onward, western moral and political philosophy has been dominated by a monist impulse manifest in a search for *the* best way of life, *the* best form of government, *the* perfect society, *the* highest human faculty, *the* highest or best religion, *the* single most reliable way to acquire knowledge of the world, and so on" (1999: 55, emphasis added). While this monism was countered early on by the skeptics and the sophists, "a systematic critique of it was not mounted until the eighteenth century" (55) and, Parekh concludes, the pluralist critiques that did emerge were weak. About Vico and Montesquieu, for example, Parekh concludes that, "although they endeavoured to lay the foundation of a pluralist moral and political theory, they remained too trapped within the dominant monist tradition to do so with much success" (56). Hence, although some European pluralist thinkers sought to acknowledge and explain cultural diversity, ultimately they were unable to escape their basic beliefs that Europe was superior to all other societies; that Christianity was the only true religion; that European culture, science, law, and manner of governing justified imperial domination of "inferior" and "primitive" peoples; and, more recently, that Western-style democracy, human rights, and economic modes of "development" are superior and should prevail globally. Thus, Enlightenment thought used to justify Euro-American imperialism assumed that European ideas "provided the model for humankind" and that European countries accordingly "had a right to guide the rest of the world" (61).[15]

Why is the simple thesis that there may be a number of equally legitimate ways to "live the good life" or "to live well together" so weakly developed in Western thought that exclusion, even extermination on the basis of "race" simply passes unnoticed in our current accounts of our own history? In this section, I explore several attempts to explain this failure of the pluralist imagination: failure in that it has been unable to understand moral and cultural difference in ways that escape the tradition of monism without adopting annihilistic relativism. It is my thesis that Western political thought cannot transcend the monist impulse that Parekh identifies, which I believe ultimately seeks to justify inequality (Vickers, 1997), because it has values embedded deeply in its tools of thinking which assume the superiority of the WE who constitute the dominant culture and the exclusion of those who are different because of their "race," sex, faith, and ethnicity. Without recognizing this, we will be unable to understand how and why fundamental political concepts support "race" doctrines and regimes.

Thinkers as diverse as Locke, Rousseau, Hegel, Kant, Marx, and Jefferson participated in the cognitive dissonance of combining universal values with exclusions based on "race" that makes pluralism so weak in the Western tradition. The tendency is so widespread (others point to J. S. Mill, Hume, Malthus, and Adam Smith) that any other approach seems improbable. Richard Day suggests that in the western tradition it can be seen first in the work of Herodotus, whom many consider the father of ethnography. Day builds on Margaret Hoden's analysis of the rules and categories in Herodotus' thought that he used to categorize "others." Hoden demonstrates that these later became the rules and categories that most Western philosophers, colonizers, and missionaries used to categorize the "others" whom they encountered through imperial expansion. A key characteristic of this mode of thinking is that it proceeds from the perspective of an *unmarked self*—WE—which becomes the norm against which all differences associated with the alienated categories of otherness are measured. Herodotus, as a Greek male, was part of the unmarked WE who got to construct the categories of otherness according to the characteristics that they chose, however superficial or erroneous. He then assigned the "others" to hierarchically organized categories with himself at the centre as the norm.

Day argues that Herodotus accordingly sought to "spy the Other through the scope of the Self" (2000: 50) and so developed techniques of thinking in which the superiority of the unmarked self is never in question. This method proceeds by homogenizing "others" in each category and by using stereotypes and reductionist formulas to describe the Other. The unmarked self at the centre was a Greek citizen whom on the Herodotan wheel of difference he contrasted to a series of "others": women, slaves, animals, and barbarians. Day renders it: "Greeks = not animal + not barbarian + not women + not slave-like" (53). The distinction between the unmarked Self (the WE who make history) and barbarians, moreover, is an "ethnic" difference; "ethnic" has its origins in *ethnos* and *ethnikos*, which Herodotus used to mean heathen and non-Greek. *Ethnos* was not used to describe Greeks, who have a *polis* (the opposite of *ethnos*). Instead, it referred to peoples who did not (and should not) have a *polis*, as ethnic group and "race" are often used in western discourse.

Larrimore's analysis of Kant's ideas on "race" (1999) suggests that many European philosophers worked within a civilized/primitive framework modelled on this ancient distinction, which assumed that only those categorized as "others" have "race" or ethnicity. So, the "WE" that the model assumes make history gain epistemic privilege by basing abstract, purportedly universal thought on our own experiences, becoming the unmarked self. Such rules were built at a deep structural level into the modes of thinking that European political theorists adopted from Greek and Christian discourses. Centuries after Herodotus, for example, Kant's account of "race" is also "definitely anti-historical" (Larrimore, 1999: 106-107). By 1785, Kant "focuses exclusively on colour as a racial marker" (106-107), theorizing four "races" (white, yellow, black, and red). But Kant's subsequent assertions such as that "[a]ll races will be wiped out, *except for the white*" (2000: 114, emphasis added), Larrimore beliefs reveals "the thought process of someone for whom 'all races' does not automatically include the whites" (114) and for whom "races" are hierarchically constructed with only members of the white "race" categorized as capable of making history and of being "human." Any people who make history (e.g., Egyptians) must be white. Much scholarship now exists that shows that the basic tools of thinking adopted by Western political thought from Greek and Christian discourses inserted assumptions about "race" into their mainly unexamined substructures. Day shows how the Herodotan wheel of difference bequeathed to Roman, Christian, and Western thought "*[i]gnorance,* in the sense of an active, willful desire not to know, [which] was paramount, and helped to maintain its complement, *xenophobia*" (2000: 59). Just as its categories and rules kept "non-Greek Others at an absurd, mocking distance" (59), inflating and normalizing the Greek self, its basic logic has also been used by most Western theories and in Canada's constructions of difference to justify its "race" regimes. It is my thesis that Western political science—including pluralist thought and analysis—uses the same logic and so assumes its biases. This weakens most pluralist approaches despite overt intentions to incorporate difference.

In Euro-American political science, pluralist thought can be explained by envisioning a spectrum with Rousseau at one end and Alexis de Tocqueville at the other. Tocqueville saw democracy as best promoted and protected through the actions of civic, interest, and religious groups all advancing citizens' crosscutting loyalties in what has come to be called civil society. Rousseau represents the monist, republican tradition and argues that citizens must be unmarked by differences, with loyalties to nothing but the polity, believing that faction within the polity threatens democracy. The bearers of some differences can become unmarked citizens by limiting their difference to the private realm. Others (e.g., women) Rousseau would exclude from citizenship, in part because they are *too* different ever to be considered equal.

Pluralist analysis in Western thought, therefore, is restricted to a rather narrow sphere to start with. Gabriel Almond, in his account of pluralist models in the discipline, notes that the concept of pluralism "entered political science as an attack on the theory of sovereignty" (1990: 82) and subsequently revolved around whether society should be viewed as "an association of individuals dominated by a central state" or "as an organization of co-equal and co-operating groups, including churches, professional associations, trade unions, local communities, as well as the state" (82). This debate reveals that pluralists, who advance a strong group-based approach, see citizens as having the same status and equal standing as citizens but differential power. Pluralism so conceived cannot explain state-administered "race" regimes that exclude groups from representation and participation altogether because of their "race." Traditional pluralist theory, moreover, assumes a homogeneity in how "interests" are advanced in civil society, while recognizing differences in their nature, content, and strength. This is seen in Ernest Gellner's assertion that civil society—defined as "a cluster of institutions and associations strong enough to prevent tyranny, but . . . nevertheless, entered freely rather than imposed"—can be operated only by "modular man" (1995: 42). "Modular man" is modern, Euro-American man who acts only instrumentally and on the basis of "lucid Cartesian thought" (42) without being encumbered by ties of blood, kinship, or intensely held faith and who acts purely on the basis of contract. Gellner further assumes that civil society "requires the substitutability of men for each other" (43) and thus a cultural homogeneity that implies the exclusion of those not "substitutable." While some other models of civil society are more open to participation by those who are too different to fit in, the very concept of "society" is a social construct that assumes homogeneity of citizens (Hindess, 2000). While we often treat "society" as if it were a natural entity, it was imposed as part of the extension of the European nation-state system and, Hindess notes, as a way of making world populations governable.

The limitations of traditional Euro-American pluralism led to the development of theories of consociational democracy from the 1960s by Arend Lijphart, K. D. McRae, and others. Consociationalism refers to regimes in which internal accommodation occurs among elites representing segments of a society that differ ethnically or in terms of language and/or religion. Following Dahl, Lijphart (1971) concludes that only three of the possible outcomes of conflict among "subcultures" or societal segments are consistent with consociational democracy—autonomy, proportionality, and mutual veto. Repression, separation, and assimilation (Dahl's other three possible outcomes)—are not consistent with consociationalism, although, historically, they have been the most common responses to differences based on "race." Elite accommodation, which is the basic mechanism of the consociational model, is possible only when the differences between or among segments are not hierarchical or based on dominance, as "race" differences usually are. The model focused mainly on smaller European countries including the Netherlands, Belgium, Switzerland, and Austria, but McRae attempted to apply it to Canada. He adopted the term *segmented pluralism* to distinguish between pluralism based on difference organized into segments or distinct communities (vertical pluralism) and horizontal pluralism, in which crosscutting loyalties and memberships in "interest" groups represent citizens' values and needs to government, as discussed earlier. To McRae, consociational democracy can involve both vertical and horizontal forms of pluralism. McRae theorized that "[t]he more completely a society is segmented around a single cleavage line, the more it is an appropriate site for the development of consociational politics" (1974a: 5). While the primary cleavages in European consociationialism are usually religion and ideology, he also suggests that segmentation based on language, race, or caste can also be managed by a consociational form of pluralism.

Both of the Euro-American approaches to pluralism discussed earlier assume that the ultimate goal is a harmonious balance in society achieved either through a market–like balancing of the diverse interests of individual citizens or through elite accommodation based on segment autonomy, proportionality, or mutual veto. The two approaches constitute what Leo Kuper describes as "equilibrium" models of pluralism. The assumptions of this model, moreover, remain compatible with the underlying values of Western political thought and of the nation-state system established by the Treaty of Westphalia and globalized through imperialism, anticolonialism and neoimperialism. Kuper introduces another model of *plural societies* in which the segments are not as equal in their relations to the state and are often in conflict. He describes this as the "conflict" model of pluralism. It was based mainly on societies outside Europe.

Kuper outlines two versions of the "conflict" model of plural societies. In the first Furnivall model (1939, 1945), the political form of plural societies is theorized as colonial domination that combines a Western sector focused on a modern, market economy and modern, rational administrative institutions, both imposed on a "native" sector in a forced union (Kuper, 1997: 222). In this model, two or more segments live side by side, but separately, in one political unit. To Furnivall, writing before the global wave of decolonization from the 1960s, any integration that occurred was imposed by the colonial power. A second model of a plural society was developed by M. G. Smith (1960), who saw it as a political form in which one unit that also is a cultural minority dominates. Smith sees plural societies as marked by cultural diversity and conflict around one or more cleavages, such that the segments would be separate societies if it were not for the fact that they shared a single polity usually established by conquest. In both models, plural societies have common *and* plural institutions with relations of superiority/dominance and inferiority/ subordination marked by "race" categories and legitimized by racist ideology. Moreover, "[t]he political significance of pluralism is likely to fluctuate with the changing conditions of domination" (Kuper, 1997: 227). Nonetheless, the assumption remains that societies should be culturally homogeneous but are prevented by the colonial power.

These conflict models of plural societies are valuable for understanding some aspects of relationships of difference in settler societies, especially the role of "race" regimes imposed and maintained by colonial rule. In a complex settler society like Canada, however, more than one model may be necessary since the issues posed by difference—even difference based on "race"—vary considerably from group to group. For example, relations between the English and French supplanting fragments may best be understood through a consociational lens. Within each fragment, moreover, the form of pluralism that begins with Tocqueville's focus on individuals' expression of crosscutting interests and loyalties is suitable. On the other hand, the conflict model of a plural society best illuminates the relationships of continuing colonialism with Indigenous nations. But it may be less useful for understanding the "race" regimes through which the white fragment societies excluded nonwhites from admission and/or citizenship.

A final pluralist model has emerged in recent years in the concept of a multicultural society. John Rex asserts that, whereas the plural society model is a model of racial *domination*, the concept of multicultural society involves the participation of peoples of different cultures in ways that combine multicultural expression and equal opportunity, especially for citizenship. The key issue for Rex is whether multicultural states should positively affirm the rights of group members to be different as *citizens in the public sphere*, thus rejecting assimilation to a homogeneous polity as the goal for the good polity. In this model, the goal is not homogeneity or equal treatment understood as same treatment but a matter of the state's providing and ensuring equal respect for different cultures treated as equally valuable. The questions also arise as to whether the cultures to be respected equally can be expressed in the public realm or only in the private and, second, whether the goal of equal respect for different cultures is to be guaranteed to groups, communities, and nations or to individuals whose basic right to cultural expression (including language, faith, etc.) is involved. This is important for "race" since even modern "race" doctrines in which "race" difference is understood as socially constructed and cultural involve visible physical markers. A model that allows only for private expression of differences is inadequate, partly because such physical markers cannot be kept hidden.

Debates about multiculturalism as a model are too extensive and complex to be considered here at length. Many "race"-minority observers, however, argue that Canada's form of multiculturalism, while promising equal respect for different cultures, fails to combat the racism resulting from colonialism and neo-colonialism. Indigenous peoples believe that multiculturalism fails to recognize the existence of ongoing colonialism and Canada's failure to deconstruct its foundational "race" regimes, while ignoring the government's role in the continuing dispossession of Indigenous peoples. For many observers, multiculturalism is consistent with democratic racism as a new "race" regime in which difference is managed by alliances of elites from English Canadian and Québec cultures. The difference is that the elite now sometimes incorporates people of "race" minority backgrounds.

FINDING SPACE FOR "RACE"

In this final section I outline several ways that we can begin to insert "race" into political science by drawing on postcolonial, plural society, and critical race theories. It is my view that the most effective way to integrate "race" and race oppression into political science is to analyse the foundational "race" regimes in settler societies like Canada and Australia. I define a "race" regime as a *political regime created and administered by state institutions for the purpose of dispossessing, excluding, or controlling some peoples while privileging and including others, on the basis of "race" or racelike criteria of difference*. I am not arguing that all states create systems of state racism or operate through "race" regimes. Establishing that proposition is beyond the scope of this chapter. My goal is to make space for "race"-conscious political analysis by making visible the phenomena represented by the concepts of state racism and "race" regimes and by providing a basic vocabulary to distinguish between European and settler societies and states. Instead of seeing regimes that oppress and privilege on the basis of "race" as incidental to the functioning of modern nation-states in settler societies, we must see the presence of "race" regimes as normal and arrange all supplanting societies—from South Africa to New Zealand—on a continuum as a common type.

We can make space for "race" in settler nation-states, first, by assessing how settler nation-states were and are affected by their roles in creating and maintaining "race" regimes, including slavery, internal colonialism, and segregation, in which racialized "others" are controlled within the state's territory but excluded from, or marginalized in, their polity by being denied citizenship, civil rights, and social benefits. Second, we can make space for "race" by assessing how each settler nation-state was and is affected by its role in imposing postcolonial and neo-imperial constraints on racialized "others" and by regulating and restricting the migration of racialized others to the polity, as in "white Canada" laws and practices. We also need to assess the implications of federalism and bureaucratic dominance in disguising such policies and practices. Third, we need to assess how each settler nation-state was and is affected by its role in the global political economy in which gross inequities between Western democratic (white, European, Christian) and non-western (non-European, non-Christian, allegedly non-democratic) countries, regions, and fractions of countries are maintained and legitimated in overt or subtle racial terms. Finally, our analyses of settler/supplanting nation-states must take into account their role in establishing and maintaining systems of colonialism, internal colonialism, and neoimperialism. Assumptions about difference, especially "race" difference, drawn from Western political theory and from equilibrium models of pluralism must be interrogated in light of critical "race," plural society, and postcolonial theories.

Adequate theoretical accounts of the persistence and rise of racism must begin by exploring the nature and roles of "race" thinking and of other forms of thinking implicated in constructing those who are different as others, including sexism, nationalism, and exclusionary doctrines based on ethnicity, faith, sexual orientation, and disability. Limiting our discussion to "race" doctrines or ideology, however, would miss what should be most important to political scientists, namely, *the role played by states* in establishing, maintaining, and enforcing "race" regimes and the impact of "race" regimes on the subsequent character and functioning of nation-states. As Anthony Marx argues, "states made race": so "[t]he key is to explain *why* states so act" (1998: 2). Racism in some form is in Western civilization, so we need to explain why some nation-states construct "race" regimes and why they do so differently, which challenges us to understand the concrete and different "race" histories of states.

Neither "race" nor racism should be seen simply as the result of psychological aberrations or characteristic only of rogue regimes, as the demonization of South Africa implied. Made by states, "race" regimes have concrete histories. A number of fruitful theories seek to explain these histories. Barbara Fields (1990), for example, theorizes that official, state-administered domination based on "race" began when the modern nation-state emerged. Balibar and Wallerstein locate the origins of contemporary racism in the evolution of capitalism, a consequence of the contradiction between universal tendencies to equal treatment and capitalism's need to make the oppression and exploitation of large groups seem natural and just because they are different. Anthony Marx locates "race" and racism in Western systems of slavery, and colonialism and in nation-state consolidation.

Brutal treatment of out-groups, however, conducted and/or sanctioned by state institutions alone or in tandem with church authorities, occurs earlier in Europe than these accounts suggest. It may be seen in the massacres of Jews in medieval Europe, in the anti-Muslim crusades and wars against the Moors, in the religious persecutions of the fifteenth century, and in the wars against women of the pre-Christian faith (wicca). In each case, differentiation was based on a conflation of faith, culture, and "race." Concerns about *limpieza de sangre,* or purity of blood, for example, motivated laws in Toledo (1449) and Cordova (1474) denying Jews access to political, military, and religious functions (Lianzu, 1999, cited in Paradis, 2000). The virulent combination in 1492 of actions by the Spanish state against the Jews, expelling the Moors and violently destroying American Indigenous civilizations, illustrates the conflation of state violence and hatred of difference that preceded the emergence and consolidation of Europe's nation-states and their globalization into the current nation-state system.

The impulse to expel or exterminate populations considered racially different—however "race" was imagined—is reflected in the modern usage of social science concepts like "society." Australian theorist Barry Hindess argues that using naturalistic concepts like "society" and "citizenship" contributed to a "global organization [based on the nation-state system] . . . rendering the global population governable by dividing it into sub-populations consisting of citizens of discrete, politically independent and competing states" (2000: 2). This partitioning into "societies" made populations governable, and, Hindess concludes, "the emergence of a world both of nations and of 'modern' or 'modernising' societies has depended on the ability of a number of states to each impose a substantial degree of exclusive control over a territory and the population within it" (8). Hindess locates the beginnings of this system of governance of populations that are to be made homogeneous in the Treaty of Westphalia, which established an international system of states wherein all agreed not to intervene in "the rights" of other states in matters of religion. Globalized through colonialism and decolonization, advocates of the framework purported to divide humanity into distinct national populations, assumed to be stable and homogeneous in terms of basic characteristics, as constructed by each nation-state. Privileged insiders of the prosperous nation-states of Europe and in the settler components of the supplanting societies gained considerable benefits from being included as citizens. But the system had few benefits for those supplanted, excluded, or marginalized or for citizens of the postcolonial states exploited in the global political economy.

CONCLUSION

In this chapter I have introduced a set of concepts borrowed or developed in an effort to create a basic conceptual map that I can use to compare "race" regimes as a way of generating theoretical insights. Embedded in this text are definitions for these concepts and several basic hypotheses about how "race" regimes structure state-society relationships in supplanting societies. Also embedded in this text are the outlines of a speculative typology that I am using to compare supplanting societies according to how their states were organized in terms of "race" regimes. This rests on the assumption, however, that there is a significant difference between the process of constructing and regulating "race" in settler/supplanting states and in the core nation-states of Europe. It also involves the proposition that our framework must centre on the settler/supplanting states as a specific type if we are to advance our collective understanding of the politics of "race."

The basic assumptions about supplanting states is that the elites of the dominant "race" or ethnic group used state institutions to create and sustain race regimes that can be defined as a symbiotic combination of force, law, administration, and ideology that practised and legitimated different treatment between the categories of people that the state constructed based on "race" categories and doctrines. Race regimes changed over time, and new regimes were created to regulate differential treatment for new "race" categories. In Canada, the founding "race" regime was internal colonialism in which "civilized, Christian, white Europeans" were set above primitive, pagan "savages." Subsequent "race" regimes addressed Asians—head taxes and "Chinese crimes" (Backhouse, 1999)—non-British Europeans including Slavs, Catholic (black) Irish, and Italians who were incorporated but discriminated against and, more recently, blacks. Moreover, the form of each regime was shaped by those already in existence, and because "race" regimes were integral to the supplanting nation-states, they are hard to undo and remain at a systemic level. This is evident, for example, in the insistence on the deeply held belief that "everybody must obey the law," such that all citizens must be treated exactly the same, despite constitutional guarantees of collective rights as in Indigenous people's collective rights and the rights conferred by the constitutional entrenchment of multiculturalism and equality based on sex and/or gender.

Traditional pluralist thought simply cannot encompass the deep cleavages in settler societies, partly because it is based on an assumption that each nation-state should govern a homogeneous society and partly because the kinds of differences that pluralist analysis envisions are not deep differences like "race." The colonial, settler state was an instrument of deliberate supplantation constructed to manage at least two legal regimes based on criteria framed mainly in terms of "race." These "race" regimes include structures, practices, and ideas used by the dominant elements of the supplanting society to administer relations between/among "races" so as to ensure dominance. "Race" regimes also extended into structures and practices in other social sites such as churches, as the current legal cases against those involved in Canadian residential schools for Natives illustrate. Education and social welfare policies and practices have also been especially implicated.

Finally, I have argued that because "race" regimes were and are fundamental to supplanting nation-states in settler societies, they are especially hard to undo. Despite conscious, good-faith attempts to dismantle "race" regimes, they persist because they remain deeply lodged at a systemic level. This is paralleled by assumptions that homogeneity and sameness are best, assumptions that are deeply lodged in Western political thought and political science paradigms. These assumptions are being challenged, however, as they must be if settler societies like Canada are to transcend the "race" scripts basic to our histories. The first step, however, is to end the denial that currently blocks clear thinking and denies "race" a place in our understanding of politics.

NOTES

I wish to acknowledge the inspiration, encouragement, and support that I received from Ken McRae as an undergraduate student and as a colleague. I also wish to acknowledge the friendship and influence of my colleague Vince Wilson. Finally I wish to acknowledge the support that I have received from the Social Sciences and Humanities Research Council of Canada.

1. I use quotation marks throughout the text to signify that the meaning of "race" is socially constructed, changeable, and problematic. While the existence of "race" as a biological or genetic fact has been repudiated, "race," nonetheless, is real as an aspect of politics, and "race" regimes are a central dimension of politics, especially in the "new,"

"settler" societies on which I focus. "Race" does not just signify the contemporary meaning of people categorized according to physical differences, primarily skin colour and hair types. As Thomas Sowell notes, "the term was once widely used to distinguish the Irish from the English, or the Germans from the Slavs" (1994: 6). Revulsion against Nazi racism and struggles against colonialism, U.S. segregation, and apartheid made older usages unacceptable, and new culture concepts have emerged that focus on "ethnicity," culture, and faith (especially the demonization of Muslims).

2. The concept of a "race" regime is based on Anthony Marx's (1998) idea of a "race order" and on the concept of sex/gender regime that I have developed elsewhere (Vickers, 1997). Marx shows that the "race" orders constructed by different states differ historically. "Race" regimes include "race" categories and doctrines, embedded in legal and administrative practices, through which the state denies or limits citizenship, civil and social rights, and physical mobility. Examples are internal colonialism, slavery, segregation and apartheid, "white Australia"/Canada, multicultural regimes, and democratic racism.

3. A number of terms are used to identify countries where descendants of white settlers dominate the political system over supplanted Indigenous populations and usually also over nonwhite immigrant populations. "New society" or "new nation" was used by Hartz, McRae, and others to signify the "spinning off" of a "fragment" of European society and the creation of a new society around that ideological/social fragment. (See Louis Hartz, *The Founding of New Societies*, New York: Harcourt, Brace and World, 1964). They failed to consider how the social and physical environment, including interaction with Indigenous political forms, also shaped these societies or how the "race" regimes put in place to consolidate the dispossession affected legal systems, state forms, and so on. More recently, the term "settler societies" is used by those focusing on the core–periphery relationships between Europeans and white Creole populations. The term is used by Daiva Stasiulis and Nira Yuval-Davis (1997) to analyse many societies, including Ireland and Israel, where settlers control the state and marginalize the original inhabitants. I have adopted Australian historian David Day's (1996) term "supplanting society," which highlights the fact that "settler colonialism" established societies that were *designed* to supplant Indigenous polities and that this could occur only through the willfull actions (force, law, social policy and education) of those in charge of the colonial state, the settler states, and the eventual nation-states. His concept accommodates the fact that the "settlers," including Australia's transported convicts, were often fleeing religious persecution, poverty, disease, and landlessness and that many were compelled to migrate or were forcibly transported. Nonetheless, the supplanting societies that they entered created these same conditions for the Indigenous peoples whom they supplanted and for other peoples subsequently racialized. Day's analysis also clearly demonstrates that the supplanting society's state continues to sustain and legitimate its claim, although not always as consistently.

4. The term "Euro-American" problematizes the case of the United States, which was "the first new nation" that best epitomized Enlightenment ideas: the brutal eliminator of hundreds of Indian nations in its drive for continental domination; the administrator of a full-fledged slave regime; and pursuers of continental and then global domination under the rubric of "Manifest Destiny." The United States is generally assimilated to European, Enlightenment political theory rather than being understood as a supplanting society. Because the United States is a major originator of one strain of pluralist thought and dominates the character of Western political science, it cannot be treated as "just one more supplanting society." Rather, it created the model and is the key link between European Enlightenment thought and the repression of conscious race doctrines in pluralist thinking and in perpetuating the myth of "the people" in a nation-state. Theories

of "plural societies," which I discuss later, give us a better handle on the United States' actual complex race regimes.

5. I also problematize the concept of "society," suggesting that it is an artefact of globalizing the nation-state system, rather than an organic cultural or social entity that entitles settlers to dispossess others.

6. Adam Kuper's *The Invention of Primitive Society: Transformations of an Illusion* (London: Routledge, 1988) explores the impact of the myth of primitive society on many Western thinkers as transmitted through the discipline of anthropology. Note especially the impact on Marxists and other political theorists who absorbed the myth in the foundations of their theories. Anthropology now largely repudiates the concept, but it remains foundational in other discourses via the concept of "development."

7. Larrimore notes that Herder, by contrast, rejects the word "race," denies the existence of "races," and pleads for an end to efforts to use "colour" for subdividing humanity (1999: 106).

8. See Crenshaw, Kimberly, Gotanda, Neil, Peller, Garry & Thomas, Kendall, eds. *Critical Race Theory: The Key Writings That Formed the Movement* (New York: New Press, 1995); and Aylward for the theoretical discussions. See Backhouse (1999).

9. The term "systemic" or "structural" racism is commonly used in sociology and "race" relations discourse to refer to seemingly neutral, universal rules and practices embedded in social systems that have racist consequences. An example would be the minimum height requirements for being a police officer or firefighter, which had the consequences of excluding Asians and women, who, on average, are shorter in stature than Caucasian men. No conscious intent to discriminate is involved.

10. The subject positions of the white settlers and their descendants where independence was gained slowly are quite confused. Some Canadian and Australian scholars, for example, use postcolonial theory as if it applied to descendants of white settlers as it does to Indigenous peoples or to Africa, Asia, or elsewhere that most of the white settlers and their descendants were forced or chose to leave. That is, white settlers of the dominant group viewed themselves as "colonized by" their European parents, hiding their role as dispossessors of Indigenous peoples and assimilators of other minorities. Members of white minority groups (Boers, French Canadians, etc.) viewed themselves as victims or oppressed by the white majority. Their role in dispossessing Indigenous nations and assimilating other minorities is hidden. Where settlers transported convicts, their position is even more complex.

11. Although immigrants, especially if not of European origin, often have been excluded, oppressed and marginalized, in the summer of 2000 Canadian Fisheries minister Daliwahl, who is of South Asian origins, acted for the government of Canada in enforcing its claim to sovereignty (dominance over territory) against the claims of Indigenous peoples of Burnt Church, Nova Scotia.

12. In both Australia and Canada, when courts have recognized Indigenous rights (as in the *WIK* case in Australia and the *Marshall* and other cases in Canada), governments have shown their loyalties by diminishing or denying even those rights of supplanted people that have been acknowledged by their own courts. The discourse of democracy is used ("everyone must be treated the same", "the interests of the majority must prevail") to justify continuing colonial supplantation. This occurs despite the fact that Canada's Indigenous peoples who live on reserves like Burnt Church have very limited access to the resources from which they can earn a living. This is reflected in an average life expectancy at least 10 years less than for "ordinary" Canadians. Moreover, those "ordinary" Canadians, whose interests are being defended, are reckoned by the United Nations (UN) to rank first on its Human Development Index, with average per capita incomes in 1998 of $19,320 compared to Indigenous peoples living on reserves who

ranked about 63rd with per capita incomes of $6,542. Nor does leaving what is left of their national homelands result in integration into white society; off-reserve Indigenous peoples remained disadvantaged, with average life expectancies five years less and per capita incomes almost $10,000 a year less in 1998.

13. Québec nationalists construct their identity mainly vis-à-vis "les anglais" and view themselves as the main victims of Canadian history because of the "conquest." There is little space in their *imaginaire* for their own participation in, or benefit from, state-administered "race" regimes or racism, a state of mind that most share with the majority of English Canadians.

14. These themes were contested from within Western thought by, for example, Marxism and Romanticism, but while they contest the dominant monist interpretations on many grounds, these theories often also assume the superiority of Europeans over racialized "others."

15. To go beyond settler states would require that we assess how European nation-states were/are affected by their role in administering colonial and abelled ial regimes in which "others" external to the core polity are racialized to legitimate and naturalize their subordination, oppression, and exploitation for the benefit of elites and citizens of the core polity.

3

The Narcissism of Minor Differences: Reflections on the Roots of English Canadian Nationalism

Stephen Brooks

We have probably all had the experience of reading or hearing something that suddenly made the lights go on or at least shine more brightly. This happened to me several years ago when I read an article by Michael Ignatieff,[1] in which he analyzed the conflict between Serbs and Croats in Bosnia using Sigmund Freud's theory that minor differences are often invested with disproportionate meaning as the unconscious' way of channelling aggressive impulses and dealing with the uncomfortable truth of resemblance. Freud called this the narcissism of minor differences.

As a Canadian who teaches American politics and who has lived in a border city—Windsor, Ontario, just across the river from Detroit—for much of his life, Ignatieff's argument and Freud's theory hit me with the force of a revelation. As is probably true of many revelations, this one struck me as being simultaneously obvious and profound. It was as though I could suddenly make sense of a whole scattered set of experiences and observations that spanned three decades as a student and teacher of politics. Books and articles that I have read over the years, conversations that I have had, and observations that I have heard from the café to the classroom acquired a more coherent sense as a result of Ignatieff's aperçu into the psychological wellsprings of a certain sort of nationalism that he argues exists in the Balkans.

The Balkans are a long way from the Canada-United States border, both geographically and in terms of the history that underpins the nationalisms that one finds in these very different parts of the world. But the difference between Ignatieff's Serbian soldier, trying rather unconvincingly to explain what he believes to be the unbridgeable differences between himself and his Croat enemy across the line, and many of my Canadian students and university colleagues, whose faith in the distinctiveness and superiority of Canadian culture is often visceral and unshakable, is not so great. I will argue that it is English Canada's own version of Freud's narcissism of minor differences and that it has existed in an unbroken line from the Loyalist emigration to Canada after the American War of Independence down to the present-day popularity in Canada of ad hominen criticisms of American culture, government, health care, foreign policy, and so on.

NARCISSUS AND NATIONALISM

The myth of Narcissus provides us with the tragic archetype of self-love. Freud used the story of Narcissus in trying to explain why a person—and a people—can hate and deny resemblance to someone who, to all outward appearances, is quite similar to himself or herself. This is a relatively undeveloped aspect of Freudian psychology but one that any student of nationalism is bound to find suggestive, as Ignatieff does. Self-love that operates to nurture and protect the individual's idea of himself or herself is, Freud argues, at the root of "the undisguised antipathies and aversions that people feel toward strangers with whom they have to do." "When this hostility is directed against people who are otherwise loved," he says, "we describe it as ambivalence of feeling [and explain it] in what is probably far too rational a manner, by means of the numerous occasions for conflicts of interest which arise precisely in such intimate relations" (Freud, 1955: 102).

Instead of trying to explain national rivalries and animosities purely in terms of respective material self-interest, strategic concerns, and other rational considerations, Freud suggests that these relations should be understood in the context of the intimate emotional and psychological sentiments that connect two people. Every intimate emotional relationship between two people that endures over time produces, Freud maintains, "a sediment of feelings of aversion and hostility, which only escapes perception as a result of repression" (1955: 101). The same is true of the relations between communal groups linked by the intimacy of their shared history and resemblance to one another. Freud writes, "Every time two families become connected by a marriage, each of them thinks itself superior to or of better birth than the other. Of two neighbouring towns each is the other's most jealous rival; every little canton looks down upon the others with contempt. Closely related races keep one another at arm's length" (101).

A theory of individual and group psychology must be part of any useful explanation of nationalism. Nationalism is about feeling that one belongs to a particular community that is different from other communities in terms of its language, ethnic roots, religion, history, customs, values, or some combination of these. It involves a communal identification, such that those who see themselves as being part of a national community identify more readily with those whom they perceive to be like them, in terms of language, ethnicity, and so on, than with others. It is not necessary that these differences be significant in the eyes of outside observers—Canadians travelling abroad are regularly irritated when they are mistaken for Americans: outside observers often fail to spot the differences—but it is important that those who share the nationalist sentiment believe that these differences are real and important.

This is what Ignatieff is getting at when he argues—no doubt to the outraged disbelief of Croats and Serbs—that the objective cultural differences between them are much less important than what they have in common. They fail to see these similarities, and even deny them at the end of a rifle, because those who interpret their respective histories and control their politics have invested their differences with a grotesquely exaggerated significance that is inherited by each generation from the preceding one, taught in their schools, preached in their churches, and kept alive over their dinner tables.

The key question, Ignatieff perceives, is "What function does this inflation of minor communal differences serve?" Leaving aside the political and economic functions that trumped-up nationalism often serves, we are interested in the psychological role that it performs at the level of the individual. It is one thing to understand why the leaders of a nationalist movement might demand independence for the community that they purport to represent, but perhaps another thing to understand why those on whose behalf they claim to speak buy into the same characterization of their nation and how it differs from that of its neighbours.

The concept of neighbour is crucial. When Narcissus looked into the pool, he saw the reflection of someone whom he believed to be another but who was also close by. Identities and self-perceptions are necessarily reflective. We understand who we are in relation to those who are close by, our neighbours or "significant others," as social scientists might prefer. Not all others are significant in terms of telling us something about who we are and who we are not. As an English Canadian, I don't make sense of who I am and what my society's history signifies by comparing myself and those who share my history to Fiji Islanders or Finns. This is not mere parochialism on my part. The sense of self is not forged autistically, free from external influences and reactions. It responds to, and is shaped by, what I learn about myself from others. Likewise, my sense of belonging to a community defined by its blood, history, language, or values is unlikely to develop haphazardly, so that the Fiji Islander is infinitely less important in telling me who I am than is my American neighbour.

Our neighbours matter in telling us important things about who we are—or think we are—as individuals and members of communities, but there obviously is more to nationalism than this. The *nature* of our relationship to our neighbour(s) is also crucial. As a Canadian, my American neighbours necessarily loom large in the reality and imagination of my countrymen and myself. Canadians, on the other hand, are of marginal significance at best in the imaginative life of Americans. To put this rather differently, it is virtually impossible for an English Canadian to talk about the culture and political ideas of his or her society without reference—direct or implied—to American society. It would be a rare American, however, who would give any thought to Canada in explaining what it means to be an American. Canadians tend to be extremely sensitive about the similarities and differences between Americans and themselves. Americans tend to be unaware and unconcerned about such putative differences, thinking of Canadians—if they think of them at all—as rather nice, inoffensive, generally similar to themselves, and certainly unimportant. This is part of what infuriates many Canadians, *the failure of the significant other to recognize them and to acknowledge their distinctiveness.* (As an aside, one of the great ironies of Canadian politics is that the same failure of many English Canadians to recognize and acknowledge the distinctiveness of French Canada helps fuel Québec nationalism.)

English Canadian nationalism is rooted in an insecurity that goes back to the origins of English Canadian society. It is, as David Bell and Lorne Tepperman argue in *The Roots of Disunity* (1979: Chapter 3), founded upon an unresolved identity crisis that requires two things: (1) denial of the fundamental cultural similarities that exist between Canadians and Americans and (2) the exaggeration of relatively minor differences and the creation of a self-image that explains and justifies why English Canada is not American.

I do not intend to argue that the cultural differences between Americans and English Canadians are insignificant, but merely that they are no more important—and perhaps less important—than the differences between New Englanders and Nebraskans or between second-generation Latino Americans and second-generation Asian Americans. It is because the real differences are comparatively small that, following Freud, they loom so large in the imagination of English Canadians. The mechanism at work here is not, however, purely psychological. The interests and behaviour of political and cultural elites in English Canada have done much to encourage a widespread belief among members of the general public that these differences are more significant than they are in reality.

Ignatieff argues that "enemies need each other to remind themselves of who they really are (1993: 14). This, he says, is a corollary of the narcissism of minor differences. But they also need politicians, historians, teachers, journalists, and other opinion leaders to keep alive the belief that the differences exist, that they matter, and indeed that they matter a good deal, lest the general population be inclined to lose focus. Nationalism must be sold and resold, particularly when the reality of the cultural gap separating two peoples is comparatively narrow.

It may not be obvious why minor differences, pace Ignatieff, should engender greater animosity and loom larger in the imagination of a people than objectively greater differences like language or religion. Freud suggests that the explanation lies in the psychic mechanism by which identity is formed and aggressive impulses are held in check. Bell and Tepperman make a broadly similar argument in characterizing Canadians' centuries-old insistence on their cultural distinctiveness from Americans as the necessary psychological denial they had to make in the face of their obvious similarities to a people and a society upon which they turned their backs and in whose long shadow they were destined to live. All of this strikes me as being close to the mark. In order to understand the ambivalence and occasional hostility of English Canadians toward Americans and, above all, the hugely significant role that the United States occupies in English Canadians' self-image, one must understand the psychology of identity formation but also the particular historical circumstances of Canada's relationship to the United States.

While in the realm of psychology, I cannot resist the temptation to introduce another Freudian concept that may be less important in explaining Ignatieff's conundrum of trumped-up differences between Serbs and Croats than it is to an understanding of English Canadian identity and nationalism. This involves Freud's theory of penis envy, a theory that is well known and so requires no explanation here. Suffice it to say that, applied to cultural rivalries and nationalist animosities, it suggests that feelings of resentment, hate, derision, or superiority may be the product of an involuted desire to be like or have something that the object of these negative projections is or has. That something may be wealth, power (or something that symbolizes power), respect, territory, confidence, achievements of some sort, or love.

This last—love—may be particularly important. Operas and literature tell us that few things hurt more than unrequited love. I have observed on countless occasions the resentment that Canadians experience when American presidents forget that Canada, not Japan or China, is and has long been the United States' major trading partner or when Americans cannot name Canada's prime minister. A popular Canadian television programme, the political satire *This Hour Has 22 Minutes,* includes a regular feature called "Conversations with Americans." The gag is simple: the Canadian host, Rick Mercer, asks Americans questions that are obviously ridiculous to Canadians and full of false information. For example, in one well-publicized case Mercer asked the Republican presidential candidate, George W. Bush, what he thought of Canadian prime minister Jean Poutine's statement that Bush was the best candidate to lead the free world. The Canadian prime minister was Jean Chretien. Poutine is a snack much loved in Québec, consisting of   abell fries smothered in gravy and cheese curds.

Canadians typically react with merriment and much head-shaking about "those stupid Americans." But the joke is funny only because of the perceived slight, the bitter hurt at the centre of the humour. Americans don't pay attention to us. They don't know anything about us. They don't love us. The Canadian reaction is to deny the injury by transforming it into a joke, the butt of which is Americans. This easily slides into a sort of humour and mockery that partake of a smug sense of superiority (we know who their president is, but they don't know our prime minister!). But an independent outside observer would find the joke much less funny and perhaps fail to understand it at all. After all, a Brit might ask, why should Americans know that the Canadian prime minister's name is not Jean Poutine?

Some will reject this argument out of hand, arguing that America has nothing that Canadians long for and that the benign ignorance that most Americans have when it comes to Canada is an indication of American selfcentredness, not Canadian insecurity. What is there to envy, they ask, in America's high crime rate, unresolved, racebased tensions, great inequality in wealth, urban decay, and swaggering globo-cop behaviour? But I suspect that even the virulence of even the most anti-American Canadian nationalist is sharpened by a subconscious awareness that Canada, for all its insistence to be a society superior to that of the United States, does not really matter much in the global scheme of things nor in the modern history of the world, whereas the

United States most certainly does. The enormous injustice of the world's failure to recognize the importance and worthiness of Canada is too much to bear. It both deepens the envy and generates a reaction in the form of exaggerated notions of self-importance and accomplishments in the eyes of others.

This is a phenomenon that is almost certainly not peculiar to Canada but is characteristic of small countries that have been destined by fate to live in the shadow of grander neighbours. For example, having lived for some time in Belgium I have noticed that even relatively modest accomplishments—being home to the cartoonist Hergé, creator of the internationally known Tintin, producing pralines and beers that are recognized abroad for their excellence, or Julius Caesar's acknowledgement of the bravery and mettle of the *Belgas,* the forebearers of today's Belgians—become sources of great pride that can be trotted out when the achievements of bigger, more powerful neighbours remind Belgians that the world tends to ignore them or at least not take them as seriously as their German, French, or even Dutch neighbours. Nonetheless, I will speak of the case that I know best, that being Canada.

RESENTMENT AND CANADIAN NATIONALISM

For many years now the United Nations (UN) has published annual rankings of countries according to its Human Development Index, a measure that combines average longevity, infant mortality, real purchasing power, and average years of formal education. Canada has been ranked first among the world's countries in most years, an achievement that invariably generates considerable publicity and pride in Canada. And why not? An educated, healthy, and wealthy population ought to be a source of pride, and it would be surprising if the politicians and citizens of the country ranked best in the world on a composite measure of such things did not crow about it a bit.

Whether Canada is the best country in the world in which to live is not the question (nor, for that matter, is it the sort of question that can be answered objectively). The question is why, beyond the normal pride that one takes in being told that one has done well, the UN's ranking of Canada on its Human Development Index assumes such great importance in Canada, being commonly interpreted by Canadians as meaning that their country is acknowledged by others as the world's best to live in. I would suggest that this is best understood as a plea for recognition that is rooted in insecurity, not confidence. "The lady doth protest too much, methinks," says the Queen when she sees her infidelity acted before her eyes in *Hamlet.* Likewise, there is probably more than a little of Hamlet's Queen in Canadians' self-congratulations over the UN ranking, as though they need to convince themselves that they are worthy and—the subtext is almost always lurking in the background—better than the brassier, bigger society to the south of them.

Denied recognition and resentment are certainly at the core of the narcissism of minor differences that is observable in the manner in which English Canadians define their identity. On a visit to one of the United States most prestigious universities, a short distance from the Canadian border, I was told by the chair of the political science department that his students know *nothing*—the "nothing" was emphasized—about Canada. He merely confirmed what most Canadians already know and resent, namely, that even well-educated Americans, opinion leaders, and policy makers typically have little information about, or interest in, Canada.

The resentment at the core of English Canadian nationalism was the theme of a hugely popular and much discussed beer ad produced for Molson Brewery's top-selling *Canadian* brand in the spring of 2000. The television ad featured a young male adult on a stage who, with a background of images showing the stereotypes that Canadians believe Americans have of them, becomes increasingly strident and forceful in declaring what Canada and Canadians are not ("I am not . . ."), and what they are ("I am . . ."). Almost all of his short speech is either explicitly or implicitly comparative, contrasting putative features of Canada to those of the United States. The ad became the centrepiece of Canadian Heritage Minister Sheila Copps' presentation at the International Press Institute's World Congress in Boston in May 2000. Copps, known to be a strong Canadian nationalist, stated that Canadians resent people (read "Americans") who do not recognize or who attach little weight to the differences between Canadians and their southerly neighbours. In this she was certainly correct. But is smoldering resentment truly proof of national identity or lack of confidence that one's identity is distinctive and secure?

The nationalist beer ad used, in fact, a familiar format. Twenty years earlier Canada's foremost popular historian, Pierre Berton, wrote a book entitled *Why We Act Like Canadians* (1982). Written as a series of letters to an imaginary uncle by the name of Sam—as in Uncle Sam—the book could just as well have been called "Why We Are Not Americans." It is an extended *apologia* for Canadian separateness and distinctiveness that is inspired by the awareness that others, particularly Americans, typically are unaware of what is special about the Canadian condition and that constantly refers to points of difference between Canadian and American society, culture, institutions, history, and geography.

Ignored and not understood by their great neighbour to the south, the resentment that Canadians feel could take various forms. One option is retreat into irony. Canadians could choose to laugh at themselves and temper their pride in their history and accomplishments and their insistence on cultural uniqueness with a self-deprecating humour that dulls the edge of their resentment. This sense of irony is found among Belgians, to some degree. The humour of having a metre-tall peeing boy—Manneken-pis—as a symbol of their country or Tintin, the journalist whose nearly featureless visage travels the globe in search of the adventure not to be found at home, is not lost on Belgians. Irony does occasionally surface in Canadians' reactions to the world's failure (or, at least, Americans' failure) to treat them as seriously as they think they deserve. The radio and television comedy of *The Royal Canadian Air Farce* and *This Hour Has 22 Minutes*—both produced by the state-owned Canadian Broadcasting Corporation—often assumes an ironic or satirical stance that pokes fun at Canadian culture. On the whole, however, irony is not the preferred method of coping with the resentment that Heritage Minister Copps correctly claims

Canadians feel when what they believe to be their uniqueness and special accomplishments are not recognized.

Irony requires the introversion of the other's reaction to oneself, transforming the pain of not being recognized or being mistaken for something/someone that one is not into a sort of self-deprecating joke. A second option that relies on an introverted response involves self-loathing and embrace of the other. Perhaps I matter as little as others appear to think? Perhaps my history and accomplishments are second-rate and undeserving of recognition? In order to be recognized and have my self-worth affirmed, perhaps I need to be more, not less, like the other. The path out of a frustrating resentment, in this case, is reached through a closer identification with the other and a denial of difference.

One of the important ways in which this second form of introverted resentment operates in Canada may be seen in the realms of popular culture, sport, and, increasingly, the job market for those with skills on which the globalized economy places a high value. It is a cliché of Canadian culture that Canadians know that one of their own is good when he or she "makes it" in the United States. This is at least as old as Mary Pickford, the Canadian-born star of Hollywood's silent era. American television, Hollywood, and the popular music industry include a large number of Canadians who have "made the big time" and whose Canadian-ness is known to almost all Canadians but seldom to Americans. By taking pride in the Canadian origins of William Shatner, Mike Meyers, Jim Carrey, Peter Jennings, Shania Twain, Céline Dion, Alanis Morrisette, Donald Sutherland, and Pamela Anderson, Canadians implicitly accept that recognition in the United States is the measure of real success. Canadians who succeed in American professional sports (except hockey, where it is expected that Canadians will excel) likewise are perceived to have achieved a level of accomplishment that is attainable only outside their country.

The pride that Canadians take when one of their own succeeds in the American market is often an ambivalent one. Success is fine, but a Canadian who makes it in the United States is expected to remember and remain faithful to his or her Canadian origins. This creates a paradox: the price of success in the United States is to hide or shed all signs of Canadian-ness and fit seamlessly into American culture, but one is expected to maintain an attachment to Canada and continue to feel like a Canadian, whatever this might mean. The paradox is usually not difficult to resolve because demonstration of a continuing attachment to Canada generally does not require more than occasional polite acknowledgment of Canadian influences on one's life and career and a willingness to accept Canadian tributes (honorary degrees from universities, interviews on Canadian radio and television, appearances at Canadian artistic award ceremonies, etc.).

It is common in Canada, as it is in many other countries, to deride American mass culture as vulgar and manipulative. Interestingly, this seems not to diminish the satisfaction that most Canadians feel when a compatriot sinks to the depths of what Hollywood can offer. It seems that the fact of recognition and success is enough to slake the thirst of nationalist resentment.

Canadians who succeed as journalists, engineers, computer specialists, scientists, or any of the other globalized professions that Robert Reich and others describe as a sort of new dominant class in the global economy are also a source of pride, and so while Canadians anguish over the "brain drain" to the United States, they are at the same time proud that Canadians can compete and scramble to the top in what they perceive to be the more fiercely competitive American market. The sentiments expressed in the following conversation between two well-educated Canadians, one of whom stayed in Canada and the other of whom had been working for ten years as a radio producer in New York at the time of the conversation, probably are fairly typical:

HER: It's interesting because I talk about you often, and I talk about you as my brother who's gone off to live in the United States, and I talk about you with a good deal of pride. People certainly respond by being very impressed, but there's that sense in which, you know, you'll be a celebrity because you're my brother who lives in the States and you live this highly sophisticated life, and you live in New York City, and everyone's deeply impressed by this, *but you wouldn't be of us.*

I think the perception would be very different if you had done the very same thing over the last ten years in London, England. I think you would be perceived as being more Canadian still, than having gone to the United States for ten years. I suspect it might even be true if you had gone to another European country, that you would still be perceived as being more Canadian than you would be perceived now.

HIM: But there's a way, because of the place that the United States has in the Canadian imagination, that going to America has a very special flavour to it. It means something.

HER: Yes, yes.

HIM: And what is that? What does it mean?

HER: Well, I mean not to put too fine a point on it, but in some ways *it is going over to the other side.* [2]

The significant other whose approval is craved and needed to provide reassurance of one's worth is embraced through a sister's pride in the success of her sibling in the United States. At the same time, the need to maintain an identity separate from the other and a loyalty to some idea of Canada and Canadian-ness, no matter how nebulous, is protected through the belief that he is still Canadian and is only in a sort of temporary exile from his proper home and condition.

A third method of dealing with the resentment that is generated by non-recognition involves an extroverted response. Anger and hatred of the other are one possibility. Ridicule and the projection onto the other of an image of stupidity or some other defect are another possibility. Both of these are encountered among some Canadian nationalists. Ridicule of Americans as stupid, ignorant, and gullible is at the heart of comedian Rick Mercer's popular "Conversations with Americans" segment of CBC television's *This Hour Has 22 Minutes.* Jokes and stories about Americans crossing the border with their snow skis in July or thinking that Ontario is an American state are commonplace among Canadians. Resentment is transformed into perceived inadequacy on the part of the other.

Dislike of Americans and things American, ranging from mild repugnance to visceral hatred, is also not uncommon among Canadians. On a personal note I can attest that I have often had Canadian students in my American politics courses tell me how much they dislike what they believe are the typical characteristics of Americans and their society. It usually turns out that their dislike is based on uninformed or wrongly informed caricatures and stereotypes that, taken together, are not much better than the absence of information and impressions that their American counterparts have when it comes to them. Anyone who has spent any amount of time in the social science milieux of Canadian universities surely knows that students are routinely exposed to a good deal of critical and negative analysis—analysis is probably too grand and dignified a word for much of it—of American society, politics, history, culture, and so on. University professors in the social sciences and humanities tend to be more liberal than most segments of the population, and in Canada the social science professoriat serves the additional function of being one of the chief bastions of nationalism (this is true in both English Canada and French-speaking Québec). Acquaintances of mine who teach secondary school tell me that a steady diet of anti-Americanism starts earlier than university, and indeed it would be surprising if those who are taught by nationalist sociologists, political scientists, historians, and communication studies professors do not absorb and in their turn impart the anti-American ideas they learned while in university.

My point here is not to rebut the arguments, correct the inaccuracies, and dispell the misperceptions that are encouraged by what I am characterizing as anti-American teaching. There is more crime in the United States than in Canada. Race-based conflict is a much more serious problem in America. Serial killers, school yard killings, and frightening cases of random violence occur more often there than in Canada. All this and more is true, and if one wishes to draw conclusions from such facts, that is fair enough.

My point, rather, is to understand the social psychological function that nationalist dislike of America serves. If we accept my premise that resentment is at the heart of Canadian nationalism, then it becomes clear that dislike of the other can be a useful response to these feelings of resentment. This may be formulated as a psychological libretto: I am ignored by the one whose attention and recognition matter most to me. Denied love, I will deny that this matters. I will transform my love into hate and protect myself from a conscious acknowledgment of my insecurity and rejection by focusing on the faults of the one who spurns me. Who would wish the attention and love of such a flawed creature?

This will strike many as being a ridiculously twisted interpretation of the dislike that many Canadians feel toward the United States. I would not argue that the mechanism that I have described operates in every case. For example, I have a university colleague whose ostensible reasons for disliking American society are not uncommon among Canadian academics and appear to be based on the gap between his own collectivist values and his perception of the United States as a place characterized by socially corrosive individualism and an unhealthy worship of private markets and profits. Nevertheless, I think that it would be a mistake to dismiss the role that sublimated resentment plays in generating nationalist dislike toward America and Americans.

The important role that resentment plays in English Canadian nationalism was recognized many years ago by Canada's foremost literary critic, Northrop Frye. In *The Bush Garden* he wrote,

> The imaginative Canadian stance, so to speak, facing east and west, has on one side one of the most powerful nations in the world; on the other there is the vast hinterland of the north, with its sense of mystery and fear of the unknown, and the curious guilt feelings that its uninhabited loneliness seems to inspire in this exploiting age. If the Canadian faces south, he becomes either hypnotized or repelled by the United States: either he tries to think up unconvincing reasons for being different and somehow superior to Americans, or he accepts being "swallowed up by" the United States as inevitable. *What is resented in Canada about annexation to the United States is not annexation itself, but the feeling that Canada would disappear into a larger entity without having anything of any real distinctiveness to contribute to that entity: that, in short, if the United States did annex Canada it would notice nothing except an increase in natural resources.* (1971: iv)

To be considered little more than real estate is the final indignity.

INTELLECTUALS AND THE NATIONALIST PROJECT

In discussing the conflict between Serbs and Croats in Bosnia, Ignatieff writes, "Ethnic difference *per se* was not responsible for the nationalistic politics that emerged in the Yugoslavia of the 1980s. Consciousness of ethnic difference turned into nationalist hatred only when the surviving communist elites, beginning with Serbia, began manipulating nationalist emotions in order to cling to power" (1993: 16-17). Particularly when peoples share a language and resemble one another in many aspects of their lifestyles, social institutions, and history, a push is needed to sharpen popular awareness of the differences between them and their neighbours. That push is regularly provided by elites who use nationalism as the vehicle for promoting their self-interested ends. In the former Yugoslavia it was the political elites who, according to Ignatieff, deliberately fanned popular awareness of national differences into inter-communal hatred. The promotion of nationalist consciousness and the vilification of the other may be encouraged by other elites as well, including economic and cultural/intellectual elites.

The important role of elites in promoting and even creating nationalism is too well known to require elaboration here. Instead, I wish briefly to sketch the crucial contribution that English Canadian intellectuals have played in defining and promoting nationalism. Indeed, I think that it is only a mild exaggeration to say that without the efforts and support of the intellectual community—I am casting this net broadly to include professors, writers and other artists, teachers, journalists, film-makers, and others involved in the production and communication of information and images about Canada—Canadian nationalism would soon wither. As it is, nationalism in English Canada is a rather fragile patient kept alive largely through a state-financed life support system.

The early history of nationalism in English Canada was dominated by economic and political elites. The industrial strategy embodied in the National Policy of 1879, including high tariffs to protect Canadian manufacturers from American competition, the construction of a railway line stretching across the country, and the populating of the west has been characterized by the historian A.R.M. Lower as a frank creation of vested business interests. Intellectuals had nothing to do with this nationalist policy. It represented, rather, a dovetailing of interests—those of the central Canadian economic elite and those of that segment of the political elite represented by the Conservative Party of Sir John A. Macdonald. This was nationalism in the service of the state elite and the dominant faction of the business class.

Early English Canadian nationalism was not entirely about rejecting the United States and protecting Canadian producers from American competition. During the first half of the twentieth century there was increasing restiveness among some members of the intellectual and political elites over the quasi-colonial ties that bound Canada to Britain. The 1926 confrontation between Liberal Prime Minister Mackenzie King and Governor-General Lord Byng was a flash point for Canadian resentment against what was seen to have become inappropriate imperial intervention in Canadian domestic affairs. The Balfour Declaration (1926), the Statute of Westminister (1931), the end of the Judicial Committee of the Privy Council's role as final appellate court for Canada (1949), and the replacement of the Red Ensign by the Canadian Maple Leaf flag (1964) all were symbolically important steps toward ending the surviving vestiges of colonialism—vestiges that almost certainly were much less important to the general population than they were to some members of the political and intellectual elites.

Both when it has been directed against the remnants of British imperial rule and when it has been targeted at American influences, nationalism in English Canada has been an affair of the elites with only tepid or, I would argue, manipulated support from the general population. As Philip Resnick observes,

> There have been few genuinely grass-roots movements to articulate English-Canadian nationalism. The Canada First movement of the 1870s was a small elite grouping of passing importance. The League for Public Broadcasting was a good deal more successful in mobilizing support for its particular objectives, establishment of the CBC, in the 1930s, but could hardly go beyond this. The Committee for an Independent Canada, while on paper a large organization, with 200,000 members at its height about 1970, proved ephemeral. (1990: 212).

Commenting on the rise of aggressive anti-American nationalism in English Canadian intellectual circles during the 1960s, the liberal historian Frank Underhill wrote,

> On this subject of continentalism, may it not be that our ordinary rank-and-file Canadians have shown a deeper instinctive wisdom than most of our leaders?

The leaders have been busy with the high mission of saving the northern half of the continent from Americanism, while thousands, millions of ordinary Canadians, French as well as English, have quietly emigrated and become American citizens. The leaders of 1867 were proud of setting up a national community that was not a populist democracy like the United States . . . [but] steadily since then, while obediently saying yes to their leaders, the Canadian people have been adopting the American way of life. (1966: xix)

Plus ça change, plus c'est la même chose. The radical disconnect between the nationalism of some parts of the Canadian political elite and the masses can be observed on a nearly daily basis. I will give just one example that strikes me as particularly revealing. For many years Canadian ministers of health have been expected to rail against the American health care system as inequitable ("two-tiered") and grossly inefficient, compared to Canada's allegedly more egalitarian, less wasteful system. Under Liberal Minister of Health Alan Rock, known to be a left-of-center Liberal, this art was perfected. It is doubtful that a week went by during his tenure as health minister when Rock did not warn Canadians of the dangers of "American-style two-tiered" health care. At the same time as Rock was issuing these dire warnings on the health care front, and his nationalist cabinet colleague, Heritage Minister Sheila Copps, was calling for greater protection of Canadian culture from American influences, thousands of Canadians continued to emigrate to the United States in what most observers acknowledged was a serious brain drain.

Of course, one can assume the high intellectual ground that nationalist intellectuals favor and regret the cupidity and Philistine insensibilities of those who see themselves as economic refugees fleeing higher taxes and lower real incomes in Canada. My point is not to pass judgment on the nationalist project that has its greatest support in the political and intellectual elites of English Canada but simply to point out that it does not ignite the passions of most Canadians nor even interest them particularly. The resentment that causes Canadians to laugh at Rick Mercer's "Conversations with Americans" and to shake their heads when it comes to light that yet another American political leader does not know the name of Canada's prime minister—and may not even be aware that we have a prime minister and not a president—is not easily mobilized by nationalist elites into policies that restrict popular access to American culture or require that Canadians pay a premium for the preservation of their putative distinctiveness.

CONCLUSION

Nationalism in English-speaking Canada has existed for over two centuries, since the Loyalist emigrants from the United States to British North America struggled to reconcile the psychologically inconvenient facts of their decision to reject American democracy and independence from Britain and, on the other hand, their obvious and undeniable similarity to the American society that they spurned. This nationalism lives on today in the form of sentiments ranging from visceral dislike of American society and values, to a mild belief in the superiority of Canada as a gentler, more tolerant, more egalitarian place than its southern neighbour. At the popular level these feelings of dislike and belief in Canadian superiority are based largely on resentment, a seldom acknowledged anger that the uniqueness and worth of Canada and Canadians are not recognized and appreciated by the significant other in whose shadow Canadian history has unfolded and to whom Canada has always been linked by ties of both material interest and emotional intimacy.

At the level of elites and, in particular, important segments of the political and intellectual elites, this nationalism is no less generated by unconscious resentment. However, the anti-Americanism of these elites serves the additional self-interested function of affirming their own importance and that of the institutions and policies that represent and nurture the nationalist project in English-speaking Canada. They are the priesthood of this nationalism, but their ability to inspire fervour among the faithful has never been strong, and the church shows signs of finally crumbling under the pressure of spiritual defections to what one Canadian aptly describes as "the other side."

NOTES

1. Ignatieff's analysis was subsequently republished (1993: Chapter 1).

2. From Act 4 of "Who's Canadian?," an episode in National Public Radio's *This American Life* series, produced by WBEZ Chicago and first broadcast May 30, 1997. All episodes of *This American Life* may be accessed free of charge over the Internet.

PART II

CONSOCIATIONALISM REVISITED

4

Accommodating Multinationality: Is the European Commission a Case of Consociational or Weberian Administration?

Liesbet Hooghe

The tension between majority rule and nonmajoritarian rule is present in every plural democracy. Yet students of divided societies have rarely ventured outside the traditional boundaries of national politics to study the conditions of rule in transnational settings. Kenneth McRae's recent work on linguistic politics in the European Union is the exception that proves the rule.[1] Conversely, only recently have European integration scholars begun to apply in any systematic fashion concepts and categories developed in the rich literature on plural democracies. In this chapter I draw from the plural democracy literature to shed light on the accommodation of multinational diversity in the European Union.

More than twenty-five years ago, Ken McRae wrote in his introduction to *Consociational Democracy* that "Canadians, whatever their other advantages and providential blessings, do not possess the best political system in the world.... [U]nquestioning acceptance of Anglo American norms in the Canadian political system has not served Canada well, and closer study might suggest modifications that would make that system more responsive to Canada's diversified social structure. Many Canadians have envisioned a political system that would fashion a more integrated Canadian society; the real problem is to find one that will reflect and support its continuing diversity" (McRae, 1974b: vii). Questioning the usefulness of majoritarian institutions for a bilingual, increasingly binational Canada, McRae invited his country fellows to examine the merits of nonmajoritarian rule, more particularly; consociationalism, for the accommodation of Canada's two nascent nations.

The European Union (EU) is the first serious candidate to become a democracy beyond national boundaries. It is also a plural polity where politics is, to a significant degree, shaped by institutionalized conflict among fifteen nationalities. The notion that the European Union has been transformed from a mere regime for economic collaboration among sovereign states into a polity is of recent vintage (see Caporaso, 1996; Hix, 1994; Hooghe and Marks, 1999; Marks, 1992; Risse, 1996; Sbragia, 1992, 1993; Schmitter, 1996, 1999). This different starting point explains partly why, contrary to Canadians in the 1960s, EU observers have rarely seriously considered a strict majoritarian model for the European Community, at least up until now. Nonmajoritarian models have always seemed more appropriate and desirable. Some students have applied the theory of consociationalism (Chryssochoou, 1998; Gabel, 1998; Taylor, 1991, 1997). Indeed, many EU features resemble those found in national consociational democracies (McRae, 1974a for an overview): highly institutionalized national segments; elite accommodation facilitated through vetoes, grand coalitions, and segmental autonomy; a historical inclination among elites to avoid the majority principle. More often, though, scholars use the concept of nonmajoritarianism in the pluralist or Madisonian sense, which aims to share, disperse, limit, and delegate power rather than concentrate unlimited power in the hands of the (elected) majority. Applying insights from federalism, Alberta Sbragia has drawn attention to territorial forms of nonmajoritarian rule in the European Union, intended to ensure to diverse territorial interests decisional participation and autonomy (Sbragia, 1993). Philippe Schmitter has proposed a complex patchwork of practices that would streamline citizenship (through, e.g., an explicit bill of rights), structures of representation, and decision making in primarily nonmajoritarian fashion (Schmitter, 1999; see also Grande, 1998; Scharpf on decision making, 1999). To lighten the decisional burden in the multinational European Union, Giandomenico Majone has made the case for devolving certain decisions to politically independent institutions such as courts, a central bank, or regulatory agencies (Majone, 1996, 1998).

However, with the European polity coming of age, some reforms for remedying Europe's democratic deficit appear inspired by a majoritarian logic. For example, according to the Amsterdam Treaty (1997), the commission president and the commission as a whole must have the confidence of a majority of the European Parliament. The bulk of legislation, including all internal market legislation and much of environmental and regional policy, is now codecided between a qualified majority (70 percent of votes) in the Council of Ministers and a majority in the European Parliament. A number of proposals currently debated have a majoritarian tinge, most prominently, suggestions to limit the presence of small countries in the commission and the council presidency so as to enhance efficiency (see Dehousse, 1995; Majone, 1998). As the European polity deepens and pressures for democratization grow, contestation about the desirable balance between majoritarian and nonmajoritarian properties of rule is likely to increase.

Considerable scholarly capital is being invested in how the tension between majority rule and nonmajoritarian rule is to shape the EU democracy to be. These system-level issues are important, but they lie mainly in the future. In contrast, this very same tension has dominated now for almost fifty years the working of the EU's central state institution: the European Commission. In the commission, two opposing conceptions of political-bureaucratic organization have struggled for dominance, each of which can be interpreted as the functional expression of a majoritarian and nonmajoritarian logic. The Weberian ideal-type articulates majoritarian principles. Merit shapes personnel selection and task organization, and legal-rational criteria guide policy making. Administrative relations are primarily hierarchical as power and direction emanate from the top. In this world, civil servants' attitudes and behavior are expected to reflect a uniform, general public interest rather than sectional interests. The second ideal-type may be abelled consociational, and it reflects nonmajoritarian standards. Jobs and tasks are distributed according to the principle of proportionality among constituent segments, while a concern for consensus and recognition of each group's vital interests shape policy making. Relations among civil servants are not based on hierarchy but are characterized by deliberation. In such a system, civil servants essentially act as "umpires" in a political game among segmental elites, or, more often, they are sounding boards—perhaps even ambassadors—for the beliefs and desires of "their" segment. Few national bureaucracies fit either one type perfectly, but it is clear that some—say the British or French—lean to the Weberian end, while others—the Austrians or Belgians—resemble the consociational type.

In the European Union, the clash between consociational and Weberian principles of political administrative organization is nowhere as acute as in the European Commission, the EU's executive-bureaucratic core. How do commission officials deal with the fact that their colleagues have different national backgrounds and that their main clients are national governments with divergent interests? Do senior commission officials consider themselves guardians of a general European interest that transcends national particularities? Or do they regard themselves as responsive to, and representative of, contending national concerns? I examine these questions with the help of data collected between July 1995 and May 1997 from interviews with 137 senior commission officials of Al or A2 grade and mail questionnaires from 105 of these people. These are the director-generals, deputy director-generals, directors, and principal advisers.

Disagreement about Weberian or consociational principles of organization in the commission is not new. The commission, or more accurately its European Coal and Steel Commission predecessor, the High Authority, was originally conceived as an unambiguously Weberian organization (Coombes, 1970; Duchêne, 1994). The first president of the High Authority, Jean Monnet, crafted a small, highly professional team of permanent officials who were to embody a higher European interest, formulate common problems and solutions to the College of Commissioners, and persuade on their behalf national representatives to adopt supranational arrangements (Monnet, 1962).[2] However, in line with consociational theory, as EU competencies have grown, national governments have become increasingly reluctant to let control over European governance slip. This is reflected in the growth of the council machinery to counterbalance the commission's organizational resources and in the expansion of comitology in the 1970s and 1980s to curb the commission's executive autonomy. It underlies more recent attempts to control the commission from the inside through national quotas for recruitment, influence on the appointment of top officials (most particularly, through parachutage, discussed later), by questioning tenure for commission officials and by encouraging their substitution with seconded national officials.

Against the backdrop of this ongoing tug-of-war between institutions, how do we explain where current top officials stand on merit versus national representation in the commission? The next section describes in a nutshell Weberian and consociational principles in the commission's rules of operation, and it presents top officials' views on these. I then develop hypotheses to explain variation in orientations. One line of theorizing explores to what extent officials' pro- or con-orientations to Weberian/consociational principles in the commission may be the result of socialization. For example, one may expect nationals from countries with a "Weberian" tradition to have internalized Weberian values. Similarly, it seems plausible that longer-serving officials have learned to defend the EU public interest, while recent recruits are probably still steeped in national identities and interests. A second approach rests on the assumption that officials are rational actors who bring their beliefs in line with the institutional opportunities that are available to them. In other words, officials' orientations on the consociational character of the commission may be a function of their utility to material goals, most particularly, professional success. When I test these hypotheses against the interview data, I find socialization to be a surprisingly weak influence on officials' orientations. Whether officials support a consociational or Weberian commission is more strongly associated with how these principles affect their career chances.

THE COMMISSION AND NATIONALITY

The organization of the commission reflects primarily consociational principles. For recruitment and promotion at top levels, proportionality and extensive consultation of national representatives prevail. Senior posts are divided among nationalities according to quotas that roughly reflect the distribution of votes in the Council of Ministers, although in reality the larger countries receive a somewhat larger proportion. A subset of these top positions is de facto reserved for particular nationalities. In commission-speak, these positions have a "flag." Furthermore, external candidates may be attracted for top bureaucratic positions if no suitable internal candidate can be found. This is called parachutage. While this practice has declined over the last decade, still, nearly half of senior appointments are recruited through parachutage ; the other half are career commission officials. The influential role of national governments in the selection of these parachutists is well documented (Ross, 1995; Nugent, 1995; Page, 1997). Finally, commission cabinets broker senior appointments. Each political commissioner—two each for the five largest member states and one for small member states—has a group of five to ten political aides, who are almost always of the same nationality as their commissioner. Negotiations for top appointments tend to take place between the cabinet of the commissioner with functional responsibility over the vacant post, the cabinet of the commissioner for personnel (or, for the most important positions, the commission president's cabinet), and the cabinet of the commissioner of the nationality of the applicants. The role of cabinets in recruitment and promotion of senior officials has increased over the last decade (Nugent, 1995; Ross, 1995). The influence of the cabinets reaches also beyond personnel policy deep into the policy-making process. Because of their unique consociational characteristics, commissioners and their cabinets have been described as "national enclaves" (Michelmann, 1978; see also Egeberg, 1995; Nugent, 1995; Peterson, 1997; Ross, 1995). So even though, in principle, top officials are appointed on the basis of merit, in practice they need the right nationality, support of their national commissioner, and (preferably) the blessing of their national government.

Consociational principles—proportionality and mutual veto—are also present in the administrative organization of the commission. As a matter of principle, the most senior civil servant of each directorate-general (DG), the equivalent of a ministerial department, must have a different nationality from that of the responsible commissioner. Officials in adjacent positions in the chain of command are generally not of the same nationality. All directorate-generals, directorates (large subdivisions), units (smaller subdivisions), and task forces (temporary units) have a policy of maximizing "geographical diversity" among their personnel, which means that they aim to have a variety of nationalities and, in addition, often a balance between north and south.

The explicit recognition of national diversity in the administrative organization of the commission restrains national bias in policy making. Multinational balance in units and across hierarchical levels makes it difficult for individual officials to bestow favors on their nationality. It also discourages colonization of particular units by a nationality or group of nationalities. These structural features do not prevent officials from promoting the interests of their nationality, but they make such national-interest behavior less effective. This conclusion finds support in systematic empirical research on nationality in the commission. Edward Page, comparing the actual distribution of nationalities in DGs with what one would expect in noncolonized DGs, has detected no general evidence of colonization, at least not at the level of directorate-generals (Page, 1997). Morten Egeberg, focusing on national favoritism by individual officials, has found limited traces in less than one-quarter of commission units. How does one interpret these findings? Egeberg concludes from these that the commission has significant Weberian qualities: "What has emerged seems to be more than just a secretariat to the Council, or a neutral broker. Intentionally or unintentionally shaped, the services seem to have achieved some autonomy for promoting common European interests" (Egeberg, 1995: 28). My reading is, however, that these findings are also perfectly compatible with a working consociational system, where segmental elites zealously guard the "neutral" status of the central state apparatus (Taylor, 1997). There is no reason that one should infer from the absence of effective national favoritism or colonization

that the commission advocates the general European interest. A seasoned top
official comments on the weakness of shared objectives:

> There is a clear difference between national administrations and the
> Commission. In a national administration, there is a broad consensus on the
> objectives. All are more or less interested in pulling the same cart and know
> in which direction and when to pull the cart. There may be disagreement, of
> course, about marginal adjustments, or about speed, but basically all agree on
> where they want to go and what the national interest is. To use the word
> national interest gives away immediately why this cannot be the case inside
> the Commission. Even though we are supposed to be working for the
> common interest of the Community, nobody forgets his background, his
> nationality. Much of the conflict between national interests has been
> transferred to the Commission. Some [officials] are almost unashamed of it;
> they go straight for it and make no secret of it. Others—and I think this is
> also a question of how long you have been in the Commission—are much
> more working for the common benefit. They tend to take first of all a
> rational-reasoned balanced Community approach, whereas others go for a
> total national-interest approach. So, national tensions are transferred to the
> Commission, and that makes it impossible to have everybody agree *ex ante*
> on the common objectives because there are no common objectives. This is
> still a relatively young institution, which is expanding and maturing. But it
> has not yet found its own identity. There is no common identity. Instead,
> Commission struggles reflect opposing approaches among member states,
> with the so-called British liberal free trade approach versus the more
> centralist Benelux approach. Those two are at odds with each other. You
> have then the French approach, which is a combination of a nationalist and
> strong integrationist approach. The Germans with their federal system are of
> the view that you can combine shared rule and self-rule. There is no common
> objective; there is no identity. This identity will have to be forged through
> many years of collaboration. (Interview with senior commission official, July
> 1995)

How do these consociational principles of organization affect Commission
officials' perceptions? Table 4.1 shows responses on two questions. The first
question taps into the national colonization issue, and the second deals with
national favoritism by individual officials. Thirty-nine percent of commission
officials think that national colonization is a problem. Individual national
favoritism is perceived as somewhat less problematic: close to 30 percent
believe that too many commission officials let their nationality interfere with
their policy decisions. So a substantial minority is not happy with current rules
that subordinate merit to nationality, and 12 percent protest unequivocally.
These officials seek to strengthen rational-legal principles of organization in
the commission. But that does not alter the fact that the majority is satisfied
with the current consociational setup, and 27 percent candidly reject concerns
about national capture. As a group, then, top commission officials seem bent
to the consociational status quo end of the scale.

Table 4.1
Top Officials and Nationality in Commission

Items	Yes (4)	Yes, but (3)	Neutral (2.5)	No, but (2)	No (1)	Mean*
It hurts the Commission's legitimacy that certain DGs tend to be dominated by particular nationalities, such as agriculture by the French, competition by the Germans, regional policy by the Spanish, environment by the north, etc.	12 11.4%	29 27.6%	2 1.9%	34 32.4%	28 26.7%	2.25
Too many Commission civil servants let their nationality interfere in their personal judgments.	10 9.5%	21 20.0%	3 2.9%	48 45.7%	23 21.9%	2.19
Weberian (4) versus Consociational (1) attitudes	12 11.4%	16 15.3%	18 17.1%	30 28.6%	28 26.7%	2.22

* Responses range from 1 to 4. Neutral position would be 2.5; an average below 2.5 indicates disagreement with the statement.

TOP COMMISSION OFFICIALS ON NATIONALITY

Imagining a European public interest requires a leap beyond the real world of diverse nationalities. Conversely, accommodating national diversity in consociational fashion presupposes the relaxation of modern Weberian conceptions of bureaucracy. Why do officials display one or the other disposition?

The first approach to understanding varying views among top officials, rooted in a sociological model of belief system constraint, emphasizes socialization. Individuals are shaped by their experiences, and those who have spent time in institutional environments supporting Weberian or consociational principles may have internalized these norms (Converse, 1964; Mughan, Steffensmeier, and Scully, 1997; Rohrschneider, 1994, 1996; Searing, 1986, 1985; Verba, 1965). I hypothesize that officials may be influenced by experiences abroad, in the commission, in the cabinet, or in state administrations. A second line of theorizing begins with the assumption that rational individuals seek to maximize their utility under institutional constraints.

In doing so, they adjust their preferences to achieve material goals more efficiently. A key postulate is that institutional rules have calculable consequences for the ability of individuals to realize their goals (Hall and Taylor, 1996; North, 1990; Ostrom, 1990, 1991; Steinmo, Thelen, and Longstreth, 1991). Consociational and Weberian criteria of organization have measurable professional consequences for top officials. Weberian criteria insulate them from political and national manipulation; consociational criteria increase the likelihood that nationality trumps merit in career and policy decisions. I discuss how three institutional settings may affect professional opportunities: rules for recruitment, rules and practices related to particular positions and tasks in the Commission, and characteristics of the nationality to which officials belong.

Prior Transnational Socialization

Officials' views on the consociational/Weberian principles of bureaucratic organization may result from prior transnational experience. Students living abroad are part of cosmopolitan communities that have distinct transnational norms and rules. They often return home with beliefs that do not sit well with local ways. For similar reasons, officials who previously worked for international organizations are likely to be more open to conceptions of a public interest above and beyond national concerns. In short, the transnational socialization hypothesis predicts that officials who have studied or worked abroad are less likely to be consociational than those exclusively bred in their home country. The measure "Transnational Experience" is a dummy variable, where commission officials who studied or worked abroad are assigned a value of 1.

Hypothesis (H)1: Transnational Socialization. Transnational experiences (study or work abroad) encourage resistance to consociational attitudes.

Prior National Socialization

A previous career in a national administration may influence officials' orientations in two ways. A simple version links prior national civil service to resistance to consociational principles. Most national bureaucracies in Western Europe rest on Weberian principles in which professionalism, merit, and impartiality outweigh particularistic connections and partisan judgments. National civil servants have been trained to develop a sense of public service. A socialization logic would predict that they are likely to extrapolate these national experiences to the commission. My indicator is *State Experience,* a dummy that takes on the value of 1 when officials spent time in the national state sector prior to joining the commission.

A *qualified socialization* argument emphasizes that Weberian principles are not entrenched equally in all national bureaucracies. It seems reasonable that former national officials of non-Weberian bureaucracies would have internalized different values than did their colleagues from Weberian bureaucracies. I use multiple indicators to divide bureaucracies into least, medium, and strong Weberian administrations. On the basis of these data I produce two dummy variables: *Strong Weberian* and *Weak Weberian.* The reference group consists thus of former state officials from medium Weberian administrations.

H2a: State Socialization. Former national officials are less likely to support consociational principles.
H2b: Type of State Socialization: *Weberian versus non-Weberian.* Former national officials from weak Weberian administrations will give stronger support to a consociational commission, while their colleagues from the strongest Weberian administrations will reject a consociational commission.

Commission Socialization

The founder of the High Authority/commission, Jean Monnet, originally conceived of top officials as a handpicked team of independently minded professionals without ties to member states. In this Weberian institution, commission officials were expected to espouse a sense of mission to transcend interstate relations and construct "an ever closer Union." To the extent that these values are embedded in the commission as an institution, one may hypothesize that the longer that officials work in the commission, the more that they should internalize these institutional norms and reject consociational principles. This socialization thesis is echoed in anthropological studies of the commission (Duchêne, 1994, on Jean Monnet; Abélès, Bellier, and McDonald, 1993; Bellier, 1995; McDonald, 1997). The indicator *Commission Career* is the number of years served in the commission until the interview.

H3: Commission Socialization. The longer an official has worked in the commission, the less he or she is likely to support consociational principles.

Commission Cabinet Experience

A final socialization hypothesis links cabinet experience to consociational principles. In his study of the Delors period, George Ross describes the role of cabinets in balancing national interests, party-political priorities, and European political goals with technocratic policy making (Ross, 1995; see also Grant, 1994). One may hypothesize that officials with cabinet experience are more consociational. The measure *Cabinet* is a dummy with a value of 1 for officials who served in a commission cabinet.

H4: Cabinet Experience. A previous cabinet member is more likely to support consociational principles.

National Control over Recruitment

One utility hypothesis links national control over recruitment to officials' orientations. In the U.S. political system, control over the bureaucracy is ensured through the spoils system combined with mandatory approval of top federal administrators by the Senate. National governments in the European Union do not have formal control over senior commission officials, but they are usually consulted informally on top appointments. This national leverage is reputedly strongest for appointments through *parachutage*, the recruitment of externals for A1 or A2 positions. Many (though not all) of these external candidates have ties with the national government that proposes them; more than half are former national civil servants or diplomats.[3] It seems plausible that officials who owe their appointment to their national government will be more inclined to be responsive to national concerns. My measure *Parachutage* is a dummy variable that takes on the value of 1 for parachuted officials.

H5: Parachutage. Parachuted officials are more likely to support consociational principles than nonparachuted officials.

Positional Interest

The argument that bureaucrats have an interest in expanding their positional power is at the heart of much public administration literature; but how to strengthen one's professional position is likely to differ from position to position. Officials in areas of strong EU competencies are not very much dependent on national governments' consent to get things done. However, they need ongoing regulatory or financial autonomy, and these resources are better guaranteed in a Weberian administration. In contrast, officials with limited regulatory responsibilities often find other attributes more essential than competencies or funds: access to information, mediation skills, capacity to use persuasion, and credibility to exert social pressure on national governments. For them, close interaction with governments through consociational mechanisms is often beneficial. The measure *PowerDG*, a composite index of formal and reputational measures, is a ranking from 1 (weak DG) to 8 (powerful DG).

H6: Positional Interest: Resources. Commission officials in positions of greater policy autonomy will be less consociational.

Substantive Policy Interest

A third utility hypothesis links substantive policy tasks with officials' views. There are several reasons that consociational arrangements appear particularly conducive to dealing with quality-of-life issues, and so officials working on environmental, cultural, and consumer issues may be induced to support consociational principles to enhance professional success. The fact that competencies on quality-of-life issues are usually shared between national and European levels creates incentives for cooperation between officials from the two levels. Preferences and institutional arrangements also vary significantly across countries, as rational actors, officials in charge of policy making on these issues, should expect better policy results if they take these national sensitivities into account. From their side, national policy advocates of quality-of-life issues have strong incentives to use the EU arena to achieve policy goals that are difficult to obtain domestically, and this should encourage close links between national and European policymakers. (On EU environmental policy, Sbragia, 1996; on EU social regulation, Eichener, 1992.) One may therefore hypothesize that officials dealing with quality-of-life issues have particularly outspoken professional incentives to favor consociational principles. My measure *Quality of Life* is a dummy with a value of 1 for officials in charge of these issues.

H7: Positional Interest: *Substance.* Commission officials dealing with quality-of-life issues will be more consociational.

Nationality

In an administration where nationality is a powerful principle of organization, certain nationalities may have better career opportunities or weigh more effectively on policy decisions. For officials from "weaker" nationalities, the rational strategy is to pursue a commission administration that is relatively insulated from national influences. Nationalities that do not benefit from current consociational rules should therefore prefer a Weberian commission.

The utility of nationality for professional life is influenced by two factors. First, a promotion system that gives priority to nationality over merit creates the perception of severe career constraints on officials from small countries. This is a direct consequence of the proportionate *size of national quotas.* Small nationalities like the Danish or Belgians, for example, are allocated between seven and ten top positions, while the four largest nationalities claim between twenty-seven and thirty-two. Though this quota is in reality a little higher than their proportionate share in the population, it nevertheless exacerbates for small nationalities the rigidity of the promotion system. With an average annual turnover rate of fewer than ten top commission positions (and fewer still in years of enlargement), it can take several years, sometimes over half a decade, before just one position opens up for small nationalities. Under a merit system talented Danish or Belgian officials could compete annually; under a consociational system based on nationality, they have to wait until a vacancy for their nationality comes up. One may therefore hypothesize that officials from smaller countries are less likely to support the consociational status quo. For *National Quota* I allocate to each official the number of votes in the Council of Ministers for each country of origin, which range between two and ten.

A second factor concerns the *effectiveness of national networks.* Some nationalities have a strong reputation of "clubness," which may be defined as a set of formal and informal networks within which members tend to act in concert. A variety of resources may contribute to clubness. One resource, often mentioned in anthropological research on the European Union, is national sociocultural cohesion. Cut off from their home environment, individuals with strong national identities tend to socialize with compatriots. These informal national networks on golf courses, in bars, or during literary evenings easily become invaluable venues for professional contacts among compatriots (Abélès, Bellier, and McDonald, 1993). Clubness may also be a by-product of organizational and financial resources. The sheer concentration of administrative-financial resources in the larger national communities enables them to better monitor and lobby commission personnel policy. This argument is similar to that made by research on the presence, cohesion, and effectiveness of state delegations to the U.S. Congress, which has found strong associations with population size, size of state bureaucracy, and professionalism (Morrisroe, 1998). Finally, clubness may be the result of a deliberate policy by national governments to strengthen networks among expatriates in Brussels. Strong clubness—and more precisely, an active role of national governments in career decisions—turns nationality into an asset for officials competing for professional advancement. Officials from strongly networked nationalities should be best placed to excel professionally in a consociational system. I divide the nationalities in three categories for *National Clubness* ranging from weak (1) to strong (3) clubs on the basis of values for cultural cohesion, financial and organizational resources, and intentional government policy.

H8: National Quota: Officials from nationalities with small personnel quota are less likely to support consociational principles.
H9: National Clubness: Officials from strongly networked nationalities will support consociationalism, while those from weakly networked nationalities will support a Weberian commission.

Dependent Variable: Orientations to Consociationalism

To measure top officials' stance to the commission's consociational solution to deal with multinationality in the commission, I combine the two items of Table 4.1 (with reversed coding) in an index for *Consociationalism*. Item 1 focuses on individual national favoritism; item 2 asks officials to take a stance on national colonization.[4] Values range between 1 (Weberian) and 4 (consociational). The mean is 2.783 out of 4, with a standard deviation of 0.795. I have included details on the operationalization of this and other variables in the appendix.

EXAMINING THE EVIDENCE

To explain officials' divergent views on how the commission deals with nationality, I find that utility arguments pack considerably more power than socialization. Three sets of factors account for 40 percent of the variance (adjusted R^2 = 37 percent). By far the most powerful association is with the pair testing the nationality utility hypothesis, which jointly explains 24 percent of the variance in the bivariate association (Table 4.2, column 3: R^2 for nationality). They also dominate the multivariate analysis (models 1 and 2). Officials competing within the limited promotion opportunities of small national quotas are more resentful of nationality as an organizational criterion in the commission. Even more persuasively, officials are much less likely to embrace consociational principles when they belong to a national group that supports its members ineffectively (National Clubness: $R^2 = 0.209$). A second set pertains to the opportunity structure within the Commission. Officials dealing with quality-of-life issues are most consociational. Among the socialization variables, state socialization is most powerful. All other things being equal, former national officials want a Weberian commission, though that is not true for former officials from Weberian national administrations. Contrary to the expectations of a socialization logic, they are more likely to champion consociational principles. I discuss this apparently counter-intuitive finding later. A secondary socializing influence comes from cabinet socialization.

So the supporters of the consociational status quo are likely to be found among officials who are able to fall back on strongly networked nationalities in Brussels and enjoy the greater range of career opportunities that come with larger national quotas. They tend to deal with the softer quality-of-life issues in the commission. It is unlikely that they have ever served in a state administration, but they may very well have worked for a commission cabinet at one point in their career.

Top officials are perfectly aware that the commission's consociational approach to nationality determines their professional opportunities in very direct ways. Career concerns color their views on the larger issue of how the European Commission should accommodate multinational diversity. The professional utility model explains 36 percent of the variance, which is considerably more than the 17 percent for the socialization model.

To dig deeper in the causality of what makes some top officials greater supporters of a consociational commission than others, I carve up the group of 105 officials according to recruitment to a top career. I contrast "consociational products," who achieved top positions through the consociational channel of parachutage, and "Weberian recruits," who reached the top through internal promotion. Common wisdom has it that parachutists are Trojan horses sent by member states to undermine the European Commission's autonomy from within; they are likely to favor consociationalism. In contrast, internal recruits are often portrayed as the most "European" officials. As we will see, the results of this study reject this wisdom unambiguously. Parachutists are significantly less keen on consociational principles than internal recruits (bottom row of Table 4.2). Parachutists are relatively unaffected by the fact that professional opportunities vary by nationality. Contrary to internal recruits, they were catapulted into the top commission administration over and above national competition.

Table 4.2
Multivariate Analysis Explaining Orientations to Consociationalism

	Corre-lation (R)	All Officials (Full Model 1)	All Officials (Parsimonious Model 2)	Para-chutists (Model 3)	Internal Recruits (Model 4)
Transnational Experience	-.188*	-.053 (.137)	-	n.s	-.035 (.212)
State Socialization	-.165*	-.228* (.208)	-.232** (.159)	-.027 (.264)	-.159 (.302)
State service	-.217**	.005 (.228)	-	n.s.	-.207* (.489)
Weak Weberian Tradition	.210**	.169 (.227)	.161 (.206)	.159 (.254)	.139 (.359)
Strong Weberian Tradition					
Length of Service in the Commission	.153	-.088 (.011)	-	n.s.	n.s.
Cabinet Experience	.183*	.153* (.141)	.149* (.134)	n.s.	
Power DG	-.235**	-.099 (.032)	-	-.194* (.043)	.231** (.178)
Quality of Life DG	.221**	.317*** (.163)	.333*** (.157)	.336** (.207)	.268** (.248)
Parachutage	-.164*	-.104 (.192)	-		
Nationality	.293**	.161 (.028)	.156 (.026)	n.s.	.303** (.040)
National Quota	.457***	.356*** (.097)	.383*** (.089)	.424*** (.150)	.230 (.130)
National Clubness					
R^2		.41	.39	.46	.46
Adj. R^2		.34	.36	.38	.37
Durbin-Watson		2.13	2.06	2.41	2.15
N of observations		N=105	N=105	N=44	N=61
Consociationalism (mean on scale of 1-4)		2.78	2.78	2.63	2.89

Notes Multivariate linear regression (constant included in equation, pairwise deletion of missing values). Standardized coefficients (betas); standard errors in brackets.
   *   significant at 0.10 level;
  ** significant at 0.05 level;
 *** significant at 0.01 level (one-tailed; but two-tailed for correlations). n.s.= bivariate correlation not significant at 0.10 level (one-tailed). A dash indicates that a variable was dropped from the multivariate analysis according to preset criteria (stepwise procedure: entry p< .15, removal p>=.15).

Nationality, therefore, is not an important constraint on their career chances. One may therefore expect their views to be shaped by other factors than nationality. This is all the more likely if parachutists are high quality professionals—and there is evidence that most national governments put forward strong candidates for top commission posts, particularly since the deepening of European integration in the late 1980s. Such professionals could be expected to be motivated primarily by professional self-esteem derived from achieving their professional goals, not by loyalty to a particular nation-ality or to the commission. Table 4.2 presents the analysis for all officials, for parachutists, and for internal recruits. The remainder of the chapter examines key results in order of prominence.

Nationality

The hypothesis that officials' views on consociational principles in the commission are influenced by the utility of national citizenship for career purposes finds overwhelming support. The two variables are highly significant in bivariate and multivariate models (combined $R^2 = 0.24$). Aspiring top officials from small countries experience *national quotas* more often as negative constraints on their professional progress than do their colleagues from larger member states. The "sense of having the wrong nationality" is particularly salient among internal recruits because their chances for promotion are most sharply circumscribed by the national quota system. Parachutists, who are usually asked to apply for a position reserved for a particular nationality, are much less sensitive.

The most powerful association is with *national clubness*. National networks shape top officials' career opportunities, but they also matter in subtle ways for people at the top. Abélès, Bellier, and McDonald (1993) emphasize the social support provided by national networks, but they also recognize more instrumental functions. Such networks are invaluable nodes for information exchange, contacts with influential compatriots in and outside the commission, and political opinionating.

> Each nationality has its club, its network, its association of European officials, its "church," and they are especially frequented by those officials who are most destabilized by the multinational work environment. These happen to be more often Irish or Danish than German or Italian. Not all officials have a need to come home. Membership of the Irish club provides gossip, makes it possible to keep up with local news. Equally so, the Dutch, the Danes ... try to find in Brussels the pubs where they can bump up against one another without having to make prior arrangements: a national habit. The Portuguese club groups ambassadorial diplomats and permanent representatives to NATO (North Atlantic Treaty Organization) and the European Community. With its thematic dinners spiced up by reputable speakers, it performs a social and intellectual function. The French participate in political associations or, for the products of the Ecole Nationale d'Administration, in "old boys networks." The Spanish form a small colony,

but the nocturnal social life has had to give way to the exigencies of the [Brussels] climate and the work rhythm in the Commission.

The British, members of a club in London, do not see the need to belong to a club in Brussels. (my translation from French, 25-26)

National networks do not only have social and professional use for officials but also are transmission belts between the commission and its political partners. Many officials play a role as "points of access" for governments, firms, and other interest groups of their country of citizenship (Egeberg, 1995). An experienced official who had served in multiple cabinets depicts the role of a good commission employee in this sense:

The Commission's best advisers on the impact of policies in a particular country are its commissioners from that country. They spend a long time saying to each other, "the specific situation in country X is the following..." It is their job to explain to the Commission the politics involved. So, there is nothing wrong with explaining the context of the impact of a Community policy on a particular country. But if you intervene on purely nationalist grounds to say "we are against this proposal because, say, we have 30,000 tons of rice exports," or alternatively, "this does not please our shippers," people will not in the end deal with you on a regular and sound basis. Your credibility is definitely reduced because, after all, everyone is conscious that we have to explain Community policies to national audiences. That is our role and we fail at it mostly. Most of the hostility is not so much in the Commission between Commissioners, but vis-à-vis the outside audience. And no doubt Spanish Commissioners spend more time explaining at home why the Commission has to be tough on state aids than they do telling us that the Spanish are worried about the impact of the Iberia decision on Spain. Being the mediator, the two-way go-between, is extremely important, and on balance, we would all find that we are most beleaguered by our own nationality and not by each other. (Senior official)

In a polity where successful policy making often depends on the quality of intelligence, officials with weak national networks are at a disadvantage.

State Socialization

The simple state socialization hypothesis, which predicts that former state officials favor Weberian principles, finds support. Though the effect is modest in the simple regression, it grows for the total sample (models 1 and 2). This effect is amplified for ex-civil servants from weak, incohesive, highly permeable, and politicized administrations (models 1 and 2). The negative effect of state socialization is reversed to a positive one for officials from strong, cohesive, impermeable administrations with limited politicization. So the qualified socialization hypothesis, which argues that officials extrapolate norms and practices from their home administrations to the European Commission, is soundly rejected; while the relationship is present and strong, the sign is opposite to the one predicted. Officials from consociational as well as those from Weberian heritage tend to support principles that run counter to their national experiences. The overall explanatory power of the three state variables in the simple regression is larger than the sum of its parts, which suggests that one logic, not three separate logics, seems to drive this factor (R^2 = 0.131). These conclusions hold for parachutists and internal recruits separately, though a different mix of state variables does the explanatory lifting.

The theoretical implication of these findings is that socialization for these elite actors is not a mechanistic process. Though they internalize norms and practices from previous settings, they reevaluate them before applying them to a new institutional context. Hence, the bottom line is the same for all: prior state service makes them less likely to support consociational principles. But, all other things equal, they draw lessons from their particular administrative experiences.

Officials from consociational national administrations know full well that consociational practices have often led to severely restricted policy capacity, low status, and alienation for civil servants, and so it seems sensible for them to prefer a Weberian commission. Officials from Weberian national administrations may realize that such traditions rest on conditions absent in the European Commission: a homogeneous cultural and educational background of civil servants, broad consensus about grand objectives ("national interests"), and the presence of a unitary political principle, and so they appear willing to endorse the consociational status quo in the commission. At work is not merely passive socialization; lesson drawing complements it.

Positional Interest: Power and Substance

Professional opportunities may be influenced by officials' work environment in two ways. The *positional interest hypothesis* predicts that the more officials that have policy autonomy, the less that they will support consociational arrangements. This hypothesis finds modest to weak support in bivariate and multivariate regressions, though it is somewhat stronger among parachutists. The *substantive interest hypothesis* suggests that officials who deal with quality-of-life issues are more likely to favor consociational principles. There is strong support in the regressions and across the two subgroups.

Cabinet

The hypothesis that officials with cabinet experience are more responsive to nationality finds support, though it is only moderately strong in the multivariate analysis. The subgroups show why the effect appears modest. Cabinet experience does not affect parachutists' views on nationality at all, but among internal recruits, ex-cabinet members are far more accommodating to nationality than those without cabinet experience.

A major reason for this differential result has to do with the divergent relevance of cabinet service for career advancement. For ambitious middle-management officials, cabinet service is an important stepping-stone to a high-flying career, because that gives them a chance to get noticed by commissioners. About 40 percent of internal recruits take this route.[5] Commissioners tend to select compatriots who understand the interests of the commissioner's country of origin and are willing to balance European concerns with national sensitivities. Once immersed in cabinet politics, officials become further attuned to diverse national interests. A mixture of self-selection, selection by commissioners, and learning—within severe nationality constraints on career advancement—explains why ex-cabinet members are more open to consociational principles: their score is 2.98 out of a maximum of 4 as against an average 2.78 for all officials and 2.63 for parachutists. Parachuted officials make very different calculations. By the time that they join a cabinet—and 30 percent do—they have already landed a top job. A cabinet posting is not a stepping-stone to a more senior position but a political interlude in an already successful bureaucratic-executive career.

Parachutage

Parachutage gives national governments the illusion of consociational control, but it tends to strengthen the camp of those defending the European public interest. Contrary to expectations, parachutage is not positively associated with support for consociational principles. If anything, the simple regression suggests the opposite association, though the variable drops out in the presence of controls. This finding goes against the dominant view among EU scholars, but it is not surprising for students of consociationalism. It is fairly easy to restrict positional access to individuals with the appropriate characteristic—party membership, ethnicity, language, religion, or national citizenship; it is much more difficult to control views and decisions of appointees on an ongoing basis. This is particularly so when appointees are protected by restrictive tenure regulations, as is the case for senior commission officials. A very senior top official, questioned about parachutage, minimizes the effect on policy making:

> It is quite true that you have a certain number of de facto national flags. But you have to look and see what is actually happening. For example, would DG IV's policy [competition, reputedly dominated by Germans] be very different if it had, say, a Frenchman and not [a German been director-general]? I don't think that the nationality difference is very strong at all in terms of how people act... [National governments] exaggerate the real effect of the decision, but let us recall that it can be very popular *chez eux*. On their home base it is important that they can point at Mr. X as "one of ours." But in the reality of the day-to-day work, does it make a lot of difference? Quite frankly, it probably does not. (Senior official)

Another official emphasizes that national governments' insistence on being able to fill senior posts with their nationals is much more driven by habit and status than by a rational concern to maximize national interests:

Official: These [national-specific appointments are the product of] *traditions* rather than anything else.

Interviewer: So there is a French tradition in agriculture . . .

O: For example. And a German tradition in competition, and so on. Strangely enough these traditions are always out-of-date. They probably reflect to a certain extent interests of the past. For example, there is a strong French tradition in DG VIII [development], which is understandable because at one point there was a *grande politique africaine de la France.* But these times are long gone and I am not sure that preserving this tradition is good for French national interests.

I: Do you think that it may actually work against French national interests?

O: Probably. Or it is indifferent to French interests. . . . I am simply suggesting that these traditions perpetuate regardless of real interests. And if you were absolutely materialist [*sic*] you would probably conclude that the French should not stake so much on development but would be advised to concentrate their efforts somewhere else. (Senior official)

Commission Socialization

Proponents of the strong socializing capacity of the commission will find little solace in this study. The variable drops out in all multivariate analyses. To the extent that length of service in the commission matters, it encourages officials to be responsive to nationality. It is possible that officials learn that it is difficult to get things done if one ignores national sensitivities. The bottom line is that the commission finds it hard to mold the orientations of its top employees to its institutional self-interest. Elsewhere, I have argued that the contemporary commission is a greenhouse neither for supranationalism nor for a particular ideology (Hooghe, 1999). It is certainly not a breeding place for a European public interest that distances itself from national sensitivities.

Transnational Socialization

Finally, the transnational socialization hypothesis predicts that officials who studied or worked abroad should be less responsive to nationality. The bivariate analysis gives moderate support, but when one controls for other, more powerful factors, the variable drops out. Living abroad does not appear to shape one's views on how to accommodate diversity in any given direction.

CONCLUSION

This chapter examines how elite officials in the European Commission conceive of the role of nationality in the commission. At stake are two distinct conceptions of political-bureaucratic organization. According to the Weberian ideal-type, merit rather than nationality shapes personnel selection and task organization, and officials' attitudes are expected to reflect the general European public interest. In a consociational model, the diversity of the European polity is reproduced in the commission's organization, and officials are counted on to be responsive to various national views. This chapter argues that, as a group, top officials are bent to the consociational status quo end of the scale. Yet there is considerable variation in their orientations to nationality. So why are some officials consociationalist, while others call for a more autonomous European public interest?

The search for sources of variation is set up as a contest between socialization factors and factors related to the professional utility function of officials, and utility packs far more power than socialization. Nationality shapes professional opportunities profoundly. The greatest support for consociational principles is to be found among officials from large nationalities and from nationalities with strong supportive networks in Brussels. Nationality figures thus prominently for instrumental reasons: support for a consociational commission depends on whether one's nationality is associated with better career opportunities and greater effective weight in policy making. In an administration where nationality is a powerful principle of organization, officials with the "right" citizenship have compelling incentives to reinforce the role of nationality. This is, of course, not surprising for students of plural societies, particularly of consociationalism, who have noted the self-reinforcing qualities of consociational practices (McRae, 1974a). Elites and, to some extent, masses used to consociational practices often have strong incentives to preserve the existing structure of rewards (Lustick, 1997; Nordlinger, 1972; Tsebelis, 1990; for an EU application, see Taylor, 1997).

Yet professional opportunities are also affected by one's position in the work environment. Being in a position with weak regulatory autonomy or dealing with quality-of-life issues induces officials to support a more consociational, responsive approach to nationality. To some extent officials' views are also shaped by experiences inculcated over time: prior experience as national civil servant reduces consociationalism, and prior cabinet experience increases it.

I have found not one but at least two different types of officials: parachutists and internal recruits. Different causal processes underlie variation in their orientations. As one moves from internal recruits to parachutists, nationality factors increasingly give way to influences having to do with life and work in the commission. Remarkably, then, parachutists are not the national governments' Trojan horses that many commentators have presumed them to be—at least not as far as their views on nationality in the commission are concerned.

Many studies of European integration have assumed that the commission is intent on substituting diverse national concerns with a uniform European interest. This chapter disconfirms this assumption for the commission's elite officials. There is a surprisingly great acceptance that Europe's diversity should be explicitly recognized in the commission. In the words of one official: "I like my service to be a microcosm of the Community. I like my colleagues to reflect the diversity within the Community. There is a certain mystery as to how people with such different backgrounds can work together" (Senior official).

NOTES

1. A few years ago, Ken McRae began to extend his interest in linguistic conflict and language policy to the European Union. His venture into EU politics was impeded, though not aborted, by the dearth of existing research and the paucity of primary data on language policy and/or linguistic politics in the European institutions.

2. For Jean Monnet, a supranational authority transcending sectional diversity was critical to the new method of common action, which he described as the core of the European Community. In an article published in 1962—after the High Authority had been replaced by the European Commission—he characterized this new method of common action as common rules which each member is committed to respect, and common institutions [i.e., first of all, the European Commission, and second, the European Parliament and the European Court of Justice] to watch over the application of these rules. Nations have applied this method within their frontiers for centuries, but they have never yet been applied between them. After a period of trial and error, this method has become a permanent dialogue between a single European body, *responsible for expressing the view of the general interest of the Community,* and the national governments expressing the national views (emphasis added).

3. Fifty-five percent of parachutists were in paid national service as civil servant or diplomat before entering the commission, against 27 percent for nonparachutists.

4. These items are randomly distributed on a list with thirty-two items. A scale reliability test produces a Cronbach's alpha equaling .63 (standardized: .63).

5. Senior officials consider cabinet service as the most effective route to higher administrative echelons. Yet nonparachutists have two other important venues to the top: support from one's national home base (national government, party connections, national administration) and recognition of one's policy expertise or managerial excellence. A prominent way to demonstrate the latter is by serving as assistant, a middle-management position, to a director-general.

5

The Consociational Theory and Deliberative Politics: A Conceptual Framework for Cross-National Analysis

André Bächtiger, Markus Spörndli, and Jürg Steiner

Contemporary political theory confronts us with an argument for a more deliberative mode of decision making. Deliberative politics implies that political and societal actors, instead of merely aggregating their initial preferences and isolated interests and forging majorities, should listen to each other, show mutual respect, reasonably justify their policy positions, and be ready to reevaluate and eventually revise their initial preferences in a reasonable deliberation or discourse about validity claims (Chambers, 1995, 1999; Gutmann and Thompson, 1996; Habermas, 1992, 1996). From a philosophical point of view, reasonable deliberation or discourse ethics is seen as a necessary means to arrive at legitimate decisions in modern pluralistic societies where a transcendental point of reference is capable of telling actors which of their perspectives is the right perspective (Chambers, 1995: 233).

Yet it is far from certain whether a conception of deliberative politics could realistically come into operation or whether it would remain a purely utopian affair. Fritz Scharpf (1997: 166), for instance, sees a practical incompatibility between the consensual ideal of deliberative politics and the electoral implications of competitive democracies. Why, Scharpf contends, should self-interested political actors enter into a decision-making process that redistributes power to the other side? In an explorative cross-national research project, we want to investigate whether there are chances for deliberative politics in current democratic systems and, if so, what could bring them about. Our basic claim is that there might be specific institutional settings that are more conducive to deliberation than others. One such favorable institutional setting, we propose in this chapter, could be consociationalism. The key feature of consociationalism is that it encompasses a set of institutional devices (proportionality, grand coalition, mutual veto) as well as cooperative and respectful attitudes of political elites in segmented societies, leading them to transcend the borders of their own groups, to be receptive to the claims of others, and to accommodate the divergent interests and claims of the segments (Lijphart, 1969: 216; Steiner, 1998: 2). We thus assume that elements of deliberative politics—such as listening, showing respect, justifying positions in cases of dissent, and finding consensual solutions—are embedded in the very structure of consociational democracies. With its basically institutional orientation, the research project attempts to develop a constructive theory of the state bridging the preserves of philosophical theory and empirical-analytical political science (Rothstein, 1998: 6-18).

When one is concerned with a more deliberative mode of decision making in real-world politics, at least two limitations have to be made. First, as one should expect self-interested political actors in democratic systems to primarily focus on the will of their constituents, probably any deliberation in real-world politics will fall short of the ideal discourse envisioned by Jürgen Habermas: one cannot assume a constraint-free communicative environment in politics, nor can one posit that only the force of the better argument will prevail or that a "rational consensus" can be found. This limitation has also a normative twist: as a citizen, one can expect that elected representatives do not just substitute their deliberatively gained judgments for those of their voters (Gutmann and Thompson, 1996: 128; see also Tullock, 1990: 136). The Habermasian ideal discourse, therefore, must be conceived as merely a regulative idea. Yet this does not invalidate the basic intent of our research, as there may be more or less reasoned deliberation and more or less of a reasoned consensus (*verständigungsorientiertes Handeln*) in different institutional settings. A second limitation refers to the vision of comprehensive deliberative politics, implying that the whole citizenship is taking part in the deliberative venture. In mass democracies, however, such a participative conception of deliberative politics runs up against severe problems of efficient decision making and also against the problem of assuring the willingness and resources of citizens to participate. However, as it is difficult to imagine that deliberation could reach all citizens, one can, on normative grounds, expect at least professional policymakers to get involved in some level of a reasoned deliberation. The research project toward which this chapter contributes follows precisely this logic and focuses on one political arena where deliberation might have its greatest potential in real-world politics: the parliamentary arena (see also Habermas, 1992: 210). We investigate debates on major social and regional conflicts in parliamentary committees as well as full sessions of Parliament in ten countries. The countries range from the consociational to the majoritarian pole: Switzerland, Belgium, the Netherlands, Austria, Italy, Germany, France, Canada, the United States, and the United Kingdom.

In this chapter we proceed as follows. The first section reviews the concepts of deliberative democracy and develops an analytical framework that explores potential links between normative theory and empirical-analytical science. In this context we also substantiate our claim that consociational democracies may have better prerequisites for deliberative politics than majoritarian democracies. The second section presents and justifies our selection of countries and debates.

In the third section we develop a "Discourse Quality Index" (DQI), representing an attempt to assemble and operationalize the diverse concepts of deliberative politics.

TOWARD AN INSTITUTIONAL CONCEPTION OF DELIBERATIVE POLITICS

The ideal of a deliberative democracy can generally be defined as "an association whose affairs are governed by public deliberation of its members," an association whose members "share a commitment to the resolution of problems of collective choice through public reasoning, and regard their basic institutions as legitimate insofar as they establish the framework for free public deliberation" (Cohen, 1989: 17, 21). Common to all conceptions of deliberative democracy is the ideal of a "talk-centric" style of decision making instead of a "voting-centric" style: outcomes should be determined by reasons rather than numbers (Chambers, 1999: 1); they should be "qualitative" rather than "quantitative" (Perczynski, 2000: 1-2).

Many central aspects of deliberative democracy originate in the republican view of democracy, with which communitarians challenged the predominant liberal model of democracy. Yet Habermas (1992: 324-398; 1996: 277-305) introduces a procedural model of deliberative democracy by placing it in the middle ground of the liberal and republican alternatives of democracy.[1] His deliberative model shares with communitarianism the vision of an active, talk-centric participation of possibly all citizens. However, Habermas believes in a pluralistic character of modern societies and thus rejects the communitarian premise of a citizenry united and actively motivated by a shared conception of the good life as being unrealistic. He shares this criticism with liberalism and promotes liberal neutrality: "The state should not act in ways intended to promote a particular conception of the good life since that would constitute a failure to show each citizen equal concern and respect" (Baynes, 1995: 223). In turn, Habermas rejects liberalism's interpretation of the political process as being primarily the competition among, and aggregation of, private and fixed preferences. In terms of deliberative democracy, preferences are usually neither fixed nor exogenous to the political process but are adaptive to a wide range of societal influences (see Sunstein, 1991). In contrast to liberalism, deliberative democracy claims that the participants of a discourse may transform their preferences in deliberation and that this is one of the most essential features of democracy (similarly Manin, 1987; see also Chambers, 1999).

Even though Habermas (1992: 369) opposes the universal character of Joshua Cohen's (1989) deliberative democracy, he basically accepts his ideal deliberative *procedure* (Habermas, 1992: 370-372).[2] It mainly consists of the following principles. Deliberation is held argumentatively; that is, "the parties are required to state their reasons for advancing proposals, supporting them or criticizing them" (Cohen, 1989: 22). Ideal deliberation is inclusive and public, and it is free from external coercion. It is also free from internal coercion; that is, each participant has an equal chance to put issues on the agenda and propose solutions and criticisms, and each has an equal voice in the decision. Ideal deliberation "aims to arrive at a rationally motivated consensus" (Cohen, 1989: 23).[3] Thereby, justifications must focus on the common good: "The interests, aims and ideals that compromise the common good are those that survive deliberation, interests that, on public reflection, we think it legitimate to appeal to in making claims on social resources" (25).

The deliberative conception of democracy is thus a participatory model of democracy as opposed to the inherent elitism of most existing representative political systems. It is basically input-oriented: most important is the *legitimacy* of a decision process, less so the substantive outputs (critically, see Rawls, 1996: 421-433). While in the conceptions of Habermas and Cohen an ideal discourse leads—through the "non-coercive coercion of the better argument"—to a reasonable, genuine consensus, less ambitious conceptions of deliberative democracy accept disagreement, as long as it is conducted in an atmosphere of mutual respect: "Mutual respect...requires an effort to appreciate the moral force of the position of people with whom we disagree" (Gutmann and Thompson, 1990: 85). This demands more than mere toleration: "It requires a favorable attitude toward, and constructive interaction with, the persons with whom one disagrees" (85). Being aware of the limits of practical discourse in terms of time and space (Müller, 1993: 70-71), a final vote is usually considered necessary in order to come to a decision. A vote after reasonable discourse should be acceptable even to the losing minority, because the winning majority was forced to show respect and empathy toward the interests of the minority.

However, even moderate conceptions of deliberative democracy are not immune to substantial criticisms. Jack Knight and James Johnson (1994: 278) argue that both preference aggregation and deliberation are vulnerable to distortion resulting from exogenous sources. They thus conclude that "the argument for deliberation is stronger if we see it as aiming not for preference transformation but for the relatively more modest goal of establishing agreement over the dimensions of conflict" (285). This is a normative criticism. Yet it still implies that deliberation even with a reduced goal leads to better results than voting-centric styles of decision making. This is precisely what we want to investigate empirically in our project. Representing another line of criticism, Lynn Sanders (1997: 350) states that the prerequisites for deliberation are unevenly distributed among the participants: "Deliberation requires not only equality in resources and the guarantee of equal opportunity to articulate persuasive arguments but also equality in 'epistemological authority,' in the capacity to evoke acknowledgement of one's arguments." By considering deliberation merely at an elite level in our project, we can assume these prerequisites to be distributed more evenly.

A fundamental criticism on the empirical level comprises the question of whether the conception of deliberative politics is realistic after all. Since most theorists of deliberative democracy stress the voluntaristic character of a reasonable discourse (e.g., Chambers, 1995: 240-241), a constructive theory of the state needs to question why presumably instrumentally rational actors—that is, actors who "take actions not for their own sake, but only insofar as they secure desired typically private ends" (Chong, 1996: 39)—would take the trouble to engage in deliberation. Potential participants know that politics is about "who gets what, when, how" (Lasswell, 1936) and that "different policy choices will have different distributive consequences, and they know that there is no preexisting rule that would neutralize unequal allocations of costs and benefits" (Scharpf, 1997: 164). In a more general perspective, the implementation of deliberative institutions would run counter to the interests of at least some powerful societal and political groups. Thus, it would be opposed, no matter if such opposition could be reasonably justified or not: "[T]he basic contradiction here is that coercion would be needed to arrive at Habermas's non-coercive *(zwanglos)* communication" (Flyvbjerg, 1998: 227). Amy Gutmann and Dennis Thompson (1996: 3) claim to be—in contrast to other deliberative theorists—sensitive "to the contexts of ordinary politics: the pressures of power, the problems of inequality, the demands of diversity, the exigencies of persuasion." Yet, as Shapiro (1999: 36) rightly assesses, even they pay too little attention to exactly these features of real-world politics.

But the prospects for more deliberation in real-world politics need not look too bad either. The behavior of self-interested political actors is not fixed but varies according to the institutional settings within which individuals must act. Following Douglass North (1990: 3), institutions are "the humanly devised constraints that shape human interaction." Including formal organizations as well as informal rules and procedures (Thelen and Steinmond, 1992: 2; also Hall and Taylor, 1996: 938), institutions structure the costs and benefits that an actor can expect when following a certain course of action. Yet, drawing on historical institutionalism,[4] (Hall, 1986; Thelen and Steinmond, 1992; Hall and Taylor, 1996), the scope of institutional analysis goes beyond such a mere calculus approach and entails a cultural and historical dimension, too. On the one hand, institutions are not just intervening variables capable of altering actors' predetermined choices and actions; they can also affect and reshape the cognitive scripts as well as the very goals and basic preferences of actors (Thelen and Steinmond, 1992: 27; Hall and Taylor, 1996: 939; see also March and Olsen, 1989: 126). By influencing the worldviews of actors, their habitual strategies, their norm system, and their preference structure, institutions become part of the cultural setting. This cognitive or cultural aspect of institutions is of particular importance when it comes to their effective functioning and their legitimacy, as related norms and interests can greatly reinforce (or undermine) the original institutions. On the other hand, institutions, often introduced at critical historical junctures to further the interests of certain actors, can also have path-dependent effects: their establishment creates commitment, and subsequently actors may be faced with sunk costs and enhanced benefits, which in turn push their individual behavior onto a path inhibiting quick institutional change (Pierson, 1996: 144-146; 2000). Path-dependency, however, may also arise from the cultural setting: when institutions are deeply embedded in the cognitive scripts of actors, they are hard to redesign because they have already structured actors' basic choices about reform (see Hall and Taylor, 1996: 940). Thus, initial institutional choices can yield longer-term effects by conditioning subsequent political behavior and policy choices (e.g., Putnam, 1993: 121-162). The seeming *aporia* of deliberative politics now seems more surmountable: one can conceive of specific institutional designs and of related cognitive scripts of actors—both embedded in specific historical paths—that create settings that make actors more conducive to deliberative politics. In respect to such an institutional conception of deliberative politics, Bo Rothstein (1998: 117-118) notes that the establishment of democratic institutions per se institutionalizes elements of a deliberative political setting: democratic institutions force actors to justify their positions publicly and at the same time let them discover the common good more easily. This is certainly true, but the additional requirements of deliberative democracy, such as respectful treatment of others and the search for consensual solutions, may not necessarily be present in majoritarian democracies with strong electoral competition. Instead, we propose that consociational democracies, both from a calculus perspective as well as from a cultural and historical perspective, may engender a greater potential for deliberative politics.

According to Lijphart's definition (1977: Chapter 2), consociational democracy comprises the following four characteristics: (1) grand coalition where all segments share power in the cabinet, (2) the principle of proportionality used for elections and appointments, (3) mutual veto granting each group the right to veto decisions involving its vital interests, and (4) segmental autonomy. Though criticized for being too restrictive (we return to this issue in the next section), these four criteria can still be considered the standard defining characteristics of consociational democracy (Andeweg, 2000: 6). While the principle of proportionality in consociational democracies provides for the equal representation and participation of all segmental groups and thus approximates a basic precondition of deliberative politics, the criteria of grand coalition and mutual veto seem to be the "lubricants" most conducive to its establishment. They create a logic of decision making that virtually forces actors to include the standpoints of others, as otherwise policy goals cannot be realized. Or, put differently, they force self-interested actors to engage in deliberation until unanimous consent is reached (Steiner, 1974: 5). However, while consociational settings undoubtedly further talking in decision-making processes, they do not necessarily make actors comply with the principles of deliberative politics. First, as George Tsebelis (1990: 159-172) points out, segmental leaders in consociational democracies can also initiate political confrontation to signal that the issue is salient or to discourage potential rivals inside the segment. Second, institutions requiring unanimous decisions—such as the mutual veto—might induce status quo defenders either to block decisions or to use confrontation strategies to impose their own point of view (Scharpf, 1994: 31). Third, the necessity to include the preferences of other actors and reach unanimous consent can also be achieved by bargaining techniques such as logrolling, pork-barreling, or buying-off groups; yet bargaining is a purely strategic, voting-centric mode of decision making that falls short of the communicative ideal of deliberative politics (see Avio, 1997: 544-551). Nevertheless, there may still be a number of instances in consociational democracies where self-interested political actors have incentives to get involved with deliberative politics, engage in true "problem-solving" activities (Olsen et al., 1982; Scharpf, 1994: 30-39), strive for common understanding, and find a reasoned consensus. This may be the case, for instance, when actors are confronted with fundamental or highly symbolic issues, which—contrary to distributive issues—can hardly be solved by bargaining techniques and require that the position of the other groups is respected and included in the decision. Furthermore, if actors want to achieve optimal rather than "lowest common denominator" solutions, they need to learn from each other and build up common knowledge, which again necessitates communicative action. Or, as negotiation theory and practice suggest, successful bargaining often depends on a prior, communicatively reached agreement about principles, norms, and rules (Risse, 2000: 20-21).

Besides this calculus aspect, the consociational theory encompasses a historical and cultural aspect. Critical junctures in history can make elite actors understand the perils of fragmentation (Lijphart, 1969: 216), leading them to strive for new institutions to contain these conflicts. This was, for instance, the case in the Westphalian Peace Treaty in 1648, in which political elites, in view of the ravages of the preceding religious wars, adopted the formulas of "parity" and "amicabilis compositio." These two formulas implied that certain essential interests of religious minorities had to be protected both by granting them equal representation and by suspending majority voting. Such institutions, in turn, can ossify into the cognitive scripts of actors, and, at the same time, they may exhibit path-dependency. This is the argument that Gerhard Lehmbruch (1993, 1996, 1998) puts forward for countries like Switzerland, Austria, and Germany: according to Lehmbruch, the two Westphalian formulas of "parity" and "amicabilis compositio" turned into actors' habitual strategies of how to cope with conflicts, and this early institutional innovation prefigured later negotiation and consensus practices in these three countries. Hans Daalder (1989) develops a similar argument for the Netherlands: he draws a parallel between the characteristics of modern consociationalism and the way that politics was conducted in the much earlier days of the Dutch republic. In both periods, Daalder argues, actors abstained from majoritarian decision making and played the political game in a cooperative way. Although one has to be wary of such continuity theses—continuity over such long periods and in changing historical circumstances requires explanation itself (Andeweg, 2000: 24)—one can still hold that traditions of conflict resolution shade into future arrangements and practices because proven and successfully working repertoires of conflict management and policy making let actors perceive the potential benefits of such arrangements, enhance the legitimacy of respective practices, or make them so conventional that they escape the direct scrutiny of actors.

Another aspect of consociationalism is that its institutional arrangement (particularly, the feature of grand coalition) can also further the recognition of the other groups as equal partners, improve the understanding of their standpoints, and, by creating positive trust spirals, foster cooperative attitudes (e.g., Linder, 1999a: 309; 1999b: 26). With an eye on deliberative politics, we assume that, on the one hand, historical insights of elite actors into the unsettling nature of the cleavages as well as cooperative and respectful attitudes emerging from consociational arrangements might create essential prerequisites for a more deliberative mode of decision making—and at the same time strengthen the deliberative assets of the formal institutional framework. Actors thus might be more willing to treat the claims and arguments of others respectfully and to find consensual solutions. On the other hand, the long historical roots of consociational practices might render such a cooperative style of policymaking a legitimate, familiar, and—in the eyes of the participants—also a potentially beneficial pattern of behavior.

Such cooperative behaviour seems to depend heavily on the political security of elites, that is, the absence of significant challenges to their leadership positions (Nordlinger, 1972: 64ff.). To be sure, we do not claim that consociationalism, is the only device to achieve a more deliberative mode of decision making. First, there may be other institutional settings and mechanisms with similar effects on deliberation than consociationalism, for instance, neocorporatism with its goal to forge compromises in tripartite negotiations among employers' organizations, trade unions, and the state, or presidential systems with less party discipline and thus more leeway for parliamentary actors to transcend party boundaries and to strive for consensual solutions; or there may also exist informal rules in committees and parliaments regarding the treatment of one another. Second, from a rational choice perspective, one can argue that self-interested actors, devoid of institutional constraints, might be interested in entering a discourse to correct false information, to enlarge their cognitions about the outside world, and to learn the preferences of their interaction partners (Risse, 2000: 12). More specific to the parliamentary arena, one can also argue that professional lawmakers with the prospect to stay in office for a relatively long term may see it advantageous to take one another's points of view seriously and seek mutually agreeable solutions (Nelson, 2000: 198-199). Third, one might conceive of political constellations in which electoral constraints are low, creating latitude for political actors to be more responsive to claims of other groups. Fourth, deliberative politics may also be influenced by socioeconomic factors such as economic growth and the financial resources of the state.[5] In the research project, we keep such factors as additional explanatory and control variables. Finally, one has always to keep in mind that institutions are not the sole causal force in politics, since they only *structure* actors' choices but do not *determine* them (Mayntz and Scharpf, 1995: 43). Self-interested actors, for example, may always face a trade-off between their narrow self-interest (e.g., short-term electoral goals) and their enlightened self-interest (e.g., to uphold the stability of the country). Or we might find actors who, during their socialization process, have acquired truly discursive attitudes and abilities. This may make outcomes indeterminate to some extent.

THE CHOICE OF COUNTRIES AND DEBATES

At first glance, the choice of the consociational countries might seem unproblematic since the literature considers Austria, Belgium, the Netherlands, and Switzerland the classical consociational countries. Looking at the history of the consociational theory, these four countries had paradigmatic status and were the empirical basis on which the theory was developed in the 1960s (Lehmbruch, 1967; Lijphart, 1968; Huyse, 1970; Steiner, 1970; for an excellent synthesis, see McRae, 1974a). Yet this classification has been severely criticized (Barry, 1975; Halpern, 1986; Lustick, 1997). In a nutshell, the critics doubted whether the four classic consociational countries did properly square both with the assumption of deeply segmented societies and with Lijphart's four defining characteristics. Another line of critique is that consociationalism had its heyday in the late 1950s and has been gradually fading since (e.g., Kriesi, 1995: 328-329). We elaborate on these criticisms for each of the four countries in turn and argue that—with some relaxing assumptions—there are still indications of marked differences between the universe of the classical consociational countries and the universe of the classical majoritarian democracies.

With regard to the Netherlands, the original interpretation of Dutch consociationalism has been challenged on the grounds that there was no real grand, all-inclusive coalition and that the Dutch society was not as deeply divided as Lijphart presents it to be (van Schendelen, 1984). The subcultures— the *zuilen,* or pillars—were not as far apart, and the religious and class cleavages were actually crosscutting. In a recent analysis, van Waarden (1998) stresses that the Calvinist, Catholic, and secular *zuilen* have lost most of their salience so that today the country is culturally quite homogeneous. Therefore, it is no longer necessary for the leaders to practice consociationalism in order to hold the subcultures together. Yet, consociationalism continues to be practiced in an alternative form. Although the political leaders no longer represent the classical subcultures, they continue to play the political game in a relatively cooperative way (Lijphart, 1989). The development of the Netherlands seems to be path-dependent in the sense that the old forms of political accommodation continue to have their effect (van Waarden, 1998).

Conceptually, one may ask whether it is still appropriate to label the Netherlands as consociational since the country has become culturally quite homogeneous. The label would no longer be appropriate if cultural heterogeneity is part of the definition of consociationalism. But, as argued elsewhere (Steiner, 1998), the social structure of a country can be treated as a separate variable from consociationalism, and it is then an empirical question what the relationship is between the degree of consociationalism and the degree of heterogeneity. With this approach, it is possible to have consociationalism in a homogeneous country like contemporary Netherlands. Of course, it would be possible to find a new label for consociationalism in homogeneous societies, for example "depoliticized" (Lijphart, 1968) democracies. In our view, it serves conceptual clarity if we use the same term for elite accommodation, whether it happens in a heterogeneous or in a homogeneous country.

As for Switzerland, the criticisms take a similar turn as in the Dutch case. It is argued that Switzerland was never a deeply divided society, that religious and class cleavages crosscut linguistic divisions. Others have gone further by suggesting that Swiss politics is not consociational in design (e.g., Lehner, 1984)—the Federal Council is not really a grand coalition because its members do not act as leaders or representatives of the subcultures—and there are majoritarian devices such as binding referenda (e.g. Barry, 1975). Yet, the Swiss polity undoubtedly has strong consociational devices, but these do not function in the way postulated by the theory. Consociationalism in Switzerland rather stems from the institutions of direct democracy. The referendum not only acts as the functional equivalent of the minority veto,[6] but it also produces a steady danger of a veto in a popular vote. This, in turn, forces political actors to adopt cooperative strategies and build large supporting coalitions for policy proposals (Neidhart, 1970; Barry, 1975: 483-485; Linder, 1994: 118-126; 1999: 295-297). On the other hand, the "trench" between German- and French-speaking Switzerland has become deeper in the last decade—at least in the perception of many French-speakers—and recent referenda indicate the existence of persistent strong differences in political attitudes among the linguistic groups (Lehmbruch, 1993; Kriesi, 1995; Steiner, 1998: 9-11; Linder, Riedwyl, and Steiner, 2000). Yet efforts are continued and even strengthened to handle these cleavages in a consociational way (see also Kriesi, 1995: 332).

Criticisms have also been raised for the Austrian case. Although Barry (1975) agrees with Lijphart and others that in the period after World War II, Austria did conform closely to the elite cartel model, he challenges the proposition that consociationalism was a necessary condition for Austrian political stability (Barry, 1975: 498). The "Lager" were not so far apart from each other, and the level of hostility was quite low between them. According to Barry, it was rather economic prosperity and a European environment that contributed to a stable parliamentary democracy in Austria after World War II. This was furthered by a general willingness of the party leaders to cooperate, a fact that has held true in Austrian politics until recently (Crepaz, 1998). With the coalition of the People's Party and Jörg Haider's Freedom Party, however, consociationalism in Austria may have come to an end. This makes Austria an all the more interesting case for our project since it allows us to study parliamentary debates in the era of consociationalism compared with the most recent time period.

Belgium, in turn, comes closest to a "classical" consociational polity. After World War II, the strong and potentially unsettling language cleavage between Flemish and Walloons gave rise to a full-fledged consociational regime including all of Lijphart's standard defining characteristics. Though consociationalism has seen a shift toward its federal component in recent years, the other consociational devices for managing conflicts under shared rule— proportionality, grand coalition, and veto points for the two linguistic groups— are still effective in the Belgian polity (e.g., Deschouwer, 1998).

Although there may be other or additional causative agents for cooperative behavior at the elite level than the criterion of segmented societies and Lijphart's four defining characteristics, the strong persistence of cooperative patterns of decision making supports the argument that Austria, Belgium, the Netherlands, and Switzerland may still be considered "consociational" countries for most of the time period under investigation. Ultimately, the critique of consociationalism can boil down to a question of adequate labeling: if the term "consociationalism" is stripped off its original connotation with segmented societies and includes other non-majoritarian techniques in its definition—as we propose— then the classical labeling might be appropriate; otherwise, it might be more appropriate to classify these countries with other labels such as "power sharing" or "consensus democracies."

How did we make the choice of the majoritarian countries to be included in the investigation? The United States and the United Kingdom are "natural" candidates since there is general agreement that they are the classic majoritarian countries (Almond, 1956). Especially the United Kingdom is the paradigmatic case of the "Westminster model": Parliament is elected by a first-past-the-post system, and the winning party forms the cabinet. Since the opposition has no veto rights, and since the country is strongly centralized, the winning party has all the power and can impose its will by majority votes in Parliament. Recently, with devolution in Scotland and Wales, the United Kingdom has taken up some cooperative features, though the effects are still indeterminate. The United States, although commonly considered a competitive majoritarian system, always had some cooperative elements, for instance, the two-thirds majority rule in the Senate for some important decisions.

Canada is an interesting case to be included in the study because it is generally competitive and has a language cleavage like Belgium and Switzerland (see McRae, 1974b). France has many competitive aspects, especially in the cleavage between the right and the left. It seems appropriate to include also two intermediate countries that we may call semi-consociational democracies. Germany combines competitive and consociational features and is labeled by Lehmbruch (1998) a semi-consociational country. Italy is classified by some as consociational (Pappalardo, 1980), and by some others as competitive so that it may well serve as another intermediate case.

A further and different check on the validity of the preceding classification is offered by the second edition of Lijphart's *Democracies* published under the title *Patterns of Democracies* (Lijphart, 1999). As in the first edition, Lijphart distinguishes majoritarian versus consensus democracies. His concept of consensus democracy is more flexible and wider than the concept of consociational democracy, as used here. It encompasses a larger number of institutional variables than consociational democracy. Lijphart looks altogether at ten institutional variables. He finds that these ten variables cluster along two separate dimensions, which he calls the executive-parties and federal-unitary dimensions. He calls the former also "the joint exercise of power dimension." This dimension of consensus corresponds closely to the concept of consociational democracy as used in our present project. The degree of consensus on this dimension is measured with regard to the following five variables: (1) effective number of parliamentary parties, (2) minimal winning one-party cabinets, (3) executive dominance, (4) electoral disproportionality, and (5) interest group pluralism. Consensus on this dimension is considered high if the first variable has a positive value, and the other four variables a negative value.

Lijphart classifies a large number of countries, including all ten countries of our current project, on both of his dimensions for the time period 1945-1996 and, separately, for the periods 1945-1970 and 1971-1996. On the dimension that comes close to our consociational-competitive dimension, our four competitive countries (US, UK, Canada, and France) are for both time periods clearly distinguished in the expected direction from our four consociational countries (Austria, Belgium, the Netherlands, and Switzerland). This gives additional validity to our classification. The situation is more ambiguous for Germany and Italy, which we classified as semi-consociational countries. Germany is in both periods rather in the middle but closer to the consensus than to the majoritarian pole. Considering also the analysis of Lehmbruch noted earlier, we feel comfortable classifying Germany as still a semi-consociational democracy and not consociational democracy. Italy is in both time periods quite close to the consensus pole. We think, however, that there is great uncertainty on how to classify Italy, which makes it all the more interesting to include it in our study.

For each of the ten countries, we select decision cases for two time periods: the 1950s as the heyday of consociationalism and the 1990s. In one set of cases the major conflict pits regions against each other. Such *horizontal* conflicts were always topical in the consociational literature and are therefore critical for our theoretical question. The second set of cases deals with *vertical* conflicts among social classes; such conflicts were traditionally the domain of the corporatist literature. But the consociational theory has also been applied to conflicts that were primarily vertical in nature, for example, the conflict between the *Lager* in Austria.[7] Thus, the results of our study will have a bearing on the corporatist literature as well.

As to the selection of the decision cases, we ensure that for regional conflicts not much more than region should matter and, for the social class conflicts, not much more than social class. Ideal-typically, region and social class should be the only considerations in the two types of conflict. In reality, these ideal types probably do not exist, but the decision cases to be investigated should approach the ideal-types as much as possible.

OPERATIONALIZATION OF DISCOURSE QUALITY

Systematic empirical studies of deliberative processes are not yet common in the social sciences. One of the few exceptions is Jürgen Gerhards' (1997) quantitative investigation of the public discourse in German mass media on abortion. He tries to observe whether the public sphere functions in terms of Habermas' discourse ethics or rather according to the liberal model. He does this by measuring and evaluating three indicators of *"Diskursivität"* that he distilled mainly from Habermas' work: mutual respect of the participants, response and justification of statements, and the level of rationality in the discourse.

Our own project involves a more complex conceptualization of deliberative politics. As we have shown, deliberation, especially in existing democratic institutions such as parliamentary committees and full sessions in Parliament, must be seen as determined both by formal institutional factors and by actor-related influences. The institutional level of deliberation in a real-world parliamentary setting differs substantially from the ideal of a Habermasian "unconstrained discourse." A reasonable consensus is probably quite rare, and concluding majority votes as well as the representation of group interests are perfectly legitimate and necessary elements of any basically representative democracy (see Habermas, 1990: 42; 1992: 210, 371; Chambers, 1995).

We intend to develop a system of indicators to judge the quality of deliberation in a given debate independently of the institutional particularities; that is, we want to measure the discursive quality of a debate as purely as possible on the actor level. On the one hand, the system of indicators should be complex enough to capture the concept of deliberation in its most important dimensions (internal validity). On the other hand, the indicators must be observable in the debate itself, in an intersubjective manner (reliability).

In our attempt to pursue these elementary goals of any operationalization, we developed seven indicators. They are based upon broadly shared key concepts of the theoretical literature on deliberative democracy and discourse ethics and are focused on the parliamentary arena. Despite the considerable complexity of parliamentary debates, we attempt to keep the coding instructions relatively easy, so as to ensure a high level of reliability. The following is an elaboration on these indicators, followed by an overview of the indicators and their codes. It is the foundation for the development of the Discourse Quality Index (DQI). We discuss the seven indicators under four headings.

1. Fundamental for a deliberation to develop is *participation* within the debate. In Western democracies, this type of basic participation can usually be seen as given in a parliamentary setting. Normal participation is assumed to be impaired only if a speaker is cut off by a formal decision, or if she or he feels explicitly disturbed in the case of a verbal interruption by other actors.

2. A more complex concept is the type of *justification* offered to defend a conclusion of content. In order to understand the rationale behind this concept, we have to characterize speeches in the parliamentary context in linguistic terms. Such a speech can be seen as an *argumentation*, that is, a process in which "someone tries to convince someone of something by citing evidence and drawing, or suggesting, inferences from this evidence and from other beliefs or assumptions (hypotheses)" (Sebeok, 1986: 50-51). Within this definition, *inference* means a "semiotic process in which from something given (the premises), something else (the conclusion) is derived on the basis of certain relations between premises and conclusion" (Sebeok, 1986: 51). In a speech in the parliamentary context, the crucial conclusion is not so much the final conclusion to vote yes or no with respect to a certain demand but the conclusion of content—which is in itself part of an inference toward the final conclusion. In short, at the center of our concept of justification is the inference in which the conclusion of content is derived from the premises (i.e., primarily

reasons). The relations (links) between premises and conclusion may contain argument connectives such as "since," "for," "so," "therefore," "because" (Angell, 1964: 4-15). Yet argument connectives can also be made implicitly. "Economies of speech" may lead speakers to leave out even other elements of an argumentation, since they may be so obvious that it is unnecessary to state them (Angell, 1964: 368-369). This is the main reason that we ignore the inference toward the voting decision (i.e., the final conclusion): it is such an obvious part of a parliamentary speech that it is often only latently made.

2.1. Thus, the first indicator of the concept of justification—the *level* of the justification—follows from the preceding linguistic characterization of parliamentary debates, applied to the guidelines of deliberative theory (e.g., Cohen, 1989: 22; Chambers, 1999). Reasonable deliberation is fostered if speakers offer a conclusion of content that is embedded in a complete inference as previously defined. This is what we call a qualified justification. Reasonable deliberation is fostered in that case, since rational critique by other speakers is easily possible.[8] A qualified justification can be topped with what we call a sophisticated justification: multiple conclusions of content, each embedded in a complete inference. On the other hand, a justification is inferior if the inference made lacks either (1) reasons (premises), or (2) relations between reasons and conclusion, or (3) both. Inferior justifications inhibit reasonable deliberation, since rational critique is hardly possible.

2.2. The second aspect of the second key concept is the *content* of the justification. This indicator measures whether the argumentation within a statement is cast in terms of a conception of the common good or in terms of narrow group or constituency interests. The importance of referring to the common good is mainly stressed by deliberative theorists drawing on John Rawls (e.g., Cohen, 1989; Gutmann and Thompson, 1990, 1996). According to Rawls (1971: 65-83), a utilitarian conception of the common good with its inherent idea of Pareto efficiency is morally inferior to his second principle of justice with its inherent difference principle. The latter states that "social and economic inequalities are to be arranged so that they are ... to the greatest benefit of the least advantaged" (Rawls, 1971: 83). In our view, however, it would contradict the principles of discourse ethics to assume a priori one conception of the common good to be superior to another. We should not normatively judge these conceptions independently of the context. Finally, we have to be aware that a given reference to the common good may be not much more than "cheap talk," being purely rhetorical and intended to attract potential voters. It should also be noted that the reference to even narrow group interests is perfectly legitimate in a deliberative arena.

3.   The third key concept of deliberative politics is *respect*.

3.1. First, it is important to see if speakers show respect toward the groups, which would be helped with the demand under discussion. This indicator is a translation of Habermas' (1991: 73) postulation of empathy into the parliamentary context: here, empathy toward the other participants of the debate is less significant than empathy toward the social groups that have a right to be represented in Parliament.

3.2. In a similar sense, deliberation requires, second, that both sides respect the *demands* under discussion, at least as long as they can intersubjectively be seen as justified. Macedo (1999: 10), for example, regards the recognition of the "merit in [the] opponents' claims" as being one of the principal purposes of deliberation. Of course, it is useless to apply this indicator to speakers who argue on behalf of a certain demand in the first place.

3.3. Third, discursive participants need to respect the *counterarguments* to their own position. As the actors can usually exchange their points of view before the debates, and since these debates are usually rigorously structured, we should not merely measure responses to counterarguments expressed in the debate itself. Instead, we also have to measure respect toward long-standing counterarguments brought forth in other settings before the current debate. Our measure is an indicator for Gutmann and Thompson's (1990: 85) concept of "mutual respect."[9] In important (i.e., conflicting) debates, there are always substantial counterarguments to one's own conclusion of content. Thus, it can be expected of a discursive actor to include in his or her own argumentation at least one such counterargument without degrading it immediately. Since the critique of a counterargument often becomes an element of justification of one's own position, the level of rationality of the critique is measured within indicator 2.1 (level of justification).

4. The last indicator is *constructive politics*. It is, on the one hand, based upon the principal goal of Habermasian discourse ethics to reach a genuine consensus. Translated into real-world politics, this means that discursive participants should at least attempt to reach a general agreement. In this respect, actors proposing mediating arguments and solutions would qualify for the fourth and highest level of rationality within the concept of Gerhards (1997: 22).[10] On the other hand, positional politics, in which actors do not actively search for consensus or compromise, can be seen as perfectly legitimate as long as participants show respect to the people with whom they disagree. This is the position of Gutmann and Thompson, who argue that seeking agreement is not always possible, whereas mutual respect is possible and desirable in any debate (Gutmann and Thompson, 2000: 243).

Based upon the preceding elaboration, we derive the Discourse Quality Index (DQI), which we use to investigate the debates. It consists of seven indicators measured in dichotomous and multichotomous, ordinal and nominal scales Table 5.1.[11]

We intend to disaggregate the parliamentary debates into smaller units, to code these smaller units, and then to reaggregate these codes for the parliamentary debates at large. The smaller units into which we disaggregate the parliamentary debates are the speeches within a debate. The seven indicators of deliberation are conceptually independent from each other. How exactly we can combine them to construct a single-dimensional variable to measure the deliberative quality of a debate must be left open at the present stage of the project. In addition, we are aware that it is not unproblematic to compare these measures across different debates. No claim in the real world is exactly the same as another, and thus it is natural that, for example, the indicator "respect toward the demand" will correlate strongly and negatively with the perceived extremity of the claim. It is thus important to choose debates that include fundamental claims of a certain extremity so that comparisons across debates are easier to make.

Table 5.1
Discourse Quality Index

---

1 Participation
  0: interruption of a speaker: a speaker feels explicitly disturbed, or interruption occurs through a formal decision.
  1: normal participation is possible.

2 Justification
  2.1 Level
  0: no justification.
  1: inferior justification: conclusion(s) embedded in (an) *in*complete inference(s).
  2: qualified justification: one conclusion embedded in a *complete* inference; additional conclusions embedded in *in*complete inferences may be present.
  3: sophisticated justification: more than one conclusion, each embedded in a complete inference.

  2.2 Content
  0: explicit statement concerning constituency or group interests.
  1: neutral statement: no reference to constituency or group interests nor to common good.
  2: explicit statement in terms of a conception of the common good:
       2a: explicit statement in utilitarian or collective terms.
       2b: explicit statement in terms of the difference principle.

3 Respect
  3.1 toward group in general ("empathy")
  0: no respect: explicitly negative statement concerning the group that would be helped.
  1: implicit respect: no explicitly negative statement concerning the group that would be helped.
  2: respect: explicitly positive statement concerning the group that would be helped.

  3.2 toward demands
  0: no respect: explicitly negative statement concerning the demand.
  1: implicit respect: no explicitly negative statement concerning the demand.
  2: respect: explicitly positive statement concerning the demand.

  3.3 toward counterarguments
  0: counterarguments are ignored.
  1: counterarguments are included but explicitly degraded.
  2: counterarguments are included, but neither explicitly degraded nor valued.
  3: counterarguments are included and explicitly valued.

4 Constructive Politics
  0: positional politics: speaker sits on his or her position.
  1: alternative proposal: proposal for a different agenda.
  2: mediating proposal: proposal within the same agenda.

CONCLUDING REMARKS AND OUTLOOK

In this chapter we sketched a conceptual framework, arguing for a certain causality between institutional settings and the mode of decision making, namely, between consociational institutions and deliberative politics. It must be stressed, however, that this framework is far from being a model with clearly hypothesized causalities. Thus, the framework is speculative to a certain extent, and the project must mainly be seen as exploratory in the sense that it attempts to incorporate the presently rather isolated conceptions of deliberative politics into more traditional frameworks of political science.

As a consequence, the project is to maintain a considerable conceptual elasticity. As elaborated in this chapter, we expect the institutional setting of consociationalism to be an important influence on deliberative practices. However, we have to be prepared that, empirically, the deliberative quality has alternative influences, maybe even influences that are constant across all countries. It is quite possible that deliberation rather stems from broader "complex political institutions" (Colomer, forthcoming). One even cannot rule out the possibility that pure self-interest may lead a majority to allow for deliberation.[12] A central part of the project is the empirical analysis of these supposed institutional influences on deliberation. This is going to be done by the means of the Discourse Quality Index (DQI). It is developed on the basis of a broad range of indicators that capture the principal dimensions of several conceptions of discourse ethics and deliberative democracy. The index is independent of cultural and institutional peculiarities and thus enables a relatively undistorted comparative—cross-national and temporal—and causal analysis.

In a later stage of the project, the conceptual framework will include a further link: the nexus between the quality of deliberation and the actual political decisions made. This can be seen in the light of Lijphart's conclusions concerning the higher qualities of consensus democracies: are "kinder, gentler" political decisions and outcomes the direct result of consensus institutions (Lijphart, 1999: 300), or can they be better explained with the additional link of deliberation? This would be an especially interesting question in the case of a low correlation between consociationalism and deliberation. Normatively, this leads again to the ancient philosophical question of the "good life" (Plato) or, in accordance with the premises of discourse ethics, the question of a "*better* life" brought forth by fairer decisions, by which we mean decisions that respect and substantially include the legitimate demands of weak minorities. Our project is set to explore the links between some of these vital aspects of democracy.

NOTES

1. The remainder of this paragraph draws on Baynes (1995: 215-216).
2. Hence, the principal currents of deliberative democracy, which are usually based upon either John Rawls (e.g., Gutmann and Thompson, 1990, 1996; Nelson, 2000) or Habermas, (e.g., Chambers, 1996, Bohmann, 1996) but only very rarely on both, maintain a common core after all. This is so, since Cohen based his conception of

deliberative democracy on Rawls' (1971) "Theory of Justice." Additionally, Habermas and Rawls themselves have approximated their respective conceptions in a dialogue (see Habermas, 1995; Rawls, 1995).

3. This is what Habermas calls a "rational consensus" following a "rational discourse" (Habermas, 1992: 138-139). To rule out confusion with the liberalist meaning of the notion of "rational" (see later), we replace the former with the notion of "reasonable." By doing this, we incorporate the differentiation between the two notions brought forth by Rawls (1996: 48-54). Rawls' definition of the reasonable (which is based upon Kant) seems to be similar to Habermas' conception of the rational.

4. Sociological institutionalism, however, is omitted from our analysis: by integrating symbol systems or cognitive scripts in the definition of institutions, it breaks down the conceptual divide between institutions and culture and thus involves the danger of tautology when taken as an analytical tool.

5. Linder (1999a: 304-305) argues for Switzerland that the economic crisis of the early 1970s put considerable strain on the smooth functioning of consociationalism.

6. Historically, it helped Catholics to make their claims heard in the national arena.

7. Consociational decision making and corporatist decision making were always correlated (e.g., Lane and Ersson, 1997).

8. *Rational critique* as defined by Angell (1964: 23): "Provided that the conclusion is meaningful and self-consistent, rational critique of an argument is directed towards (a) the acceptability of the reasons and/or (b) the connections between the reasons and the conclusion," thus not toward the conclusion itself. Thereby, Angell's notion of "argument" is comparable to Sebeok's (1986) notion of "inference," and the notion of "connections" is interchangeable with Sebeok's notion of "relations."

9. It would be problematic to include *personal respect* as another aspect of respect. This would have to be largely based upon indicators of politeness. In most Parliaments codes of conduct are institutionalized, such as the expressions "My honourable Gentleman" and "My honourable friend" in British debates. Yet the more a formulation of politeness is used in a setting, the less it represents genuine respect (see also Haase, 1994: 98).

10. Gerhards' levels of rationality draw heavily on Rainer Döbert (1996), who in turn developed his conception on the basis of Jürgen Habermas and Jean Piaget.

11. For a fuller description of the DQI with illustrative examples, see the Web site of the project: www.ipw.unibe.ch/discourse.

12. According to Chwe (1999), a purely self-interested majority might allow the minority to sometimes "enforce" its favored decision, since this provides greater incentives for the minority to participate and thus leads to an accumulation of information, which, in turn, makes the majority better off.

6

From Jean Bodin to Consociational Democracy and Back

Can Erk and Alain-G. Gagnon

In this chapter we argue that the career of a concept that is currently receiving serious attention from intellectuals and policymakers in much of the Western world, that of divided sovereignty, may be charted in the work of one of the foremost contemporary students of cultural pluralism, Kenneth McRae. His extensive writings on consociationalism, federalism, and the accommodation of ethnolinguistic differences in democratic society have been widely acclaimed for their empirial richness, but his explorations in cultural pluralism have always been guided by normative concerns.

McRae wants to understand how linguistically divided societies can best manage and solve their problems. In his series *Conflict and Compromise in Multilingual Societies*, McRae wrote on Switzerland, Belgium, and Finland, but a case could be made that all these works are, in fact, about Canada. McRae was looking for a way to keep the Canadian experiment going and searching for ideas and practices from these countries. It is not entirely clear if he found the magic formula in the end. Maybe it was not a magic formula that he was after, but from the way that his work looks from Québec, the preoccupation seems to be stability and continuity. To be fair, his attachment to stability did not corrode his inquiry or the way that he dealt with facts. One rarely feels that there is an agenda forced down the throat of the gullible and willing reader. Basically, McRae is after understanding and explaining the tensions that characterize multilingual societies. He has often remained reticent about volunteering to concoct prescriptions for Canada. Even when he served as a research supervisor for the Canadian Royal Commission on Bilingualism and Biculturalism, he retained his characteristic cautious erudition, but one element distinguishes his work from that of most other English Canadian scholars and, we must add, from many Québécois scholars nowadays. He has a normative attachment to a vision of Canada that is increasingly being discarded on both sides. Despite many setbacks and disappointments, McRae continues to believe in dualism. We will now briefly cover some of his important works in light of the preceding arguments.

It is quite surprising to note that McRae's doctoral dissertation at Harvard was on Jean Bodin. His first important work was, consequently, on this philosopher, who was an advocate of royal absolutism and who is often considered to be the principal architect of the modern state. McRae's (1962) work is an edition of Jean Bodin's *The Six Bookes of a Commonweale* translated by Richard Knolles in 1606 together with revisions based on Bodin's Latin and French originals. McRae compared the Latin and French editions of Bodin's *Six livres de la République* and combined various parts of the two editions and eliminated the contradictory sections in order to come up with one coherent, English-language version.

We have to admit that McRae's choice of Bodin is rather puzzling. Bodin is known as one of the philosophical forefathers of the strong state along with Thomas Hobbes. In fact, Bodin predates Hobbes in his absolutist line of thinking. Bodin's ideas of a strong monarchy, common public interest, and absolute sovereignty have provided the theoretical foundations of a unitary central state. However, McRae's subsequent work on Canada and other multilingual societies, in contrast, is characterised by an implicit acceptance of divided sovereignty. Given his research interests, one would have assumed that McRae's choice of a classical theorist would be someone like Johannes Althusius rather than Bodin. In fact, McRae himself admits the incompatibility between federal ideas and those of Bodin when he states that "there is nothing in Bodin's theory to enable him to explain a federal state" (McRae, 1962: 21). But at the same time, maybe it is precisely Bodin who influenced McRae's thinking the most. Facing the strength of an argument for a strong sovereign state for the common good and recognising the attractiveness of such idea, arguably McRae wanted to show the limits of such an ideal in the Canadian context. In due course, this probably led to a decades-long quest to demonstrate that democracy and stability can very well be attained in divided societies without a strong central sovereign. Put differently, McRae's entire career can be seen as an attempt to prove Bodin wrong. This agenda is most visible in his series *Conflict and Compromise in Multilingual Societies*, but elements concerning divided sovereignty and an endorsement of dualism can be found in his earlier works as well.

McRae's brief overview of Canadian history, in particular, that of Québec, in an edited volume published in 1964 is one of the most comprehensive accounts of a complicated past and certainly the most pleasurable read on what would have otherwise been a very tedious subject matter. Here he lays down the groundwork of a dualistic concept of Canada that will mark his future work. The historical survey is rich with details and comprehensive in its scope. It shows a deep knowledge of French Canada, and, written during the Quiet Revolution, it includes insights that have remained surprisingly solid despite the massive changes in Québec since then. This knowledge and his insights have remained the defining cornerstone of his subsequent inquiries. McRae's work is remarkable for its understanding of French Canada's discontent. He does not explicitly empathize with the historical grievances of the French Canadians, but he covers the issues in such a way as to leave no doubt where his sympathies lie. One of the best examples of this is the way that McRae covers the history of the Red River colony that later became Manitoba (for a discussion of Manitoba's official duality, see McRae, 1964: 255-258). We believe that the failure of a bicultural and bilingual Manitoba epitomizes McRae's vision of a federation that has recklessly wasted opportunities. To be fair, he never puts it the way that we do, but it seems clear that the fate of the Red River colony is a recurring theme in his work. As it is the case in this historical overview, his subsequent works on Canada often include lengthy sections on the disappointing fate of this bicultural experiment. It represents what McRae probably wished Canada had become, a bilingual and bicultural country from coast to coast. Twenty-five years after the historical survey on the Canadian federation, his views have hardly changed. Writing in 1990 on Manitoba's original official duality, he provided the following observation: "Even though [the] linguistic and religious guarantees were constitutionally entrenched, both were swept away in 1890 by provincial statutes inspired by the rising tide of anti-Catholic and anti-French sentiment imported from eastern Canada. In just two decades, a consociational replica of Québec had been refashioned into a hegemonic replica of Ontario (McRae, 1990: 210).

In 1974 McRae brought together leading scholars on divided societies for an outstanding edited volume entitled *Consociational Democracy: Political Accommodation in Segmented Societies*. To this day, this book remains the best collection put together on consociational democracy. The volume is separated into three sections, a theoretical one, a comparative section covering the divided societies in West Europe, and a final section on Canada. The theoretical section is an impressive collection of the top theorists of consociational democracy, including Val R. Lorwin, Arend Lijphart, Gerhard Lehmbruch, Jürg Steiner, and Hans Daalder. The comparative section includes the case studies of Austria, Belgium, Switzerland, and the Netherlands. In the last section McRae's reasons for editing such a book become visible. This section on Canada, especially McRae's own contribution, searches for signs of consociational democracy in the Canadian context and seeks to explore if such consociational practices deliver the same mollifying political effects as they do in Europe. In fact, in his preface to the volume; McRae makes explicit that the whole project was put together to help find solutions to the problems that the Canadian federation was facing: "I do accept that it is imperative to explore, with urgency, imagination, and willingness to innovate, just how [the Canadian] federation may be continued and adapted so as to accommodate and reconcile forces that are threatening to tear it apart." (McRae, ed., 1974: viii).

In his chapter on consociationalism and the Canadian political system, McRae seems to have recognized the limits of a consociational solution in the Canadian context. Once again, after lamenting the termination of official dualism in Manitoba in 1890 and the Northwest Territories in 1892, McRae turns to the most important actor in English Canada: "In place of bicultural accommodation, the move to abolish French-language schools in Ontario in

1913 and the wartime conscription policy of 1917 led to further and sharper polarization" (McRae, 1974a: 259). His conclusion is indeed a very bleak one: "In retrospect, the quest to accommodate linguistic diversity in Canada may be viewed as a series of lost opportunities" (259). But this article—and in fact, the whole volume—is not a conclusion for a research project. Indeed, this work is only the beginning of a research agenda that would mark the coming twenty five years of McRae's career. His attention from this moment onward seems to be toward finding a way to solve, or at least manage, the divisions in Canadian society. It comes as no surprise, then, that following this poor 1974 report card on the Canadian federation's inability to accommodate linguistic-cultural diversity, McRae embarked upon his massive project on *Conflict and Compromise in Multilingual Societies*, where he sought answers to the question of stability in divided societies. In this series, McRae covered some of the most important examples of divided societies in the developed world. In particular, his focus was on Switzerland, Belgium, and Finland. A fourth volume on Canada is due to follow these three case studies. The subject of the series is self-explanatory, that is, conflict and compromise in multilingual societies. Nowadays, such themes are increasingly occupying centre stage in political science, but for many decades studies on linguistically divided democracies were left on the fringes of the discipline. In this respect, McRae is a very different political scientist who has distinguished himself by continuing to write on societies with divided political sovereignty.

During the 1960s, 1970s and 1980s any deviation from the Westphalian/Hobbesian unitary state was seen by mainstream political science as an anomaly. Divided or partial sovereignty was perceived to be a transitory phase in a journey toward state consolidation or eventual breakup. Theories of consociational democracy were dealing with political order in divided societies, but they stopped short of combining their insights with constitutional and, in particular, federal arrangements. Consociationalism dealt with divided societies, not with divided sovereignity. McRae's work is unique in the sense that he wanted to translate theories of consociational democracy in divided societies into workable solutions. In other words, his concerns were beyond theoretical formulations. However, he was always to retain his scholarly caution before jumping to prescriptions. Yet, the one common, underlying point is glaringly visible in all of his work: an acceptance of divided political authority. Looking back at McRae's work spanning more than forty five years, he seems to be one of the few political scientists who saw continuity and stability in divided authority. Knowing the Canadian case by heart, he turned his attention to other successful experiences with divided political authority to seek answers and insights. Now that studies on deviations from the Westphalian/Hobbesian unitary state are in vogue, students of federalism and nationalism find his work on divided societies to be of immense use. His series *Conflict and Compromise in Multilingual Societies* remains an indispensable contribution to the field. The series carries with it a quality that is characteristic of McRae's work; that is; it is a rare combination of a historian's attention to detail with a political scientist's concern for generalizable observations.

At the end of the day, there is one major front on which we believe McRae has fallen short. He has not yet provided us with the formula for the stability and continuity of the Canadian federation. Once dualism is out of the picture and all historical opportunities for a consociational accommodation have been squandered, there is not a lot left to do. His suggestions for restraint and understanding have been overlooked by English Canada, a conclusion that he readily admits: "To any dispassionate observer it must be evident that throughout Canadian history the English fragment everywhere has shown itself coldly unreceptive to the idea of dualism outside Québec and often violently hostile to the values of the French fragment" (McRae, 1992: 151). For the success of his version of a bilingual and bicultural Canada, English Canada had to recognize French Canada as an equal partner. This has clearly not been the case. For a scholar committed to duality, the remaining option is to support Québec's demands to opt out from this union when it is clear that a partnership is not on the table.

There was one rare moment when he came out in full force to argue Québec's case. This was during the chaotic ratification process of the Meech Lake Accord. In a tributary volume to his colleague at Carleton University, Khayyam Zev Paltiel, McRae abandoned his academic detachment and berated English Canada for its intransigence: "If Canada should fail to survive the next few years as a political entity, historians will seek the causes not so much in the dream of Québec nationalism as in the failure of our collective political leadership to find a place for this nationalism within a tolerant Canada" (McRae, 1992: 145). In this article, he criticized the constant references to "equal rights" in English Canada. He warned that such "equal rights" discourse eerily resembled the anti-French and anti-Catholic backlash against the 1888 Jesuit Estates Bill and did not hesitate to bring in his comparative experience: "My own studies of several plural societies over many years suggest that any appeal to majority rule generally means that somebody's rights are in imminent danger of being overridden" (145). Moreover, McRae seemed to be ready to dispose of the prudent optimism of consociationalism in favour of the radicalism of the control model. He argued that the situation in Canada was better described as the dominance of one linguistic group over the other rather than a compromise to coexist. McRae considered English Canada's attachment to majoritarian liberalism to be an impediment to harmonious coexistence. This, he argued, rendered unattainable a partnership based on consociational principles. Instead, McRae saw signs of Ian Lustick's (1979) sceptical and pessimistic control model where the dominant group establishes control over the weaker group through the workings of the political structure. "The very least that one can say is that this Anglophone view of Canada comes closer to a control model than to a consociational one" (McRae, 1992: 146).

Lustick had developed the model in the context of the Arab minority in Israel. His model replaced some of the basic points of the model of consociational democracy, where power is shared between the elites in divided societies, with one where one dominant group uses the political system to "control" the weaker side and thus attain political stability and avoid disorder.

Clearly, this is not a normative prescriptive model but one that seeks to supplement consociational democracy in explaining stability in divided societies. At the same time, it has to be admitted that it is a more radical model with built-in assumptions concerning injustice and the potential for explosive tension. Considering his usual scholarly distance from the subject matter in his other works, this article is somewhat of an anomaly for McRae. It is interesting to note that this outburst of indignation was a one-off thing for McRae. The Meech Lake debacle had compelled him to put his professional detachment on hold, and he had delivered this scathing critique of the narrow-mindedness, even hypocrisy of English Canada. But he would never repeat this. The coauthor of this article tried to convince him at that time to expand on the control model and explore the further implications of this idea, but McRae simply refused. Maybe this is the main theme that will be in the fourth volume of the study *Conflict and Compromise in Multilingual Societies* on Canada.

However, we believe that neither consociational democracy nor its control variant can help to solve or even explain the problems facing the Canadian federation nowadays. Things have changed considerably since the days of the Red River colony and countless other missed opportunities for a consociational settlement through the recognition of duality. With its national assembly and government, Québec society can now lay claim to a state that has many of the trappings of autonomous states in the modern world. Models that offer prescriptions for divided societies within single electoral systems, such as the theory of consociational democracy, have little contemporary applicability. A workable model has to acknowledge Québec as an autonomous national state, not a consociational pillar of a divided society.

The attractiveness of a theory that explains political stability in deeply divided societies is understandable. Particularly in response to the dominant Anglo-American view that associated stable democratic government with social homogeneity and majoritarian democracy, the experiences of European countries with deep divisions like Switzerland, Belgium, Austria, and the Netherlands presented interesting theoretical and practical questions for political scientists during the 1970s and 1980s. A group of prominent scholars, including McRae, formed an epistemic community around the theory of consociational democracy that used notions of an elite cartel, proportional representation, grand coalitions, and depoliticization to explain political stability in divided societies. Consequently, consociational democracy spurred a research agenda around this core question and gradually became a part of mainstream political science.

In its most basic form, consociational democracy is a theory that seeks to explain how some small European states have avoided the shortcomings of majoritarian democracy through accommodation and power-sharing between the political elites representing the constituent social groups; but an often overlooked component of this theory is a single electoral system. In a system of proportional representation, a so-called elite-cartel is formed by means of a grand coalition. Consequently, political stability is attained through this somewhat secretive collusion among elites as they avoid confrontational politics. In a federal system, however, with separate orders of government and elected parliaments, such secretive accommodations are not possible and, we believe, not desirable. Separate parliaments with their own oppositions and separate governments with their own bureaucracies bring an element of democratic accountability and transparency that does not exist in a pillarized social structure. Any prescription that seeks to eschew confrontation and decrease tension between Canada and Québec should recognize the existence of these separate orders of government. Of course, it is still necessary to seek ways to avoid inflating the divisive issues to the point of no return between the two sides in a federal system, even if the dual nature of the system is not officially recognized. While the theory of consociational democracy is inapplicable to this situation in many ways, its core premise of attaining stability despite deep divisions is still relevant, but the existence of political institutions in a federal arrangement produces a system considerably different from a divided society within a single electoral structure. On the one hand, a high degree of institutional autonomy in a federal structure, as opposed to a pillarized society, allows constituent units a much higher degree of self-rule over many issues that would have otherwise become controversial at the center. When real disagreements arise, the existence of separate political institutions can exacerbate the conflict by transforming the issues into a confrontation with "interstate" characteristics. Consociational democracy might have played an important role in solving problems over confessional schools in the Low Countries, but it has little applicability to circumstances when the disagreement is over the very nature of the political community. The present problem facing the Canadian federation is precisely that. Duality is not recognized, the distinctiveness of Québec is not accepted, and Québec has not given its approval to the changes to the country's Constitution adopted in 1982. But certain insights from the theory of consociational democracy can still be useful in devising workable solutions. In order to find means to minimize confrontation in federal structures, we have come up with a model that seeks to combine some elements from consociational democracy with a compact theory of federalism (see Erk and Gagnon, 2000).

Our model developed as an outcome of a comparative analysis that we carried out on Canada, Spain, and Belgium. In these three federal states we found that ambiguity had been an important factor in managing the differences between the federal partners. It appeared that in federal partnerships based on a compact between the constituent units, constitutional ambiguity had become a sign of a broad consensus to eschew polarization. When parties to the federal compact could not agree on the exact terms of the union, they left the question about the nature of the political community unclear. Compact between the provinces or compact between peoples; in a way, they have been agreeing to avoid having to agree. At the same time, the successful continuation of these arrangements was dependent on the overall federal trust between the partners. This notion of federal trust is not about a common position and consensus. It assumes the absence of a clear-cut consensus over issues, yet this coexists with a feeling of confidence between federal partners that they will work together in good faith. As we have put it: "It is our contention that constitutional ambiguity in the federal division of competences is a sign of a desire to avoid potentially divisive issues. Such ambiguity, however, cannot function in the absence of an overall trust between the federal partners (i.e. orders of government).... Believing that the others will act in good faith, thorny issues are left aside" (Erk and Gagnon, 2000: 94-95). The findings of our inquiry suggest that when important differences between the constituent nations of a federal partnership exist, ambiguity can be a potential source of longevity for the federal arrangements; but it is important to stress that by itself constitutional ambiguity is no panacea. The benefits of constitutional ambiguity can be reaped only if it is underscored by a feeling of solidarity among the constituent nations, or if trust in the mutual willingness to work to sustain the federation exists. In the absence of trust, constitutional ambiguity could stir latent tensions in multinational federations by blurring the rules of the game and thereby increasing the issues of contention. The outcome would then be a protracted and divisive process toward the codification of exclusive competences.

The implication of this argument is that in federal systems with deep disagreements over the nature of the political community, there might be no common ground to establish a consensus. Consequently, quests for legalistic precision can only aggravate the conflict. This would then render a legalistic clarification of the federal arrangement an inappropriate measure to ensure the stability of multinational federations. Moreover, obsessive constitutional precision may actually work to undermine a potential source of longevity for these federal partnerships. That is, intentionally leaving the constitutional definition of a federal arrangement ambiguous may, under certain circumstances, promote the durability of federations as each side can interpret its membership in the association differently, rather than being forced to accept the legally defined interpretation of the federation favoured by one side of the partnership. When important differences between the constituent nations of a federal compact exist, constitutional ambiguity is a way to keep the federation going. Initiatives like the Clarity Act, introduced by the Canadian government in 1999, might appear as strong preemptive tactics for Canadian federalists. The federal Clarity Act aimed to interfere with the drafting of a referendum question in Québec to ensure "clarity." But such federal initiatives are perceived as intrusions into Québec's prerogatives by all sides in Québec, federalist and sovereignist alike. In the long run, there is a danger that such risky policies could eliminate the remnants of federal trust and constitutional ambiguity at the same time.

By no means do we claim to have found the magic formula for longevity and stability; in fact, the climate created by the Clarity Act looks pretty gloomy. At the end of the day, we sincerely believe that only a solution that recognizes Québec as an autonomous state has chances for success. In this respect, consociational democracy is unsuitable as a guideline to solve Canada's problems. Following a decades-long exploration of various forms of consociational democracy, Kenneth McRae eventually gave up on this theory. It could have been useful in the past, but the history of the Canadian federation reads as one long, frustrating record of lost opportunities and missed chances for a consociational settlement and the recognition of duality. Like a full circle, it all comes back to Jean Bodin. The federation has bifurcated into two sides that have separately moved closer to Bodin's concept of a sovereign state. Recognition of the Québécois as a people within a dual Canada has not been accepted by English Canada. Many historical chances to settle the issue within the context of a Canadian society have unfortunately been wasted. It should come as no surprise that this has pushed Québec toward consolidating its separate "statehood." This is also reflected in the changing discourse of the Québec nationalists; the nationalist movement has increasingly adopted the position of Québec's right to self-determination as an institutional entity within the Canadian federation rather than the previous position based on a compact between two peoples, an approach that has run through Canadian history from Georges-Etienne Cartier and Henri Bourassa, to André Laurendau and Pierre Trudeau. Things are now much closer to Jean Bodin's conception of the sovereignty of the state. English Canada's unwillingness to compromise within the framework of the Canadian state has created the political necessity for an independent Québec state. The way forward lies in the recognition of this fact.

7

Althusian Federalism for a
Post-Westphalian World

Thomas O. Hueglin

> Have we, under the 400-year-old spell of national sovereignty, unwisely
> neglected other sectors of Western thought . . . ? Should we devise an
> alternative curriculum in political thought that would stress Althusius over
> Bodin, Montesquieu over Rousseau, Gierke over Hegel, Karl Renner and Otto
> Bauer over Marx and Engels? In short, have we been studying the wrong
> thinkers, and even the wrong countries?
>
> McRae, 1978

It can been said that Carl J. Friedrich's entire work was a lifelong footnote to his
early preoccupation with Althusius. For Althusius, politics is the art of
consociation, of building a plurality of narrower and wider communities for the
sake of organizing a just and rewarding social life. Literally translated, the
German title of one of Friedrich's most important works reads: politics as a
process of community building. The title of the American original, of course,
had to be *Man and His Government*. That my own work to date has been a
footnote to the passage from Professor McRae's presidential address previously
cited would be an overstatement. But it has been an ongoing inspiration to take
seriously those thinkers and theorists in Western political thought who have
remained neglected at the margins, not only Althusius but also Montesquieu,
Gierke, the Austro-Marxists Renner and Bauer, and the French school of
integral federalism. In fact, it is my contention that these theorists, who have
been neglected because they do not conform to the dominant modern
juxtaposition of territorial state and liberal society, will gain in importance as
this modern world draws to a close under globalizing conditions. In what
follows, I attempt to demonstrate why and how the political theory of Althusius
strikes me as a singularly appropriate historical starting point to rethink politics
and governance for the twenty first century.

THE CENTRAL ARGUMENT

Althusius' theory was written before the modern Westphalian state system
became the dominant model of political order, and it was in fact explicitly

opposed to its central political premises. It may therefore be of heuristic value in the search for a post-Westphalian political theory of governance *beyond the state*[1] for which ongoing processes of globalization in general and of European integration in particular have been specific points of reference.

Johannes Althusius (1557-1638) lived through dramatic and traumatic times. As a second-generation political Calvinist, he was witness to the religious wars in France and the Dutch Revolt against Spain. Explicitly opposing Jean Bodin's epochal concept of absolute sovereignty as the only way out of political, economic, and cultural factionism and strife, he designed an alternative political system of shared sovereignty in which a plurality of partially autonomous communities or consociations would cooperate in multilevel governance on the basis of negotiation and consent. At the beginning of the seventeenth century, this was a political theory that had not yet ceased to resemble widespread political practice. Althusius still lived through the first twenty years of the Thirty Years War as well, that first great European war, but he died ten years before the Peace of Westphalia would bring the old order to a definite end.

What this peace treaty meant can be best appreciated by taking a look at the polarized juridical discussion about the nature of the Holy Roman Empire, which had taken place ever since the Reformation had begun to destroy its religious and—however precarious—political unity. At one end of the spectrum and based on Bodin's absolute sovereignty formula, there was the new idea of the empire as a unitary and centralized political system from which all intermediary political powers had to be excluded. At the other end and naturally centred in the anti-imperial camp, there was the insistence on the continued existence of the empire as a plural system of governance shared between emperor and estates. This second view took its cue almost exclusively from Althusius (Hoke, 1997). Only after the Peace Treaty of Westphalia did the former view begin to triumph over the latter. Without a unifying religious bond, however, the claim to absolute sovereignty passed on to the lesser territorial princes.

The political theory of Althusius marks the early modern beginning of an alternative tradition in Western political thought in several ways. On the one hand, it constructs political order as a compound or federal commonwealth on the basis of a social contract the members of which are not individuals but collectivities. On the other hand, these collectivities or members are not only territorial units but sectoral-functional interest communities as well. Finally, the process of governance does not follow the majoritarian parliamentary tradition of government and opposition but is based on multilevel negotiations aiming at mutual consent and solidarity among a plurality of autonomous collective actors. To be sure, elements of such a political order can be found throughout the history of western political thought, most prominently in Montesquieu's federal principle and doctrine of checks and balances, in Proudhon's vision of agroindustrial federation, or in Petr Kropotkin's grand account of mutual aid as a natural principle of social organization (Montesquieu, 1748; Proudhon, 1863; Kropotkin, 1902). Moreover, Althusius' theory is based on the three broad themes of federalism, social contract, and popular sovereignty, which have been central throughout the history of political thought. However, it is Althusius' unique early modern combination of these themes in a grand federal design from which emerges the kind of affinity claimed for a late modern, post-Westphalian world.

FEDERALISM

Althusius wrote his book at the beginning of the seventeenth century, during a time of transition from the medieval plurality of rule to modern state sovereignty. The old order had proven unstable. A new generation of political thinkers, from Machiavelli to Bodin and Hobbes, identified power fragmentation as the root cause of this instability. As Hobbes would put it half a century after Althusius: "a Kingdome divided in itself cannot stand" (1651: 93). Consequently, all these thinkers rejected the old plural order of overlapping and largely uncoordinated powers, pleading instead for a centralized, exclusive, and absolutist system of governance. It did not occur to them to search for general principles of a political order that might have preserved the old plurality yet constitutionally stabilized it in a federal organization of joint governance. This is precisely what Althusius aimed at.

However, caution is required. Althusius did not develop anything like the model of a modern federal state. He did not even use the word "federal" except in a brief passage in which the possibility is discussed of linking several existing polities in a larger confederation (Althusius: Vol. 17: 24ff.). Rather, by tying the plural elements of the old order into a novel constitutional order, Althusius developed the general contours of a political system based on federal principles in a much wider sense. The most important of these are *pluralization of governance, consent requirement, subsidiarity,* and *mutual solidarity.*

PLURALIZATION OF GOVERNANCE

The first of these principles can be described as *pluralization of governance.* This means more than just vertical power separation among two or three levels of government. Rather, it denotes a system of multilevel governance among a plurality of spatial and social-functional collectivities comprising cities and provinces but also family clans, guilds, and estates. One can therefore speak of a kind of "societal federalism" (Hueglin, 1991). The federal structure of governance further requires that the lower and smaller units both retain substantive powers of self-governance and be collectively represented in the legislative processes at higher levels.[2] Such rights of legislative codetermination had typically existed only as contested rights from case to case in the old order; they had not been a constitutional right for all members of a commonwealth.

At least in principle, Althusius suggests a much more inclusive approach to multilevel governance: It is a matter of liberty that all affairs should be conducted with the counsel and authority of those bearing the risk (Althusius, Vol. 33: 30). Because the lawful conduct of affairs differs for each kind of consociation according to its specific nature and necessities as established by its members (Althusius, Vol. 1: 19-21) and because, further, the construction of the commonwealth thus proceeds from the simple and private to the mixed and public consociations (Althusius, Vol. 17: 60), all societal groups are included in the process of political participation, even though not necessarily at all levels of the federal commonwealth. Guilds and professional colleges mainly participate in the governance of cities and regions, whereas the counciliar legislative body in the universal commonwealth comprises the representatives of these larger spatial collectivities. One can speak of an ascending system of consecutive federalization. Consent requirement and an organized commitment to mutual solidarity are its mechanisms of cooperation and coordination.

CONSENT REQUIREMENT

The second principle is the *requirement to reach consent*. This is the main difference between federal governance and parliamentary government on the basis of the Westminster model. Since all constituent members of a commonwealth possess a right of self-governance, the vital interests of one or several of them cannot be subjected to a majority vote. In modern federal states, this consent requirement has typically found partial expression in bicameral legislative systems and qualified majority voting procedures. Obviously, this is only a rather mechanical and approximate realization of the consent requirement and a concession to the prioritized efficiency requirement of modern statehood.

For Althusius, consent more generally means that what pertains to all must also be approved by all: *quod omnes tangit, ab omnibus approbetur* (Vol. 17: 60). This was, of course, a venerable Roman law formula that in medieval political practice did not always amount to very much. If the princes did not consent, they would typically have to resort to war and insofar as these princes or estates claimed to represent their lands on the basis of consent, this consent was simply presupposed because the estates *were* the land. On the other hand, as Althusius notes, an effort was made at the Imperial Diets to bring the assembled members to one opinion before the various colleges and benches delivered their final vote (Vol. 33: 18-20), and it is this practice from which Althusius drew in constructing the entire political process in a universal commonwealth as a multilayered chain of organized deliberation with the sole purpose of reaching consent through communicative action.

It is here that Althusian federalism intersects with *consociational democracy*, a term that Arend Lijphart (1977) originally took from Althusius, who calls all social communities *consociations*, from the family to guilds, colleges, cities, provinces, and the universal commonwealth itself. Modern consociationalism, however, as Lijphart distilled it from political practice in the same countries that had also inspired Althusius, the Netherlands and Switzerland, rests on political accommodation among historically contingent elites. As in the case of the Imperial Estates in the Holy Roman Empire, these elites communicate, deliberate, and negotiate with one another by taking for granted that they do so on the basis of their constituencies' consent.

Governance in the Holy Roman Empire obviously was not based on democratic accountability, and Althusius was not a democrat, but the way that he described and defined politics as the mutual communication of goods, services, and rights (Vol. 1: 7) throughout society, at least in principle, went far beyond elite accommodation, and it turned the mere supposition of consent into an organized process of consent *finding* and community *building*. All members of a commonwealth should have the right to participate in this process, and all should have a collective veto against decisions violating their basic interests. To this effect, governance was to be organized as a pluralized chain of legislative councils. At each level of consociation, these councils were to be composed of representatives of all consociations at the preceding lower level. Since this chain was to begin with families, guilds, and colleges at the bottom of the societal pyramid, it was to include each and every person, even though representation higher up would be indirect rather than immediate. This is a matter of radical federalization on the basis of subsidiarity.

SUBSIDIARITY

Different from the North American *juridical* concept of residual powers, subsidiarity essentially denotes a *political* commitment to allocate all powers at the lowest level of government possible. Lower levels also retain residual powers and therefore decide for themselves what they consider possible or not. For Althusius, this is nothing other than expression of the fact that all communities possess a natural right of autonomy.[3] He also seems to assume that reaching consent is easier in smaller communities than in larger ones. In the city, for instance, he insists that the particular interests of one group or a minority cannot be overruled by a majority (Althusius: Vol. 33: 64). For the conciliar deliberations at the level of the universal commonwealth, this unanimity requirement is not mentioned (Vol. 33: 18). However, his faith in consensual politics at the local level of governance is by no means carried by a naive assumption of social harmony, and neither does it allow for a local tyranny of conformism. Consent—and this seems to be his central modernizing message directed against the older medieval world of organic communities—can never simply be presumed but needs to be facilitated and organized within an open dialectic of those particular *and* universal ties that determine the integral personality of individuals as well as of groups.

It is in the interest of all groups that more specific interests are left to self-governance in more particular arenas of decision making, whereas more general and common interests are delegated to larger ones. When lower levels of governance can deal autonomously with those political issues affecting them most directly, substantive material agreements on the basis of compromise appear plausible. Higher up, such agreements obviously can pertain only to more general standards of conduct. Consequently, legislation at the lower levels will be more specific, and it will become increasingly general higher up. Althusius describes this kind of legislation very well as framework legislation setting the general standards and conditions of political, economic, and cultural life in the entire commonwealth (Vols. 11-15), and it is for this generality that majority decisions become more feasible at this level. To this day, the German system of administrative federalism has retained this concept of power division. The bicameral federal legislature passes general bills in nearly all areas of policy making, whereas the details of implementation and administration are left to the *Länder* (Watts, 1997).

MUTUAL SOLIDARITY

Consent can be established, at least in the long run, only when the material results of the political process are acceptable to all as fair and balanced. Institutional structure, organized process, and material outcome of politics cannot be separated. The fourth principle of federalism, therefore, consists in a general commitment to *mutual solidarity*. From the perspective of the modern federal state, such solidarity typically means fiscal equalization and regional development policy. For Althusius again, it means more generally that a balance must be found between the rights of self-governance and a universal commitment to mutual aid. On the one hand, every political community should have the powers to pursue whatever goals might appear useful or necessary for the political, economic, and cultural life of its members. On the other hand, these goals must not violate general or universal standards of fairness and welfare.[4] Once more, it is the federalized participation of all communities at all levels in the universal commonwealth that ties universal governance to those general principles of mutual aid laid down and agreed upon in the original federal compact. This compact is nothing other than the plurality of those agreements by which the commonwealth is established as a consociation of consociations (Althusius; Vol. 9: 3, Vol. 19: 49). Again, it is important to note how Althusius transcends earlier practice. Solidarity and welfare had, of course, been part of medieval political culture, but they had typically existed only within particular communities and not among them.

Starting from the Aristotelian definition of man as *zoon politikon*, Althusius sees all human activity rooted in a natural inclination of community building (Vol. 1: 32–33). The process of community building is then determined as what he calls the communication of goods, services, and rights (Vol. 1: 7). What he means by the communication of rights is administration or governance, which naturally extends to the material sphere of social reproduction (Vol. 1: 10). There is no separation of state and market; both are genuinely political.[5] If the communication of goods and services is as political as governance itself, however, the principles of sharing and cooperation apply as much in the former as in the latter. Althusius' federalism is a societal or integral federalism because the open dialectic between particular and universal pertains as much to the sharing of goods and services as to administration or governance. The principle of subsidiarity also applies to the market sphere of production and consumption. Obviously, a large commonwealth will benefit from universal trade and commerce, and Althusius does understand the new epoch very well, describing at great length the administrative duties of the supreme magistrate in this arena (Vol. 11). At the same time, however, the extent of the universal communication of goods and service is limited from below, by the right of the smaller communities to determine what and in which way they may want to provide for themselves (Vol. 6: 17–27). Or, to put it differently, according to the federalized right of self-governance, all communities have a right to codetermine what is to be free in a free market and what is not.

This also requires the maintenance and protection of a pluralized system of production enabling the members of each community to decide for themselves which goods and services they consider necessary and useful. Instead of a universalized regime of trade regulation, control over the social conditions of trade must remain part of the political process. Although governance can be pluralized in many arenas of spatial and/or functional policy formation, a general commitment to solidarity cannot be maintained if the decision-making arenas concerning economic reproduction and social stabilization are lastingly separated.

Althusius does not provide a blueprint for a postmodern world of pluralized economic diversity. The communities whose autonomies he sought to preserve were, for the most part, closed and isolated hierarchical societies the vast majority of whose members had little room for choice. Only among the recognized and organized members of these communities did the experience of negotiated freedom of federated plurality exist. At the same time, Althusius was certainly aware of a new openness in European relations and transactions, which had begun to threaten this experience because it lacked a common code of conduct and governance. Before the modern state won a Darwinian struggle over all other forms of governance (Elkins, 1997), Althusius could at least envisage a system of politics in which this experience would be preserved by expanding it into just such a common code of conduct and governance. The result was a general theory of federalism from which arose the contours of the other two central themes in the Althusian *Politica*, social contract and popular sovereignty.

SOCIAL CONTRACT AND POPULAR SOVEREIGNTY

It is almost self-evident that the necessary stability and cohesion of such a complex political system can stem only from some kind of social contract, pact, or covenant (Althusius, Vol. 1: 2). It is quite remarkable indeed that Althusius developed a social contract theory already half a century before Hobbes, who is usually credited as standing at the beginning of this tradition in modern political thought (Rawls, 1971). More important than the question of who said what first, however, are the differences between this modern tradition and the Althusian approach.

First of all, the Althusian contract is not one fictitiously concluded among individuals. Contractual partners, rather, are collectivities that have in turn been constituted from previous such contracts or covenants. The federal structuration of society operationalizes civic participation. The process of community building is a real one. Second, at least in sharp contrast to Hobbes, Althusius strictly separates social and governmental contracts (especially Vol. 9). While the former establish organized social life among equal partners, the latter determine form and content of mandated governance between the people and its rulers, who are consistently identified as administrators and magistrates.

Of course and once again, Althusius was not a modern democrat. In fact, he harboured rather elitist views of who should rule and who should obey, and since he wanted his theory to be taken seriously and his book to be read, he also did not hesitate to acknowledge that these administrators would at least in part be dynastic rulers. However, his separation of the two contracts put this traditional world of rulers and ruled onto a radically changed fundament. There was to be a civil society of horizontally coordinated social life that could be private or public but was always intrinsically political, and there was necessary governance within the limits of contractual stipulations.

Moreover, within the federalist parameters of consent, subsidiarity, and solidarity, the Althusian concept of contract or covenant is not a juridical one. It does not settle the question of who should do what with legal certitude, once and for all. Instead, it commits all participants to a flexible process of political deliberation about what is fair and balanced according to time and circumstance. If these change, the partnership needs to be renegotiated. Althusius' federalism is not so much a federalism written in constitutional stone, therefore, as it is a kind of treaty federalism or confederalism among consenting partners.[6]

This, then, leads to the third and final central theme in Althusius' theory, the inevitable question about popular sovereignty. Once again, caution is required. On the one hand, based on his construction of all organized social life from contractual or covenanted agreement, Althusius' answer is perfectly clear and squarely aimed at refuting Jean Bodin's epochal definition of sovereignty as *puissance absolue et perpetuelle*.[7] He declares that while the rights of sovereignty can be administered by one or several rulers, the ownership of it belongs alone to the organized body of the people (Vol. 9: 19, 22). On the other hand, this formulation differs fundamentally from the modern concept of the people as the sum of all individuals and of popular sovereignty as expressed in general elections and plebiscites or, more indirectly, as expressed in media interpretations of public opinion.

What Althusius means by organized body of the people is entirely different from the modern Rousseauian notion of democracy. In his view, the will of all (*volonté de tous*) can never be transsubstantiated into an entirely unstructured general will (*volonté générale*). Even in the small community of a city like Rousseau's Geneva and even more so in a large commonwealth, popular unity can be generated only through adequate structuration, and it can manifest itself only through cooperatively organized multilevel governance. Nevertheless, the Althusian system of politics aims at the inclusion of everybody. Contrary to the rather fictitious all-inclusiveness of modern democratic systems constructed upon the two-dimensional juxtaposition of individual and state, this system is based on overlapping membership in an ascending order of plural communities.[8] From a modern perspective, this may appear as a rather conservative reproduction of the old order with its traditional loyalties and identities, restraining free choice and social mobility (Habermas, 1972: 67-68). Insofar as it is constructed in principle as an all-inclusive system of politics, however, recognizing every commitment to a particular type of identity, it may indeed allow more realistic choices than the centralized territorial nation-state with its universalist claim of citizenship. The distinction between closed communities of fate and open communities of choice becomes less clear-cut (Hirst, 1994: 49-55).

But it is true that popular sovereignty as democratic governance cannot become manifest as *the-people-speaking-with-one-voice* in such a pluralized context. It can be approximated only through plural processes of organized access and cooperation. One can understand the essence of Althusius' notion of sovereignty best as shared or pooled sovereignty in a mixed society (Vol. 9: 3). It exists only through its legitimate exercise, as expressed through consent among its consociated members (Vol. 9: 19). It exists, in other words, when a plurality of rulers or magistrates exercise their mandated powers within the limits of both the contractual or treaty agreements within the communities that they serve, and of those more fundamental agreements establishing the relationships among these communities. The dichotomous distinction between domestic politics and external relations is dissolved. Both appear as part of the communication of right among the members of a commonwealth, and this right in its more specific sense of civil law (Vol. 11: 2) includes the augmentation of welfare through confederation with others (Vol. 17: 24) as well as the lawful administration of the commonwealth through counciliar deliberation among its members (Vol. 17: 57–58).

THE RELEVANCE OF ALTHUSIAN FEDERALISM FOR A LATE MODERN DEMOCRATIC ORDER

The Westphalian Peace Treaty of 1648 helped to bring on its way the modern distinction between sovereign domestic politics and international relations. Internally, absolutist rulers would claim to hold all powers in unitary fashion (Hirst and Thompson, 1996). Externally, the new state system would have to rely on diplomatic relations. Eventual democratization affected only domestic affairs. The absolutist claim of princes was replaced by a likewise unitary and absolutist claim on behalf of the people. In order to make that claim credible, the unity of nation, state, and territory had to be assumed. These were the ideological foundations on the basis of which parliamentary majority rule could become acceptable as a formalized expression of democracy.

Today, the end of the Westphalian system appears in sight because the exclusivity of nation-state governance has been eroded from above and below. Above, the anarchy of international relations has become tamed by international regulatory regimes such as the World Trade Organization or the International Monetary Fund and by processes of regional integration such as the European Union and the North American Free Trade Agreement. Below, regions, organized interests, cultural minorities, and social movements have reasserted claims of self-governance.

For such a late modern world of integration and fragmentation, the Althusian multilevel construction of a federal political order might be a better intellectual starting point than the monocentred theories of Bodin and Hobbes. That was the message in Professor McRae's provocative question to his peers. His own work on multilingual societies provides hard evidence that the monocentred concept of politics has never been so adequate in the first place. The first volume, on Switzerland, begins with a reference to John Stuart Mill, who wrote that a people speaking different languages cannot be governed by representative institutions based on united public opinion. Another quotation from Dankwart Rustow goes even further by asserting that multilingual states are an aberration (McRae, 1998: 3). McRae's studies to date, on Switzerland, Belgium, and Finland, strongly suggest otherwise. Judging from recent developments in a globalizing world of migration, they might in fact become the norm.

The purpose of my analysis in this chapter has been to point out that the conceptual basis for a more complex ordering of politics and society has in fact a long tradition in the history of political thought. The federal political theory of Althusius marks an important turning point in this tradition. Its relevance can be illustrated by a comparison with the exemplary conceptual framework of McRae's own studies (1999: 1-3).

This framework is organized around four broad "headings," the first of which focuses on *historical and developmental factors*. Although the contextualization of time and circumstance is always a sign of good political science, it has been neglected far too much during the modern epoch with its tendency of generalization on the basis of universal principles and grand narratives. McRae's work on multilingual societies, while far from embracing the new postmodern discourse of radical deconstruction, nevertheless gains its strength from careful differentiation. Although sharing certain general characteristics, conflict and compromise in each case are shown to follow a specific rationale and trajectory.

This is not something that one can learn from Hobbes, Locke, or Rousseau, but it is a tradition that has intellectual roots in the early-modern rediscovery of political complexity (Wolin, 1957). Althusius very much belonged to that tradition. The general principle of social organization was for him that all communities share in the desire for a prosperous and just social life. But in order to achieve this end each community—or consociation—would require specific laws and political arrangements. His notion of federalism is treaty-based rather than grounded in constitutional certitude. The political process does not rely on general and timeless principles of power division. Instead, it is organized as an ongoing process of negotiated agreements according to time and circumstance.

The second heading is broadly concerned with *social structure*, its cleavages, and boundaries. Obviously compelled to do so by overwhelming evidence, McRae's analysis breaks wide open such cherished assumptions as national unity and unquestioned political legitimacy based on parliamentary majority rule. His studies show with great clarity and evidence that political unity does not necessarily require universal and national citizenship. Instead, it can be constructed upon concepts of pluralized citizenship, allowing for membership in plural communities with overlapping boundaries and loyalties.

The third heading has to do with *perceptions and attitudes* within and across these communities. One could also say that it has to do with ideological structures or what one might call "mind-scapes." Perhaps the most pertinent question that McRae asks is about the attitudes among different language groups about "cultural diversity itself." From the older and modernist perspective, the political goal had always been a universal solution such as official bilingualism in Canada, for instance. The focus on the difference of leading images among different groups and communities, however, strongly suggests a need for differentiated and even asymmetrical solutions.

Particularly instructive here is McRae's study on Belgium, a multilingual society with two major cultural communities (Francophone and Dutch/Flemish) and three sociohistorical regions (Wallonie, Flanders, and Brussels). Already the constitutional compromise of 1970 recognized both communities and regions as two different manifestations of overlapping loyalties and identities (McRae, 1986: 319-321). After the last round of constitutional revisions in 1993, Belgium became a formally constituted federal state (Article One), now recognizing three communities (French, Flemish, and German; Article Two) as well as three Regions (Wallonie, Flanders, and Brussels; Article Three) with different sets of self-governing powers (Senelle, 1996).

McRae notes, in his summary of the common framework for his studies, that "just how the pattern of organized and political action may be linked to intergroup differences in values and attitudes is a complex question for further study" (1999: 3). To a large extent, this is, of course, a question of political design (see later), but it is also a question of political culture and tradition. What recourse to tradition do societies have for which a predominantly statist tradition does not work? What guidelines can be recalled for the invention of adequate political design?

Again, the classical canon of political thought provides little guidance here. Perhaps the Belgians were able to find a stable solution without such a recourse. The statist tradition is not very old in Belgium, and, more importantly, it always remained challenged in a country with a Flemish majority that historically was dominated by a French-speaking elite. But the statist tradition has come under attack elsewhere, in Canada, in Spain, and even in the United Kingdom. And it does not provide much guidance at all for the European Union or the brave new world of globalization.

It therefore seems that the recourse to the prestatist early modern tradition of Althusian federalism is of some relevance, that is, as long as it is still acknowledged that intellectual history is a guiding part of human experience and attitude. Althusius' question is not who has the power to do what. He asks who *should* do what in order to achieve the most acceptable result for all. Instead of a static design, he provides guidelines for a dynamic political process. Its poles are subsidiarity, the retention of self-governance at the lowest possible level of governance, and solidarity, a commitment to common standards shared by all. Political compromise between these two positions depends on the organization of public discourse and has to be negotiated according to time and circumstance.

Under the fourth and last heading, concerning *constitutional and institutional arrangements*, McRae's inquiry does not just focus on the constitution itself, on the branches of government as well as on various forms federalism or decentralization. Rather, it includes the "widest possibilities" for institutional arrangements capable of managing linguistic conflict (1999). If we look at the Belgian case again, we find at least one such arrangement in the 1993 Constitution that exceeds not only the widest but possibly also the wildest expectations of conventional federalists (Senelle, 1996: 315-319).

There is no residual powers clause, nor a provision like Article Thirty One of the German Basic Law according to which federal law ultimately breaks Länder law. Instead, there is an unprecedented constitutional emphasis on cooperation, concertation, and arbitration among all levels of governance, the federal authority, the communities, and the regions. In essence, this means that for all practical purposes majority rule has been suspended. The emphasis on consent and strict proportionality is not without problems. The Belgian state has been rocked by scandals of corruption and inefficiency in recent years. As in the Swiss case of governance by a perpetual grand coalition, there appears to be a lack of transparency in the political process, which, in turn, stems from a lack of effective opposition.

This is why the majority principle has been triumphant in modern democratic politics. Where it cannot find unmitigated application, however, such as in the small, ethnically segmented European democracies, in the European Union, or in the emerging global order, governance by mutual agreement and compromise remains the only option. But consent cannot simply be presupposed as an act of alienation, as in the Hobbesian social contract, for instance. And neither can it be left to elite accommodation, as in modern consociational practice. Instead, consent and compromise need to be organized as the end product of a political process in which the decisions are made by those who are affected by them.

Once again, this is the Althusian tradition of pluralized governance. A merely territorial organization of politics falls short of this pluralization requirement in fragmented societies, and therefore social communities need to be recognized as well. Nonterritorial federalism based on principles of personality rather than territoriality, as exemplified by the Belgian communities, is no longer a utopian model. It has a long tradition in theory and practice.[9] For Althusius, at the beginning of the modern epoch, it still represented the normality of organized social life. There is no reason that such a pluralized system of politics cannot be as approximately democratic as has been the modern state, and it may indeed prove to be a more realistic model for a post-Westphalian world in which the approximation of nation, state, and territory increasingly rings hollow. Indeed, it may be democracy's next best option.

NOTES

1. The Westphalian Peace Treaty of 1648 is generally acknowledged as having established the modern system of sovereign nation-states, a system that now may be replaced by a new system of globalized relations without a clear distinction between national sovereignty and international relations.
2. A somewhat different angle is suggested in Giuseppe Duso (1998: 28).

3. Again, Althusius does not refer to subsidiarity explicitly, but the concept is embedded in his political theory.

4. Note Althusius' discussion of self-sufficiency or autarchy (Vol. 1: 10), assistance and mutual aid (Vol. 16: Vol. 17: 49).

5. Such a statement must not be confused with the endorsement of a socialist public economy. The conceptual inclusion of the market sphere in the political only means that political deliberation must include questions of market control.

6. Given the relatively static world in which Althusius lived, this is perhaps an overinterpretation. However, Althusius is perfectly clear in principle: the organized body of the people jointly owns the right of sovereignty and sets up those fundamental federal pacts or covenants that give the commonwealth structure and governance; and what the organized body of the people has thus set in order is to be maintained and followed, unless something else pleases the common will (*nisi communi voluntate aliud placeat*, Vol. 9: 18).

7. Jean Bodin, (1576: Vol. 1: 8); in the Latin version, which Althusius probably used, the absolute character of this definition is even stronger: *legibus solutus poetstas*.

8. The difference between the Althusian notion of organized plurality and Rousseau's essentially unitary and homogeneous vision of society best comes to the fore in the latter's objection to all *sociétées partielles*; Rousseau, (1762: Vol. 2: 3)

9. Compare Kenneth D. McRae, "The Principle of Territoriality and the Principle of Personality in Multilingual States," *International Journal of the Sociology of Language*, no. 4 (1975): 33-54; Elkins (1995).

PART III

CONSTITUTIONAL REFORM AND LANGUAGE POLICY

8

Causes and Effects of Constitutional Changes in Multilingual Belgium

Kris Deschouwer

Belgium is a divided country. That goes without saying. The comparative literature on segmented pluralism, divided societies, and consociational democracy has paid quite some attention to this small European democracy (e.g., Huyse, 1971; Lijphart, 1981). Today Belgium does hit the headlines once in a while with some political scandals, but not because of its blatant political instability or the danger of civil war. Belgium is still divided and is still apparently stable. Yet it has changed thoroughly, at least as far as its institutional organization is concerned. Between 1963 and 1993 the country was gradually transformed into a federal state, granting territorial autonomy to the linguistic groups. Indeed, since 1993 the Belgian Constitution states very officially that the country is now a federal monarchy. The general election of 1995 was the formal starting point of this new institutional design, with the first direct election of the Parliaments of the regions of Flanders, Wallonia, and Brussels.

One can consider this beginning of the federal state as the end of a story, as the culminating point of a successful territorial management of the linguistic divide. There are, however, some good reasons for not doing so. First, the constitutional changes have not come to an end. Soon after the reform of 1993, new demands were put on the agenda for institutional reform. In 1999 and again in 2000 negotiations between the language groups (i.e., the governing parties of both language groups) led to plans for a further devolution, for granting even more autonomy to the federal entities of the Belgian state. In the second place, the institutional reforms—themselves aimed at reducing the inherent political instability of the linguistic divide—have produced a number of mainly nonanticipated consequences, endangering the viability of the new institutional context of Belgian politics. These consequences of the constitutional changes are in fact the result of a combination of the constitutional changes and of a number of societal and political changes that occurred at the same time. Quite important in this respect are the split of the Belgian parties and party system and the shifting economic balance between Flanders and Wallonia.

In this chapter we first look back. We give a systematic and analytic overview of the division lines in Belgian politics and society. We will especially pay attention to the way in which the language cleavage has interacted with the other cleavages. The latter is important to see how the territorial or federal-type solution for the linguistic divide has affected the political life inside the regions and the relations between them.

THE ORIGINS: LANGUAGE AND RELIGION

Two fairly old societal frontiers cut across Western Europe. The first divides Europe into the area that was linguistically influenced by the presence of the Roman Empire and where varieties of Latin-type languages are spoken and the area that escaped from that influence and where—among others of course—a variety of German-type languages are spoken. This language border starts today in the northwest of France, just south of the Belgian border, then enters Belgium and cuts it in two while passing just south of Brussels, before going down through the Alsace to Switzerland and to the north of Italy. The religious divide, reflecting the result of Reformation and Counter-Reformation, starts in the south of the Netherlands and then proceeds to divide Germany and Switzerland. The two lines do not coincide, although at some points they come close to each other. Belgium belongs to an area where they are pretty close. Yet exactly the fact that they do not coincide is an important part of the picture.

When in 1648 the southern border of the Netherlands was fixed in the Treaty of Westphalia, it actually created a third division line, just between the language borderline to its south and the religious borderline to its north (Andeweg and Irwin, 1993). The modern state of the Netherlands was born after a long war between the Dutch Calvinists and the Catholic Habsburgs. The new Dutch state was clearly both a Protestant and a Dutch-speaking state. Especially the religious identity is more or less the raison d'être of the Netherlands. The state borderline, however, does not follow the religious divide but is situated south of it, thus creating a Catholic minority in the south of the Netherlands. Here is the origin of one of the major cleavages in modern Dutch politics. The language of the Netherlands is less problematic. It is Dutch and will subsequently be further standardized.

The Treaty of 1648 not only fixed the southern border of the Netherlands, but also defined the current northern border of Belgium. In 1648 the area south of the Netherlands was not yet called Belgium. But the separation had far-reaching consequences. One direct result of the "liberation" of the northern part of the former United Seventeen Provinces from the Catholic and Habsburg-dominated south was a braindrain of Dutch-speakers to the north and the non standardization of the Dutch dialects spoken outside the new Dutch state, that is, in the current northern part of Belgium.

South of the linguistic borderline, standardized French (from Paris) was becoming more important, without, of course, at that time eradicating the differences between the dialects spoken by the common people. In the course of the eighteenth century this French became even more important as the language of the Enlightenment, liberalism, and modernity. French had become the language of the elites, of education, and actually of court life almost throughout Europe. That, of course, became even stronger under the French rule of Napoleon, who conquered Belgium from the Austrian Habsburgs. French was now, in the area that would become Belgium, the language of the upper class, that is, the upper class both south and north of the linguistic borderline.

The French rule did not last very long. The Congress of Vienna rearranged the territorial organization of Europe and created the Low Countries, reuniting more or less the former Seventeen Provinces, but then after centuries of separation and different development. The union was not going to last very long. Three forces quickly pulled Belgium away from the northern Low Countries. The first was political liberalism. The Dutch monarchy was still fairly absolutist, and demands for a more responsible Parliament were not met. The second force was religion. The Catholic Church did not like the Protestant domination of the north and of the monarchy and saw the possibility to create a homogeneous Roman Catholic state. The third force was language. The Dutch state used Dutch and wanted to impose this language on the southern provinces. Yet the upper classes there were Francophone and did not at all appreciate this policy. We need to stress again the fact that even the population north of the linguistic borderline did not really speak standard Dutch. They spoke a variety of local dialects, only slightly affected by the cultural and linguistic homogenisation that had taken place in the Dutch state.

Here was the beginning of the Belgian state. The date was 1830. This new state was more liberal than the Low Countries, was Catholic, and was Francophone. The Catholicism soon became the source of political conflict. The will to keep the country firmly controlled by the church was not acceptable to the Liberals, and this church-state cleavage dominated Belgian politics until deep into the twentieth century. The language, to the contrary, was not an issue. Belgium was at that time not seen as composed of two different language groups. It was just Francophone, in a natural but also deliberate way. The Constitution guaranteed freedom of language, but that was meant to give the Belgian Francophones indeed the freedom to speak their own language and not to be obliged to use the Dutch imposed on them in the Low Countries from which they had seceded.

Yet language slowly but surely became an issue and even a major one (Lorwin, 1966; Zolberg, 1974; McRae, 1986). Already before the creation of the Belgian state, a small movement existed that tried to promote the use of Dutch and that resisted the too easy use of French in public life in the non-Francophone part of the country. During the nineteenth century, thus during the early days of Belgium, a mainly urban and middle class-based group of intellectuals went on promoting this use of Dutch, tried to preserve the Dutch culture, and actually started to claim the right to use that language in public life and in administrative matters. The newly born "Flemish movement" defended a non-homogeneous view of Belgium. It stated that Belgium was bilingual, and that the use of the second language should at least be allowed and respected. It asked for some individual language rights for the population of the north.

The Flemish movement did not grow very fast. It started as a very marginal phenomenon and grew into a larger and also more radical movement because of the fierce refusal of the Belgian Francophone elites to take its demands really into consideration (Reynebeau, 1995). The marginality of the movement was also due to the fact that there was no real consensus about the nature of this second language. Dutch was a possibility but also a problem. Dutch was the language of the Dutch state and thus the language of the enemy. Dutch was also the language of Protestantism, which led the Catholic Church to be rather reluctant in accepting it. Attempts were made to promote regional "Flemish" languages as the standard for the second language in Belgium. In the end the Flemish movement clearly opted for Dutch, but then that was a language that still, to a large extent, had to be learned by the population of the north. The absence of a properly standardized language was a perfect argument for the Francophones to claim that French was already available as a standardized and universal language and that the learning of French would help the population of the north to get access to high culture. The idea that Dutch was going to be used, for instance, at universities, was absolutely unthinkable.

While the tension was building during the nineteenth century, one issue within the language problem becomes very visible and very salient: the role and position of Brussels. The capital city of Belgium was situated close to the language border, but clearly north of it. As a city of government and administration and as a city close to the Francophone world it had already been slightly Frenchified before the creation of Belgium. The choice of Brussels as Belgium's capital city only increased the process. By the turn of the century the majority of its population spoke French. This was due to immigration from the south and to the rapid Frenchification of the immigrants from the north, who needed French to function in the public administration and who, of course, wanted their children to be educated in the language of upward social mobility. Not only did Brussels become a Francophone "enclave" in the Dutch-speaking part of Belgium, but it also gradually grew and expanded, just like any other (capital) city. This expansion meant the expansion of the Francophone enclave in Flanders. The pieces of a very difficult puzzle were being put on the Belgian table.

World War I was an important turning point. During the war it became utterly clear that the language issue could not be avoided anymore. Several elements contributed to that awareness. First were the problems at the war front. Flemish soldiers had complained about the language situation, and they became conscious (and were mobilized to become conscious) of the fact that they were eventually expected to die for a country that did not even try to communicate with them in their own language. Flemish elites had tried during the war (i.e., during German occupation) to obtain the right to organize some classes at the University of Gent (in Flanders) in Dutch. They did succeed but were accused of high treason, which apparently was needed to obtain such an elementary right.

Not only the language question sharpened during the war. The soldiers were lower-class people who had the right to fight for their country but not the right to vote. Actually, an imperfect system of universal male suffrage had been introduced in 1893, giving all men at least one vote and granting a second or a third vote to the property owners, taxpayers, and better-educated citizens. One of the first things to be realized after the war was the introduction of full and equal male suffrage. This would directly translate into a Parliamentary demographic situation within the country, in which almost 60 percent of the population lived in the non-Francophone part. With the language problem now clearly on the agenda, it would start producing real changes.

The most obvious and visible change that came about was the territorialization of the issue (Murphy, 1995). Territory was part of the problem from the very beginning, but the Belgian elitist perception of the problem was not territorial. Once language laws are introduced, they will follow a territorial logic. The way to boost Dutch as a full and equal second language, without introducing Dutch as a new language in the south, was the division of the country into three linguistic regions: a Dutch-speaking north, a French-speaking south, and the bilingual area of the capital city. Language laws passed in 1921 and in 1932 were clearly territorial, although they kept the possibility open for the language border to move, according to the languages effectively spoken at the local level. The consequence of this was the further gradual loss of Flemish municipalities to the bilingual area of Brussels or straight to the Francophone region. In 1963 the borderline was finally fixed (see later).

The Flemish movement came out of World War I as a political and even party-political movement. The newly created Frontpartij—referring thus to the war front—wanted to see a reform of the Belgian unitary state into a decentralized and even federal state, which would grant the Flemish region the right to organize its cultural life itself. This now-bipolar view of Belgium soon led to a new Francophone perception of Belgian. They rather had the feeling that their Belgium was gone, that there were no Belgians anymore, only Flemings and Francophones. Among the Francophones, those living in Brussels were in a different position. They lived in a former Dutch-speaking city that was claimed by the Flemish movement as being still a part of Flanders, and they therefore preferred not to be in Flanders. We thus had a bipolar logic in the perception of the problem, in which three territorial units were involved.

We have witnessed in this short overview of a long history the politicization of the language divide and its translation into a territorial definition of alternative solutions, with discussions about the exact boundaries of the territories. Belgium now contains four language regions, one of which we left out so far for the sake of clarity. The first one is the Dutch-speaking region, or the Flemish region. The second one is the region of Wallonia, which is Francophone. Actually, Wallonia includes also an area in the east that was transferred from Germany at the Treaty of Versailles in 1918 and where the population speaks German. It is today formally recognized as the German-speaking region, but for regional matters (see later) it belongs to Wallonia. The fourth region is Brussels, the limits of which were set and fixed in 1963. That region is bilingual. It is on the basis of this territorial division that the Belgian federal state was built, but in a rather complex way, since the Francophones defended mainly a division in three regions, meaning that Brussels should be a separate region, while the Flemings defended the idea of a bipolar federation, based on the language groups, which meant that Brussels belonged territorially to Flanders.

BUILDING UP THE TENSION: MUTUALLY REINFORCING CLEAVAGES

Until now we have discussed only the language question as such, although we pointed out that its connection with the religious divide has played a significant role. Yet there is more than just language. The other cleavages in Belgian politics are strongly related to the language divide, not because of the language as such but because of its territorial base. The different regions did not develop in the same way, and that makes them look different in more than just the language aspect.

We do not dwell on details here, because the point can be made very clear at once. The first cleavage to develop in Belgian politics was the church-state cleavage (Lipset and Rokkan, 1967; Lorwin, 1966). It opposed the Catholics and the Liberals from the very early days of the Belgian state. The second cleavage was the labor-capital cleavage. It developed quite early, because Belgium was one of the first European countries to industrialize, that is, the current region of Wallonia industrialized. The first industries—mainly coal and steel—were almost completely concentrated in the areas of Charleroi and Liège in the south. That part of the country therefore not only industrialized, but became more urban and more secular than the north. The north remained mainly—except for some industry in the cities of Gent and Antwerpen—a rural area.

The consequence for the other cleavages is obvious. The north is Catholic and hardly sends Liberal or Socialist representatives to the Parliament. When in 1893, after the introduction of the universal (but still unequal) male suffrage, thirteen Socialist Members of Parliament were elected, all were from the Walloon region. All the seats in Flanders went to the Catholics, which means that all the Liberals also were elected in Wallonia (and in Brussels). The south developed a worker's movement, with a strong trade unionist tradition. Wallonia was the home base of the Belgian Socialist Party. The south was also the area where the wealth was produced (and then controlled by the financial groups in Brussels), while the north remained rural, poor, and underdeveloped.

The economical and societal disparities did not disappear, but they changed. After Word War I and even more after 1945, the Flemish region starts to develop. The seaport of Antwerpen proves to be a very important asset. In general, the Flemish economy was a mixture of a few large industries (chemical plants and automobile construction) and a large variety of smaller enterprises. The Walloon economy, which was a much larger-scale industry, faced decline after 1945, just like the other old industrial regions in Europe. Toward the 1950s and 1960s the Flemish economy was clearly the most growing and expanding.

Flanders became the richer part of the country. The battle for the use of language had been fought and won, and the Dutch-speaking region became rich, dynamic, and expanding. These evolutions obviously did not reduce the tensions between the regions. These tensions became extremely important in the 1960s and then dominated the scene for more than three decades. These were the decades of the federal-type state reform but also the decades during which the main political actors—the political parties—completely fell apart, and that was another element adding to the regionalist tensions. We discuss the end of the parties in the following section.

INSTITUTIONAL CHANGE: THE SPLITTING OF THE PARTIES AND THE PARTY SYSTEM

Between 1961 and 1965 the Belgian government was a centre-left coalition of Christian Democrats and Socialists. These two parties became the cornerstones of Belgian politics. They are clearly the two large parties, both well entrenched in their network of pillar organizations and well entrenched in one of the two major regions of the country. Together they poll some seventy five percent of the votes, and this has been the case since the introduction of universal (male) suffrage in 1918. Only in the elections of 1932 and 1936, when several right-wing extremist parties experienced some (short-lived) success, did the share of the votes held by the two big parties fall back to sixty percent.

That 1961-1965 coalition can today be labelled "historical." Indeed, it was the very last governmental coalition that was able to last during the full four years of its term for a period of thirty years. Only recently, the second Dehaene government also did its four full years between 1995 and 1999. Between 1965 and 1995 all governments collapsed before the end of the term or deliberately called for early elections (1971 and 1995). The period studied here is thus a period of huge governmental instability, mainly as the result of the regionalist tensions. The 1961-1965 coalition did live until the end, although it had therefore to survive at least one major crisis. This occurred when the government tried to fix the linguistic borderline, that is, to do away with the old logic in which the borderline could move according to the language spoken by the majority of the inhabitants of local municipalities (see earlier). The government did succeed in 1963 and thus produced the starting point of the federal reform. To go further in that direction, however, the Constitution had to be changed, and the two partners agreed to do so after the next elections. Yet sine the elections of 1965 the old governing parties have not secured the needed sixty seven percent of the seats, and the reform of the state was then a long and painful process, with always the difficult search for a solid majority.

The two governing parties lost heavily in 1965 and were beaten by several new parties. There was first the Flemish nationalist Volksunie (6.4 percent in 1965), claiming a federal reform of the state that would have to include autonomous competencies for the Dutch-speakers. Next there was a Francophone "resistance" party in Brussels, the FDF, fearing the now-clear political (and economical) dominance of the Dutch-speakers and fearing especially the inclusion of the city of Brussels into a Dutch-speaking region. Finally there was the RW, a Walloon regionalist party, claiming autonomy for the southern (and Francophone) region of the country, in order to be able to take the necessary measures for the recovery of the old industrial infrastructure in that region. In other words: specific regionalist parties, putting pressure on the traditional Belgian parties, now also took up the linguistic-territorial cleavage.

In 1968 the government collapsed on the "Leuven" question. This important Catholic university was located in the Dutch-speaking part of the country and had—like all Belgian universities—been unilingual Francophone for a very long time. In 1968 the Dutch-speakers claimed that a university located in the Dutch-speaking or Flemish part of the country should be unilingual Dutch. The Francophones were forced to move out and to create the new university of "Louvain-la-Neuve" south of the linguistic borderline. The Christian Democratic Party did not survive this linguistic tension and fell apart into two unilingual parties.

The most spectacular and most relevant aspect of recent change in the Belgian parties, was the death of the three traditional parties. Christian Democrats, Liberals, and Socialists were not able to survive the growing linguistic tensions, and within a time span of only ten years, they all fell apart. The consequence of this change is the total absence now, and since 1978, of Belgian political parties, of parties defending the centre against the regionalist pulls. All parties are regional and do not even keep a federal structure of cooperation (Deschouwer, 1992, 1994b).

This falling apart of the parties did not happen suddenly. Actually, the parties were more or less prepared for this, since they had been gradually taking into account in their internal structures the differences between the Dutch-speaking north, the French-speaking south and eventually also the bilingual Brussels region. Between the wars the Catholic Party—then called the Catholic Bloc—had already virtually fallen apart, functioning as a loose federation of a Flemish wing and a Francophone wing (Gerard, 1985, 1995). When the party was re-created as a modern Christian Democratic Party in 1945, it was again more united but did explicitly take into account the existence of two "wings," each having its own president and each being formally recognized in the decision-making organs of the party. When in 1968 the question of the language status of the Leuven Catholic university came to the front, the party simply died and let each of the two wings become a full-fledged political party. In Brussels the split did hurt, since the local party sections had to be torn apart. Attempts to keep the party united in Brussels were a failure, since the language issues were especially salient there. The newly created Flemish CVP was a very large party, gathering at that time some forty percent of the Flemish vote. The Francophone PSC was much smaller, both in absolute and in relative terms. The PSC polled in 1968 just under twenty one percent of the Francophone votes.

Unlike the Christian Democrats who accepted the existence of two wings from 1945 on, the Socialist Party (BSP-PSB) always presented itself as a "strong and unified" party. The first acceptance of internal differences came only in 1963. A second difference from the Christian Democrats, was the way in which the party fell apart, that is, the number of "wings" into which it was divided. The Christian Democrats were very strong in Flanders and followed therefore the Flemish logic of a division into two wings along the language lines. The Socialist Party, however, was very strong in the Francophone electorate, which is divided between the region of Wallonia and the Brussels region. Therefore, the Socialists began to divide themselves into three wings along these regional lines. After the failure of one of the major plans to reform the Belgian state (the so-called Egmont Pact in 1978), the party died. The Flemish wing went its own way as SP, and the Francophones went their own way as PS, divided, however, in a Brussels and a Walloon wing. The PS always had to face this internal duality. Today it has not at all disappeared, since the regions, which were recognized in the party structure, are today the substates of the Belgian federation.

The strength of the Liberal Party (PVV-PLP) was more evenly spread out than that of its major rivals, being medium-size in Flanders and Wallonia and rather strong in the smaller Brussels region. Unlike the two other parties, the Liberals did not formally recognize any linguistic or regional wings, taking care only of the equal representation of French and Dutch in the executive organs. In 1972 the Flemish wing went its own way, while the Francophones fell apart in a Brussels Liberal Party (still internally very divided) and a Walloon Liberal Party. Only in 1979 were Brussels and Walloon Liberals united again in a new party called PRL.

While regional parties replaced the national parties, all the new parties are obviously regional. That is the case for the already mentioned Volksunie in Flanders, Walloon Rally in Wallonia, and Francophone FDF in Brussels. Parties that were created later were also regional parties. In the early 1980s two Green Parties were born, one for each part of the country: AGALEV in Flanders and ECOLO in the Francophone electorate. In 1978 the radical nationalists, not accepting the participation of the more moderate Volksunie in the federal government, created a new Flemish nationalist party. That party—Vlaams Blok—was not very successful, until it became in the early 1990s an extreme right-wing Populist Party, combining the radical Flemish nationalism with xenophobic and conservative ideas. In Flanders it reached its highest point in 1999, with fifteen percent of the votes. There is a less successful right-wing Populist Party called Front National in Wallonia and in Brussels. It is more straightforwardly neofascist but also badly organized. It polled five percent of the Walloon votes in 1999.

In 1961 the three traditional parties polled together more than ninety percent of the votes. In 1999 there were eleven parties represented in Parliament (thirteen in 1991), and the three traditional party families polled together sixty five percent of the votes. Yet these national figures and interpretations become more and more meaningless. The parties, all being regional, do not compete in a national arena. The Flemish parties field candidates only in Flanders and in Brussels, while the Francophone parties present candidates only in Wallonia and in Brussels. The split of the parties and the subsequent creation of two units of the new parties have ended the life of the Belgian party system. First came the language problem, then its territorialization, and then the adaptation of the political parties to the linguistic-regional divide. Each step reinforced the regional pluralism and made it more difficult to contain.

In the electoral arena the Belgian party system is definitely gone. Electoral results have to be analysed at the regional level. That is the level at which the parties themselves and the political commentators (including political scientists) are looking at the figures. Electoral results tell us (almost) nothing about what is going on and how it should be interpreted. If we break the figures down per region, we can see how different these regions are. The difference is the language but also the format and the logic of the other cleavages and therefore the format and mechanics of the party systems. All the parties are present in Brussels, but Brussels is much more important for the Francophone parties, since eighty-five percent of the Brussels electorate votes for Francophone parties. Looking at this from a different angle, it means that almost one out of five Francophone voters in Belgium lives in Brussels. On the Flemish side the balance is very different: only some three percent of all the Belgian Dutch-speakers live in Brussels.

This disappearance of the national Belgian parties and the creation of two new electoral party systems (Deschouwer, 1996) were striking and even unique and exceptional features. The differences between north and south are not new, the north has always been more Catholic or Christian Democratic, and the south has always been more Socialist. But that only meant that one regional wing of these parties was stronger. This relation is seen in the public debate as a relative one; that is, a party that improves its score is considered to have "won" the elections, while those who score less than what they did before are believed to be the "losers" of the elections. Although it is a strange way of interpreting the results, it is an understandable way of giving substantial meaning (producing a meaningful link between election result and government making power) to elections under the proportional rule. The other way of doing this, looking at the largest party, is meaningless in Belgium since there is more than one largest party in the electoral arena. Until 1999 the CVP was the largest party in Flanders, while the PS was the largest in Wallonia. Since 1999 the VLD or Flemish Liberals is number one in Flanders, with the PS still number one in Wallonia. In Brussels the PRL-FDF alliance is the largest party.

So the expected and legitimate link between electoral results and government building, a link that can produce something like a Belgian party system at the governmental level, is problematic. It assumes (or hopes) that the electoral movements up or down of the members of the same ideological family are the same. Yet this is not the case. The parties in the two party systems move in different directions. To form a government that "respects" the will of the voter is a difficult exercise, and it is bound to go against the expectations of the public. The split of the parties and of the electoral party system has therefore in yet another way increased the tensions in Belgian politics: there is no direct electoral control and sanctioning of the central government. The system heavily loses legitimacy.

The existence of two electoral party systems in a country that attempts to have one governmental party system is a feature that has furthermore not improved the stability of the coalitions. The linguistic cleavage as such has proven to be a very effective coalition killer, but the effects of the cleavage on the parties and the party system have even reinforced this killing power (Deschouwer, 1994a).

At first sight the parties might seem to have an easier job now. They do not have to seek internal compromises anymore. For the parties this is easier indeed, but for the coalitions it is a major problem. Whereas before the split of the parties a linguistic issue could eventually be solved by reaching a compromise within the parties, almost every linguistic issue that comes to the surface now after the split of the national parties ends on the table of the government. That means, then, a conflict in the governmental party system. It is impossible to avoid these issues.

Though the two major regions have a different party system, the absence of a truly Belgian party system confronts them both with a number of awkward problems. Most important probably is the lack of visibility of the regional level of policy making. So far the parties have tried to keep regional and federal coalitions "congruent", that is, producing the same coalitions at all levels. That seems to be the best possible way to manage the multilevel game by actors that are present and visible only at the regional level. Until now the regional and national elections were organized on the same day, which allowed the parties indeed to play the game this way.

The coalition building of 1999 illustrates this nicely. The core is an alliance of Socialists and Liberals. It originates at the Francophone side, where PS and PRL had a preelectoral agreement to govern without the Christian Democrats. The latter is a rather small party that could always access power because its Flemish counterpart was the largest Belgian party. The Greens had done well in 1999 and were added to the coalition. On the Francophone side they are not needed for a parliamentary majority, but they are in Flanders. In Flanders the Volksunie had to be added as a fourth partner to be able to govern without the Christian Democrats. At the federal level Liberals, Greens, and Socialists govern together, and here also the Greens are mathematically needed. The only "incongruity" is the presence of the Volksunie in Flanders, not at the federal level, but the Volksunie is not a major party and has indeed no Walloon counterpart.

The parties look at the different levels as one single reservoir of opportunities and positions and prefer to distribute them in the best possible way in one single shot. Again the distribution of the political personnel after the 1999 elections offers a very nice illustration of this. The Flemish prime minister Patrick Dewael was elected in the federal House of Representatives and was actually a possible candidate for becoming minister of justice in the federal government. The new Walloon prime minister Elio Di Rupo had been vice prime minister of the previous federal government and had also been elected in the federal House of Representatives. The PRL could fill the position of prime minister of the Brussels region, but since they could also fill the position of president of the Senate, their candidate was put in that seat. The new prime minister of Brussels, Jacques Simonet, was then picked out of the federal House of Representatives. For the position of prime minster of the French community government, the PRL chose Hervé Hasquin, former vice prime minister of the Brussels regional government and now elected in the federal Senate. Elio Di Rupo was also elected president of his party and therefore decided not to combine this position with that of prime minister of Wallonia. He resigned in April 2000 (taking up his seat again in the federal House) and was replaced by Jean-Claude Van Cauwenberghe, who had indeed been elected to the Walloon regional Parliament. This change in Wallonia led to a total reshuffling of most of the executive positions held by the PS at the federal level and in both the Walloon region and the French community. One needs to be very well informed to be able to distinguish between local, regional, and federal politics and policy making in Belgium.

Following up on this, one can indeed say that there is no real political centre in Belgian politics. Federal politics are conducted by regional parties, which also play a role at the regional level. There is no central public forum for political debates. There are two unilingual debates. Federal policy making involves dealing with the different sensitivities of the parties in both sides of the country. The media report on details of their own side and refer to the other side as the single Flemish or Francophone position. The solution at the federal level will involve and will be interpreted as an agreement between the parties of the two sides. That is what we mean when we say that there is no centre: the centre is always where the other is. Federal politics looks very much like interregional politics and is obviously conducted or opposed by regional parties.

CONSTITUTIONAL CHANGE: THE FEDERAL-TYPE SOLUTION

The actual federal state came about in five major stages, over more than thirty years of conflict, tension, and subtle conflict management (see also Covell, 1993). We do not here go into the details of each phase and into the details of the many failed attempts to get out of the deadlock. The following is thus a very general overview and looks more logical and smooth than the full story of conflicts and failures.

The first step was 1963, when the "language border" was fixed. That is important, because it confirmed the territorialization of the problem and allowed later for the mainly, yet only partially, territorial solution. The agreement of 1963 stated that the borderline would not move anymore, that is, the logic of constantly refixing it on the basis of the language census was abandoned. Thus, three territories now have fixed boundaries, which is especially important for Brussels, which will not be able to expand anymore. In a number of localities where the last census of 1947 revealed a minority of at least thirty percent speakers of a language other than the official one for the region, the inhabitants received so-called facilities, allowing them to use their language in their individual contacts with the public authorities. That is especially important for the area around Brussels, which in the old logic would have become an integral part of the bilingual area. Since 1963 this periphery has been clearly and definitively in Flanders, be it with language facilities for the Francophones in some localities.

The next step in the reform of the Constitution was in 1970. This reform formally recognized the existence of the communities and the regions and gave them their territory. The three regions obviously coincide with the three linguistic areas fixed in 1963. The "Flemish community" consists of the Dutch-speaking region and the Dutch-speakers in the bilingual region of Brussels, while the "French community" consists of the Francophone (Walloon) region (not the German-speakers) and the Francophones of Brussels. As for the German community, it is located in the Francophone area, but it is granted language facilities. During the 1970s many attempts to translate these principles into working institutions failed, because of divergent interpretations of this logic and the prevalence given by one group (the Flemish) to the communities and by the other (the Francophones) to the regions.

In 1980 a second round of constitutional reforms introduced a real devolution of competencies. For the regions of Flanders and Wallonia and for the three language communities, institutions were set up. For Brussels, however, there was no solution, and that region did not receive its autonomy yet. The institutions consisted of parliamentary councils, composed of the members of the House of Representatives and the Senate, elected in one of the regions. For those elected in the bilingual area, the first language in which they take their oath defines their linguistic identity and defines in which community council they can sit. These councils have an executive, but they do not elect it (technically, the regional and community ministers belong to the Belgian government). In other words, community and regional parliamentarians are "central" parliamentarians, sitting for certain purposes in linguistically divided assemblies, and the regional and community executives are subgroups of the central executive (the term "federal" had not emerged yet).

At this point, the Flemish institutions were merged, in the sense that there was one single council and one single executive, taking care of both the competencies of the region of Flanders and the competencies of the Flemish community. Flanders wanted indeed to be a community in the first place and did not ask for the regional logic. At the Francophone side two sets of institutions were built, one for the Walloon region and one for the French community. Again, this difference in structure continues to this day.

The next step forward was in 1988, when constitutional reforms gave Brussels its regional institutions, which also arrange the way in which both the Flemish and the French community can be present in Brussels. This is organized through awkwardly named institutions called the "French Community commission" (or COCOF as it is commonly called), the "Flemish Community commission" (VGC), and the "Common Community Commission" (COCOM / GGC). The COCOF is a real and full-fledged legislative body. The Flemish Community Commission VGC is not a legislative body, since decisions on Flemish community issues are decided by the regular Flemish institutions and merely implemented in Brussels by the VGC. As for the Common Community

Commission (COCOM), it deals with community issues relevant to both linguistic communities, such as bilingual hospitals. The reform of 1988 also transferred new competencies to the regions and the competence over education to the communities, which is a very important step. The councils now elect region and community executives, but the councils themselves are—except for Brussels—not (yet) directly elected.

In 1993, the institutions were changed again, and the Constitution now formally declared Belgium to be a federal country. The major change here was the direct election of the councils of the regions and the reform of the Senate into a house of the communities (not regions). The central province of Brabant was also split in the provinces of Flemish Brabant and Walloon Brabant, the provincial competencies being taken over by the regional authorities in the region of Brussels. The 1993 reform also permitted the transfer of powers from the French community to the Walloon region and the COCOF, in the areas of manpower training, aspects of health care policy, education, and policies toward handicapped people, to name a few. This transfer occurred in 1994. It did not happen at the Flemish side, because there was no need and especially no demand to do so. The Flemish institutions simply stick to the fusion of region and community and to the direct incorporation of the Brussels Flemish population into the Flemish community as a whole.

The 1993 changes were the last formal constitutional reforms so far. But the process of reform goes on. The elections of 1999 did not put into place a Parliament able to change much, because the tensions before the elections made it impossible to reach a compromise on the list of constitutional articles to be reformed. Especially the Francophones did not want to move anymore, while Flanders (i.e., the Flemish government and Parliament) continuously stressed its desire to regionalize parts of the social security, to get some degree of fiscal autonomy, to receive the right to organize the political institutions of local municipalities and provinces, and to achieve more autonomy in policy domains like agriculture, international relations, and aid to developing countries. At the end of 1999 and again when drafting the 2001 budget in October 2000 the Liberal-Socialist-Green government reached an agreement on a number of these points. Only the regionalization of social security was not agreed on and not even really discussed. The Francophones accepted all these changes, mainly because the French community receives more (federal) money for education. The story of institutional reform is certainly to be continued.

THE CONSOCIATIONAL NATURE OF THE FEDERATION

As already discussed, the federal state was not produced overnight. The first constitutional reform of 1970 was important because it laid down the basis for the consociational logic of the further reforms. The 1970 Constitution introduced the obligation to have an equal number of French-speaking and Dutch-speaking ministers in the government. It also introduced the principle of the "double majority" for all further institutional reforms and for all laws implementing institutional reforms. The double majority means an overall majority of two-thirds (the normal requirement for all constitutional reforms) and a simple majority in each language group. This requirement means that it has become impossible for the Flemish majority to use this majority. Majority is not enough anymore.

The threshold for future reforms was thus fairly high. That has certainly slowed down the further implementation of the reforms, but, on the other hand, it also helped to finally solve the problems. The thresholds being so high, there were many attempts to continue with the reforms, but many attempts also failed. That meant that after a few years there were many unsolved problems and tensions, leading once in a while to a very deep crisis. These crises occurred when new governments had to be formed. As we explained earlier, most governments since the 1960s collapsed because of the linguistic divide. But after a governmental crisis a new government had to be formed by parties of both sides. When things really became troublesome, the risk of a total deadlock of the political system actually helped to produce the awareness that a solution had to be found, and then a solution was found indeed.

The Belgian federation is a fairly extreme kind of federation. The federal level has been almost completely emptied, and most of the powers have been given to the linguistic communities and to the regions. That is a clear result of the double party system. All the parties are regional parties. They represent only one part of the country and compete only with the parties of their own language. This produces a very centrifugal competition, because there simply is nobody to defend the centre. All parties want, in varying degrees, more autonomy for their region and/or community. The separated electoral competition unites the parties on each side and creates a huge cleavage between the two sides. These same parties have to bridge the gap when they form a Belgian coalition government. The way to do that is by using consociational logic: waiting until there are many problems to be solved and then producing an agreement that means essentially that the nonagreement is institutionalized by letting both sides deal with their own policy. In consociational language this is "granting autonomy," and that is exactly what is done in a federal state.

The solution produced by the consociational crisis management was a consociational federal state, full of checks and balances, power sharing, and veto powers (Deschouwer, 1999). The granting of autonomy that was just discussed is probably the most obvious feature. But there is more. We already mentioned the constitutional obligation to share power in the federal government. There is either no government or a government in which parties of both sides have reached an agreement and govern together. The logic of decision making in the federal government is consensus, which means that both sides have a veto power. This is much more important than the rather symbolic obligation to have an equal number of ministers for each language group.

At the level of the Parliament, there is also a veto power. When members of a linguistic group declare (with a two-thirds majority of the MPs of that group) that a proposal is probably going to harm them as a linguistic group, they can activate the so-called alarm bell. In that case the proposal goes to the government, which has to produce an alternative proposal (by consensus) within thirty days. This guarantee for the minority—together with equal number of ministers and consensus decision-making—is also present in the Brussels region, to protect the Dutch-speaking minority in that region.

Conflicts over distribution of powers or so-called conflicts of competence are settled in a judicial way. If a conflict over distribution of powers is signaled after a law, decree, or ordinance has been issued, it is settled by the Court of Arbitration. This court is composed of twelve judges, six Dutch-speaking and six French-speaking, all appointed by the federal government, on proposal of the Senate. Half of the judges are former politicians, and half of them belong to the judicial profession.

Conflicts of interest (i.e., conflicts involving lack of agreement on the substance of laws, decrees, or ordinances), are more problematic, since they need a political solution in an institutional setting that is complex, and full of subtle equilibrium and potentially diverging interpretations. The conflicts here are likely to occur between the two poles of the bipolar federalism and then in practice have to be solved by an agreement between them. The typical case is a projected legislation or regulation by one entity or by the federal government that another entity fears will affect it negatively. In order to deal "officially" with conflicts of interest, the Concertation Committee was created. It is composed of the federal prime minister, five ministers of the federal government, and six members of the governments of regions and communities. It also needs to be perfectly linguistically balanced. Either the federal government or the government of one of the federated entities can signal a potential conflict to the committee. This move suspends the debated decision during sixty days. During that time the committee can try to find a solution by consensus. If this is not found after sixty days, the suspension is lifted, and the conflict remains unsolved.

This Concertation Committee is only the official way to deal with these problems. It is rarely used. In practice the party presidents of the governing parties, who meet regularly with the prime minister, deal with the prevention of conflicts. The absence of federal parties in Belgium obliges indeed the parties to be active at two levels (the same party governs at the regional and at the federal level) and obliges them to contain the potential conflicts between the levels among them. Other institutions for a more permanent concertation and cooperation are not available, since the fairly exclusive competencies do not imply (at first sight) a great need for this cooperation. The system, however, does generate tensions concerning the interpretation of the rules and their eventual further reform. In the absence of good institutions for discussing them, they are allowed to accumulate until there is enough (i.e., until the system blocks) for a general and broad round of negotiations.

REMAINING AND RECURRING TENSIONS IN THE BELGIAN FEDERATION

The Belgian federation is the result of piecemeal changes, constantly trying to manage the conflict between the two major language groups. The federation is still young—it was really put into place in 1995—but at the same time the gradual buildup allows us to identify a number of weak points (i.e., aspects where the conflict is clearly not pacified or where the federal logic tends to enhance the conflicts). We have organized them under four headings.

The Financial Transfers

We have already mentioned the striking differences in economic performance between the north and the south of the country. The two have a very different history and today a very different economical structure. The bottom line is that Flanders has a growing economy with a very low degree of unemployment, while Wallonia is still struggling with the reconversion of the old industrial activities and faces a fairly high degree (twenty percent) of unemployment. Wallonia needs the support of the federal state and the financial solidarity from the north.

Yet in Flanders this situation and especially the obligation to support the south are seen as problematic. After having had to struggle for its linguistic and cultural rights, it sees itself now blocked by the lack of economic dynamism in a Socialist-dominated Walloon region. This is more or less the generally expressed feeling of the Flemish elite. In the spring of 1999 the Flemish Parliament voted a series of recommendations for a further reform of the state, in which demands for more financial and fiscal autonomy were very prominent. Furthermore, the Flemish Parliament wanted to defederalize a few sectors of the social security system.

For the Francophones these demands were unacceptable. Even if the Flemish elite defends its demands by referring to a better and more logical organization and distribution of competencies, these demands are perceived by the Francophones as a clear and deliberate attempt to reduce or even to break the financial solidarity between north and south and thus as a direct attack on the viability of the Walloon region. The Francophone response to any proposal to change the current rules is a clear and loud no. This only adds to the frustration of the Flemings, who interpret this refusal as the choice for the easy solution of living at the other's expense.

In the course of 2000 and with a very regionalist prime minister in Wallonia, some steps toward fiscal autonomy were achieved, but they were merely symbolic. The regions will receive, from 2002 on, the right to increase or reduce parts of personal income taxes, still collected, though, by the federal state. The regions will then control some six percent of the total amount of these financial means. It is certainly a symbolic breakthrough, but more will be requested by Flanders very soon. The question of social security has so far not been discussed, because it is absolutely clear that for the Francophones just the idea of discussing this topic is already one step too far, and since this is a new government with a new and experimental party composition, it wants to survive in the first place. The closer to the federal elections of 2003, the more the topic of regionalization of social security and further fiscal autonomy will be put on the agenda by Flanders.

The Bipolar Logic

This kind of tension between richer and poorer regions in a federation is, of course, not at all typically Belgian. It is rather typical for federal regimes. Yet in Belgium this type of conflict occurs in a bipolar federation, and that makes it a lot more difficult to manage. The actors in any conflict are basically the same, whether it concerns the financial redistribution or not. During the first legislature of the new state structures (1995-1999) this became extremely visible. Actually, the recurring problem is the result of the fact that Flanders wants to go further in the process of devolution, while the Francophones do not have any concrete demand, except keeping the current federal system going.

There are three major explanations for this Flemish urge to receive more autonomy. The first lies in history. The drive to reform the Belgian unitary state came from the north in the first place. There is today in Flanders a stronger feeling of regional-linguistic identity than in Wallonia or in the Francophone part of Belgium. This feeling has been reinforced by the new institutions. Although the institutions are fairly complex, they are rather simple and straightforward at the Flemish side: there is one Parliament and one government working and speaking on behalf of Flanders. This has strongly reduced the strength and importance of the societal Flemish movement. Claims and requests are now put on the agenda by the official and fully legitimate institutions of Flanders. The counterpart is much more divided. Francophones have a community Parliament and government, a Walloon regional Parliament and government, and also their own separate institutions in Brussels. They perceive the Flemish requests as the deliberate attempt of a well-organized and well-oiled machine to simply break up the country. They do not like this dynamism of the Flemish institutions, which is actually not so much dynamism but simply a sharper awareness of the lack of homogeneous competencies to go forward. The Francophones function in a complex and heterogeneous institutional environment. The Flemish environment, however, is much more homogeneous, and that leads to demands for controlling a number of extra competencies, especially with respect to fiscal and financial matters. This is perceived then by the Francophones as mere greed from the richer region, and that is also a part of the explanation.

The Flemings threatened to block the formation of a new federal government after the June 1999 elections if no negotiation on institutional reforms would be possible. Yet the discovery, one week before the elections, of dioxin in the feeding of cattle and the subsequent major crisis for the Belgian economy and export obliged the politicians to rapidly form a working federal government and to postpone the institutional discussions. The hurdle of government formation was thus easily taken, and discussions on the federal institutions were postponed. The basic logic of the subsequent negotiations and of the expected conflicts to come will, however, remain the same.

The Use of Language: Brussels and Its Periphery

Earlier we discussed a very structural problem of the Belgian federation. It occurs whenever a conflict is on the table. One type of conflict comes to the front very often and is actually the original conflict that has led to the state reform. That conflict concerns the use of language. The two major languages now have officially an equal status. Yet in practice French still dominates, only because—the result of history again—the Flemings often understand and can speak French, while the Francophones are more often unilingual. Official rules on the use of language, which have mainly been put into place to protect the minority (or lower-status) language, thus often are at odds with real life.

There are at least two hot points in this respect: Brussels and its periphery. Both are the result of the fact that the rules on the use of language were made back in 1963 with the deliberate Flemish attempt to stop the process of Frenchification, while in real life it was not stopped. Brussels is the capital city and the capital region and therefore has a bilingual status. That means that all public services have to be offered in both languages. Yet today the Brussels population (of Belgian nationality) speaking Dutch amounts to only some fifteen percent of the votes. In some local municipalities it is even less. Accommodating this minority is quite a burden for many Francophones. They consider this practical overrepresentation of a small minority as nondemocratic. It obliges civil servants to be bilingual, just to serve a few people. To get and to keep the job of civil servant, one needs to be bilingual, and that is a problem for many Francophones. The language laws of 1963 seem, therefore, to be constantly on the agenda.

The same goes for the municipalities in the periphery of Brussels, where Dutch is the official administrative language. In 1963 language "facilities" were granted to the inhabitants of six local municipalities around Brussels, which would simply have been added to Brussels at that time if the old principle of the language census had still have been followed. It means that more than thirty percent of the inhabitants were Francophones. Now the Francophones are a majority in all six municipalities, but they have to administer them officially in Dutch. Only the inhabitants can use French to communicate with the public authorities (local, regional, and federal). The Flemish government has recently tried to make this use of facilities a bit more difficult, obliging the citizens to ask for a French translation every time they receive a document in Dutch. That was seen by the Flemish government as something absolutely normal—after thirty five years of facilities one should be able to understand Dutch—but the move was seen by the Francophones as (one more) attempt to simply get rid of the Francophones and especially to put (once more) into question the old agreements. As long as Brussels exists, as long as its periphery exists and as long as the language border exists and runs through the middle of Belgium, this kind of conflict will occur again and again.

The Absence of Federal Parties

Belgium has no federal parties anymore. This point was also discussed at length earlier. It makes the role of the political parties in the system absolutely crucial. They find themselves in a very awkward position. Since they are all regional parties, they are the carriers of the ethnolinguistic demands. The separation of the parties and the party systems make them mobilize in only one of the two language communities. Yet these same parties also have to govern at the federal level. This multilevel setting is not new, but the lower level at which they mobilize has now become a full-fledged political system. This situation is pretty hard to manage for the parties. The two levels of decisionmaking are very different. We mentioned earlier that the substate governments (especially in Flanders) introduce matters of conflict, which tend to be avoided by the federal government. Yet exactly the same parties are present at both levels! Especially for the governing parties and more precisely for those leading the governments, this is a schizophrenic situation. The CVP was in that position until 1999, and now the VLD has to play the double-language game.

Governing at the regional level is easier. There is no language cleavage to deal with, and the governments can be more responsive. The federal government cannot be responsive because there are no real Belgian elections and no Belgian party system, and it has to deal with the differences between the two language groups, because the two are equally represented in the government. So far the parties have tried to contain these tensions by keeping the coalitions at all levels congruent (i.e., the same parties are either in government or in opposition at both levels). The perverse effect of this attempt to manage within the regional parties the problematic effect of the absence of federal parties is that the real political autonomy of the substates is reduced. They have to form the government that is compatible with the federal government, which also tries to respond to electoral results in the other part of the country. That is again an extremely frustrating experience. A very difficult test for the viability of the system will occur in 2003. That is the normal date for the next elections of the federal Parliament and for the formation of a new federal government. These elections will take place while the competing parties have to continue for one more year at the regional level, even if the new federal coalition is not "congruent" any more. One can expect the parties to do whatever they can to keep the congruence, but sooner or later the electoral results will not allow it. That will be the day when the question of the viability of the Belgian variety of federalism will be answered. June 2003 is already marked in red in the agendas of Belgian politicians and political scientists.

9

Revisiting Bilingualism and Biculturalism in Canada

Milton J. Esman

During his distinguished career, Kenneth McRae has been the leading Canadian advocate for the consociational management of ethnic conflict. While examining and analyzing the experiences of other countries, his eyes have remained focused on his homeland and on how best to realize his vision of a bilingual and bicultural nation. As a young researcher during the 1960s for the Royal Commission on Bilingualism and Biculturalism (B&B), he was responsible for its volume on *The National Capital*, a task dear to his heart as a resident of Ottawa and faculty member of Carleton University. Moreover, he shared the commission's core philosophy that Canada must be conceived as an "equal partnership" between its two founding peoples, British and French, that Canada's survival would depend on a renewed respect for this relationship, that its implementation required a bilingual regime, and that individual Canadians would be enriched by participation in two of the world's great cultural traditions.

During the ensuing three decades, as Professor McRae pursued his analysis and documentation of other pluralistic systems, Canada only partially accepted the B&B vision. Its principal success was the landmark Official Languages Act (OLA) of 1969, which prescribed a bilingual regime for all the institutions and agencies of the Government of Canada. Any Canadian anywhere in Canada should feel at home in the official language of his or her choice; thus, all federal public services should be available in either official language. Positions that require competence in both languages would be designated "bilingual;" and incumbents would be expected to demonstrate bilingual proficiency or be trained at government expense in bilingual educational centers. The federal public services would strive for "balanced" or "equitable" participation, so that the proportion of civil servants of Anglophone and Francophone origins would parallel the nation's demographic structure. A language ombudsman, the commissioner of official languages, would call complaints of violations or nonobservance to the attention of Parliament and the offending agency and attempt to negotiate corrections consistent with the language and spirit of the

OLA. French-language units would be established within the various departments to permit members of the Francophone minority to work in their native medium. Where there were significant official language minorities, bilingual districts would be designated where all public services, provincial and municipal as well as federal, would be available.

The Official Languages Act was supported by an elite phalanx of all the parties in Parliament, though individual backbenchers opposed all or parts of it, presaging continuing opposition and protest from civil servants and members of the public who felt threatened by its specific provisions or were offended by the very notion of language pluralism for all of Canada. With the important exceptions of French-language units and bilingual districts, its provisions, elaborated and enforced by the Treasury Board, have been implemented, despite lapses by some federal agencies in the English-speaking provinces. The 1969 act was supplanted by a 1988 statute that consolidated official language practices and authorized, in addition, federal subsidies to facilitate minority official-language instruction by provincial agencies.

The commission, however, underestimated reactions from the provinces that control language policy for the many services that fall within provincial jurisdiction in Canada's federal structure. The commission expected Québec's elites and attentive publics to welcome bilingualism, since it roughly replicated for all Canada the bilingual regime that had long prevailed in Québec. They were mistaken. Five years after the enactment of the federal OLA, the federalist Liberal Party government of Québec enacted the province's legislation that declared French to be the sole official language of Québec, ordered all children of non-English-speaking backgrounds to attend French-language schools, required that members of professions demonstrate a working knowledge of French, and prescribed the conversion of most governmental, industrial, and commercial establishments to French as the language of work. The liberal principle of freedom of language choice that the commission had endorsed was decisively rejected. After the election of the separatist *Parti Québécois* government in 1976, these measures were tightened; and others were adopted to ensure that French language and culture would provide the dominant ambiance in all phases of life within the province.[1] Measures were subsequently adopted to insure that all outdoor commercial signs be displayed in French only. Only by such measures, it was argued, could the survival of French language and culture be assured in the aggressively English-speaking environment of North America, and only the government of Québec had resources sufficient to safeguard this heritage. The B&B recommendation for a bilingual district covering all of Québec was summarily brushed aside.

Though New Brunswick readily accepted bilingualism as provincial policy, English-speaking Canada was stunned by Québec's rejection. They believed that the OLA represented generous concessions by the Anglophone majority to their Francophone compatriots, only to find this generosity spurned. Ontario, with a large French-speaking minority in its eastern counties and in the national capital area, declined to become bilingual or to implement bilingual districts. It confined itself to providing a limited, but gradually expanded, range of services in French, including education from kindergarten through university.

The commission also misjudged the implications of Canada's changing demographic structure, a mistake that might have been avoided had it taken more seriously the complaint of the Ukrainian minority that the B&B formula marginalized them and demeaned their status as Canadians. Recent migration patterns have further pluralized Canadian society to the point that French-speaking founding peoples are less numerous, except in Québec and New Brunswick, than Canadians of nonfounding status. For the most part, the latter are willing to acculturate to English, since they consider Canada to be an English-speaking country, but see no reason that French should be "stuffed down their throats" or accorded higher status than their ancestral languages. Much of the resistance to Québec's demands for special status and recognition as a "distinct society" stems from the hostility of these other minorities. While he was unwilling to consider official status for any other language, Prime Minister Pierre-Elliot Trudeau in 1971 inaugurated a program of "multiculturalism within a bilingual framework" to help French-speaking Canadians perpetuate their ancestral cultures, to grant public recognition of their contributions to Canada's development, and thereby to soften their hostility to official bilingualism. The official myth that Canada, unlike the United States, is a mosaic, not a melting pot, is, however, belied by the rapid rate of linguistic assimilation, especially in English-speaking provinces, by persons of non-English-speaking backgrounds and the diminishing salience of heritage identities in the wake of widespread intermarriage and acculturation, strikingly parallel to a similar evolution in the United States.

In 1982, after tortuous negotiations energized by Prime Minister Trudeau, the Canadian Constitution was finally "patriated," an amending formula was agreed to, and a new Charter of Rights and Freedoms was entrenched in Canada's governing instrument. The Charter, emphasizing the inherent human rights of individual Canadians, confirmed the bilingual practices of the federal government and the province of New Brunswick. (It also recognized for the first time the special status and rights of the aboriginal peoples, Indians and Inuit, an important dimension of Canada's pluralism not treated in this chapter.) All that Trudeau could extract from the provincial premiers, however, was a commitment to provide public education in minority official languages to Canadian citizens, where numbers warrant. Québec and Ontario furnish a range of public services, notably, health and hospital care, to the English- and French-speaking minorities, respectively, but these are matters of provincial policy, not constitutional entitlement. The new constitutional provisions were duly ratified by the provincial, federal, and British Parliaments and came into force, but without the assent of Québec's governments, federalist or separatist, which argued that the new Constitution insufficiently recognizes and protects Québec's role as a distinct society. I do not here revisit the failed efforts at Meech Lake and Charlottetown to induce Québec to accede to the Constitution. At this stage, Québec continues to function as a component of Canada but has not adhered to its constitution and has refused to enforce important Supreme Court rulings regarding language policy.[2]

With its high standard of living and excellent quality of life, Canada is widely envied as a highly civilized society, one of the most desirable countries in which to live. Yet its very survival as a state remains precarious, and the partnership concept promoted by the B&B Commission has become increasingly irrelevant. Individual Francophones serve proudly in all of Canada's public services, including its armed forces and even as prime minister; but in a 1995 referendum, a majority of Québec's French-speakers voted in favor of a separatist resolution.[3] The present separatist government in Québec promises future referenda, threatening to keep the pot boiling.

What is evolving in Canada is a two-tiered pattern: official bilingualism at the national level, embodying the "personality" principle that individuals, wherever they may be, are entitled to receive public services in the official language of their choice. At the provincial level, with the sole exception of New Brunswick, the "territorial" principle prevails—there is one official language, and official language minorities must be content with a limited range of services in their language, including the constitutionally guaranteed right to education. But because the survival of languages normally depends on their economic viability, official-language minorities are diminishing everywhere in Canada. As it is virtually impossible to earn a livelihood in French in the English-speaking provinces, the ranks of Francophones *hors Québec* are rapidly eroding. Since French has been enforced as the language of work in Québec, the numbers of English-speakers have declined by more than half, and many of its institutions are withering.[4] Except for the so-called bilingual belt—New Brunswick, the western districts of Montreal, and perhaps the areas of Ontario surrounding the national capital—language use is gradually conforming to provincial boundaries. Persons of non-French/non-English-speaking backgrounds, the purported constituents for multiculturalism, are joining official language minorities in assimilating to the dominant language of their province and to its dominant culture.

Canada's survival as an integrated polity depends on the continuation of a vigorous bilingual regime in the federal government. Francophones, especially Québecers, could not otherwise feel that Canada is also their country. If Québec should secede from the confederation, there would be little support for official bilingualism in a predominantly English-speaking Canada, embittered by Québec's departure. But while Canada endures as a single polity, it remains bound by some of the consociational practices that Kenneth McRae has illuminated in his writings. These include official bilingualism at the federal level, balanced participation in the federal public services, a bicultural ambience in the national capital region, Francophone representation on the Supreme Court, and rotation of leadership in the main national party, the Liberal Party of Canada. The B&B Commission's broader vision of a robustly bicultural country, including provincial and municipal participation in bilingual districts throughout Canada, failed to appreciate the intensity of French Canadian nationalism in Québec and widespread skepticism, especially among non-founding peoples in the English-speaking provinces. Except in New Brunswick, its prompt and summary rejection by Québec doomed it elsewhere in Canada and led to the emergent regime of unilingual provinces with limited accommodation for official language minorities. Despite official patronage, multiculturalism remains a shallow concept as non-official language minorities are expected to adopt the official language of their province and participate in its mainline culture.[5]

The prolonged and passionate debate over the status of its largest minority community and the political turbulence that this has generated stand in strange contrast to the peaceful evolution of Canada's prosperous economy and orderly society with its international prestige and very low levels of criminal violence. The fathers of confederation, representing the two founding peoples and keenly aware of the perils of intercommunal strife, managed, in the 1860s, better perhaps than they had even hoped, to provide posterity with the institutional means to maintain "peace, order, and good government." The vision of these practical men of goodwill that Canadians of different origins could find ways to prosper together in the same political system in mutual respect remains very much alive in the writings of such scholars and opinion leaders as Kenneth McRae.

NOTES

I am grateful to John Edwards for his comments on an earlier version of this chapter.

1. The 1974 legislation by the Québec National Assembly was known as Bill 22; the 1977 measure was designated the Charter of the French Language.

2. The Charter contains a "notwithstanding" clause, which enables pro-vincial governments to opt out of some of its provisions and out of subsequent legislation and court decisions.

3. The separatist resolution was defeated by less than one percent of the total vote, and that result was achieved only by a solid negative vote by the minority of Anglophones and recent immigrants.

4. This diminishing minority is now concentrated in western Montreal. Though its younger members tend to be bilingual, the process of out-migration to other areas of Canada or to the United States continues.

5. Many members of non-French-speaking minorities regard multi-culturalism as a political sham. How, they ask, can our culture be protected when our language has been relegated to vernacular status? Québec nationalists, on the other hand, claim that multiculturalism will reduce them to the same status as that of the other minorities. Thus, they insist on formal constitutional recognition as a distinct society.

10

The Politics of Language in Québec: Keeping the Conflict Alive

A. Brian Tanguay

In this chapter, I provide an interim report on the politics of language not in Canada as a whole but in the province of Québec alone. I develop a tentative explanation of the following paradox: why are conflicts over language still so prominent in contemporary Québec when the Charter of the French Language, adopted in 1977, has apparently succeeded in eliminating the most important causes of nationalist mobilization and anger during the 1960s? At present, the French character of Québec is incontestable; French is the dominant language of the workplace; and immigrants send their children to French-language primary and secondary schools in overwhelming numbers. How is it, then, that groups such as the Brigade d'autodéfense du Français (BAF) have captured headlines with a campaign of violence and intimidation (poorly organized and somewhat farcical though it may be) directed against "Anglophone racists" and firms alleged to have infringed the spirit of Bill 101? Even if the BAF is dismissed as a ragtag collection of a few misguided zealots, how does one account for the claims of more mainstream figures like Yves Michaud, Québec's former agent-general in Paris, who has argued that any concessions to minority language groups in Québec amount to a "linguistic Munich"? The Québécois people do not have the right to commit hara-kiri, Michaud writes, and they must take all necessary measures to preserve the French language, especially in Montreal, where it is most threatened (Michaud, 2000).

In the analysis to follow, I employ Kenneth McRae's framework for studying multilingual societies in order to make sense of language politics in contemporary Québec. The first section of the chapter examines the historical and developmental factors that have shaped relations between the main language groups in Québec. In the second section, I explore the relationship between language and social structure in Québec, with a view to determining whether language divisions in the province are reinforced or offset by other cleavages; whether, for instance, there is still a linguistic division of labour in Québec, as there was on the eve of the Quiet Revolution in the late 1950s. In a brief concluding section, I examine the prospects for attenuating intergroup conflict in Québec in the near future.

The burden of my argument is that in spite of the improved status of French in Québec today, which is the direct result of the passage of Bill 101, linguistic tensions in the province have not declined appreciably. This is because new sources of conflict have emerged; in fact, some of these conflicts have been exploited by nationalist elites for their own purposes. This explains, in part, the obsession with the language of commercial signs in Québec during the past decade. At the same time, the politics of language in Québec has shaded off into the politics of immigration: many of the complaints of Francophone nationalists centre on what they perceive to be the painfully slow process of integration of immigrants—designated "allophones" in the province—into the majority culture.

A CONCISE HISTORY OF LANGUAGE POLICY IN QUÉBEC

Language policy in Canada and Québec, as Ramsay Cook has pointed out, has sought to determine who has the right to use what language and in what circumstances (Cook, 1995: 150). In Québec prior to the Quiet Revolution, the issue of language was not highly politicized, nor was it the source of open, intractable conflict. Language policy focused primarily on the educational rights of the English-speaking minority in the province and, to a lesser extent, on the language of government institutions. Policymakers and intellectuals paid scant attention to the language of the workplace or the linguistic *visage* of Québec (155). Nationalism during this period was a defensive and inward-looking ideology, preaching *la survivance*—the preservation of the rural, Catholic way of life. For the most part, the French and the English treated each other with benign indifference. The two groups lived in almost entirely separate worlds; there was in the province what Hubert Guindon called a system of "mutually satisfying, self-segregated institutions" (1964: 158). In the fields of education, religion, welfare, leisure, and residence, according to Guindon, the separation of the two cultures was "total" up to the 1950s.

Industrialization and urbanization in the early part of the twentieth century brought French and English into contact, in the mines and resource industries of Québec's hinterlands as well as in the factories of the major cities. Even here, though, Québec's clerical elites were quite successful in containing intergroup conflict, through such strategies as the creation of confessional unions. The principal function of the Confédération des travailleurs catholiques du Canada (CTCC), established in 1921, was "the defence and perpetuation of the Catholic faith and the French-Canadian cultural heritage and language of the francophone working class" (Behiels, 1985: 123). Catholic trade unions articulated a vision of social partnership between employers (English) and workers (French) and actively discouraged strikes as expressions of godless, socialistic class conflict (Rouillard, 1989: 230).

This is not to say that everyone in Québec prior to 1960 happily accepted this cultural division of labour. Conflict simmered below the surface of social relations. To rework Guindon's formula: by the 1950s, relations between French and English in Québec may well have been self-segregated, but they were not always mutually satisfying. Popular accounts of Québec society at the time capture the latent conflict between the two cultures. In the opening scene of Claude Jutra's classic film *Mon Oncle Antoine*, for example, an English foreman chews out a French worker, Joe, at a mine in the Asbestos region of Québec. Joe and the foreman are linked by mutual incomprehension and hostility. When one of his fellow workers asks him what the foreman said, Joe replies: "J'sais pas, je parle pas l'anglais!" ("I don't know, I don't speak English!")

A second example of the latent language conflict in Québec prior to the Quiet Revolution can be found in Michel Tremblay's reminiscences about his adolescence in Montreal during the 1950s, published in *Les vues animées* (1990). In one of the stories contained in the collection, Tremblay recounts one of his regular visits to the downtown Eaton's store to purchase phonograph records for the princely sum of ninety-nine cents. He asks the clerk, a young girl barely older than Michel himself, to slit open the plastic wrapping on a record so that he can listen to it in one of the booths provided for that purpose. Tremblay addresses the clerk in French. She looks at him "as if I was a dog turd on a velvet cushion" and claims not to be able to speak French. Yet Tremblay *knows* that the clerk is French: "the accent, the head, the hairdo, the clothes, the chewing gum, all came from the Plateau Mont-Royal" He persists in speaking to her in French, and the clerk, exasperated, finally lets loose an epithet in *joual*. She then asks Tremblay if he's trying to get her fired, at which point he spots a supervisor observing the two of them, "without even attempting to hide his pitiful game of the poorly paid spy, trying to catch a couple of francophones red-handed, talking to each other in their own language. I understood everything in a second: the ceaseless humiliations, the harrassment, the small and contemptible capitulations. I pitied her. And me."[1]

With the Quiet Revolution, this latent conflict over language erupted into the open with a force that shocked many observers, both inside Québec and in the rest of Canada. The Royal Commission on Bilingualism and Biculturalism, established by Prime Minister Lester B. Pearson in late 1963, issued its *Preliminary Report* in February 1965. In it, the commissioners underscored the seriousness of the ethnic and language conflicts racking the country: "Canada, without being fully conscious of the fact, is passing through the greatest crisis in its history" (Canada, Royal Commission on Bilingualism and Biculturalism [RCBB], 1967:xvii). If steps were not taken immediately to meet the demands of French-speaking Québecers, the commissioners warned, the country could easily break apart.

The demands of growing numbers of Francophones in Québec in the early 1960s centred largely on the economic and social status of their language. As Book III of the RCBB report, *The Work World*, put it, the formal equality of languages and legal guarantees of the use of both French and English in the courts and government institutions would mean very little if they were not "accompanied by equality of economic opportunity" (Canada, RCBB, 1969: 3). The commissioners noted that the dissatisfaction of Francophones in Canada stemmed primarily from "what they perceive to be their inferior position vis-à-vis Anglophones in the work world. Again and again we came across such phrases as: 'I have to hang up my language with my coat when I go to work'" (3.). The report went on to note that many Francophones resented the fact that they had little real control over many of the economic decisions that affected "both their material well-being and the capacity of their institutions (e.g., schools and the mass media) to provide for their special needs" (4).

A number of research studies conducted for the Royal Commission had an incendiary effect on the burgeoning nationalist movement in Québec in the late 1960s, providing it with ammunition for its claim that Francophones in the province were an exploited, subaltern class, an "ethnic class."[2] In a study of income disparities between different ethnic and linguistic groups in both Canada and Québec, the economist André Raynauld uncovered a highly stratified income structure. In Québec, for example, workers of French origin earned roughly ninety two percent of the provincial average in terms of labour income (salaries plus wages), while those of British origin earned approximately forty two percent more than the provincial average. As Table 10.1 indicates, the average labour income of the French ethnic group was among the lowest in Québec, surpassing that of only the Italians and native Indians.[3]

Another table in the report (not shown here) indicated that, in Canada as a whole, bilingual Canadians of all ethnic origins earned higher average incomes than unilingual Canadians of all ethnic origins, except in Québec, where unilingual Anglophones of British origin had the highest average income (Canada, RCBB, 1969: 21-22). In yet another study, Raynauld demonstrated that Francophone-owned manufacturing industries in Québec accounted for a low proportion of provincial value-added; were less productive than industries owned by Anglophones or foreign interests; employed fewer workers and paid them less; produced mainly for the Québec market rather than for export; and were concentrated in what would later be called the "soft sectors," such as leather goods, wood products, and furniture (56-60).

In sum, then, despite the sweeping social and political changes that had been ushered in the election of Jean Lesage and his Liberals in 1960 and despite the Liberals' reelection in 1962 on a platform of "*maîtres chez nous*," Francophones in Québec in the mid- to late 1960s were clearly *not* the masters of their own economic house. The federal government's response to the brewing conflict caused by this ethnic division of labour was two-pronged. On the one hand, Liberal prime minister Pierre Trudeau, elected in 1968, forcefully argued that Québec did not need any special powers in order to protect its culture and language and to thrive within the Canadian federation. Indeed, Trudeau's aggressively antinationalist posture was one of the traits that made him so attractive to voters in Canada in the 1968 federal election. Once elected, Trudeau put the notion of "French power" into practice, appointing key Francophones to the cabinet and placing his "alter ego," Marc Lalonde, in the prime minister's office (Clarkson and McCall, 1990: 116-118). On the other hand, the Official Languages Act was passed in 1969, declaring French and English to be the two official languages of Canada. The legislation also created

Table 10.1:
Average Labour Income of Male Salary- and Wage-Earners,
by Ethnic Origin, Québec, 1961

Origin	Labour Income	
	Dollars	Index
All origins	$3,469	100.0
British	4,940	142.4
Scandinavian	4,939	142.4
Dutch	4,891	140.9
Jewish	4,851	139.8
Russian	4,828	139.1
German	4,254	122.6
Polish	3,984	114.8
Asiatic	3,734	107.6
Ukrainian	3,733	107.6
Other European	3,547	102.4
Hungarian	3,537	101.9
French	3,185	91.8
Italian	2,938	84.6
Indian	2,112	60.8

Source: Canada, RCBB (1969: Table 5).

the commissioner of official languages to oversee the implementation of the law, promoted the bilingualization of the federal civil service, and, most importantly, ensured that the institutions of the federal government would provide services in either French or English, depending on the consumer's preference. These initiatives came at a considerable cost, but as the legislation's defenders argued, "We must be prepared to pay a reasonable price to keep our country from breaking up" (Forsey, 1974: 281).

More than thirty years have passed since the implementation of the Official Languages Act, time enough to arrive at an assessment of its overall effectiveness. In terms of its principal objective—moderating Québec nationalism and strengthening national unity—the policy of official bilingualism must be considered a failure. There is no doubt that Pierre Trudeau's vision of a bilingual Canada, in which Francophones would feel at home no matter where they happened to travel or reside in the country, was a noble dream that deeply touched many individual Canadians.[4] Nonetheless, the dream of official bilingualism, *a mari usque ad mare*, has foundered on Canada's stubborn demography and geography. As McRoberts (1989; 1997: chapter 4) has pointed out, formal linguistic equality of French and English has never made a lot of sense in those provinces (especially Saskatchewan, Alberta, British Columbia, and Newfoundland), where the Francophone minorities have constituted little more than one or two percent of the population—far smaller, in some cases, than other significant ethnic minority groups in these regions. In spite of the good intentions that underlay the adoption of the official languages legislation, it has been powerless to reverse or even halt Canada's evolution toward two unilingual entities, Anglophone Canada and Francophone Québec, with a small "bilingual belt" in those areas of Ontario and New Brunswick that are adjacent to Québec (McRoberts, 1989: 157; Joy, 1992: 5).

It is important to note that nationalists in Québec welcomed Ottawa's efforts in the 1970s to make the federal public service bilingual and to ensure that Francophones across the country would be served in their own language whenever they dealt with the institutions of the national government. However, the Official Languages Act, as it was implemented by the various Trudeau governments, failed to address the two issues that were of paramount concern to French-speaking Québecers in the 1960s and 1970s, namely, the language of the workplace in their province and the perceived need to channel immigrant children into French-language schools. The first concern, as we have seen, stemmed from the economically inferior situation of Francophones in their own province, a subordination that was underscored yet again by the publication of the Gendron Commission report in 1972.[5] The Gendron Commission recommended, among other things, a massive infusion of Francophones into the upper levels of management in the private sector in order to make French the normal language of communication in the business world and to bring to an end the discrimination against Francophones that had been a feature of the Québec economy up to the 1960s (McRoberts, 1988: 179-180).

The second concern, over the integration of immigrants into the French-language school system, was prompted by the rapidly declining birthrate among Francophones in the 1960s and 1970s, and the consequent need to welcome large numbers of immigrants into the province in order to ensure population growth. As demographers noted, the vast majority of the immigrants coming into Québec, upward of eighty five percent, settled in Montreal, specifically, on the island of Montreal (the downtown core of the city, so to speak). Before 1975, the overwhelming majority of these immigrants sent their children to English-language schools, partly because they recognized that "economic opportunities were greater in the English language" (McRoberts, 1988: 181) and partly because, until the Quiet Revolution, the French-language school system had not seemed interested in opening up to immigrants, preferring that the newcomers integrate into the Anglophone community.[6] Jacques Henripin, the leading demographer in Québec, predicted in 1969 that if existing population trends continued, Francophones would decline significantly as a proportion of the total provincial population, from over eighty percent to somewhere between seventy two and seventy nine percent by 2001. The situation would be even worse in Montreal, where Francophones risked becoming a minority in the province's major metropolis (McRoberts, 1988: 182; Henripin, 1993: 315).

As a result of these concerns, in the same year that the Official Languages Act was passed, the provincial government in Québec began to legislate in the area of language rights. In 1969, provincial language policy recognized the formal equality of French and English and enshrined the freedom of choice of all language groups to send their children to schools of either official language. This decision sparked a series of protests and riots by Francophone nationalists in Montreal in 1969. By 1977, French had been recognized as the only official language in the province, the rights of Anglophones and immigrants in the matter of schooling had been severely curtailed, and steps had been taken to ensure that French was the predominant language of commercial and economic affairs (see Table 10.2 for a chronology of the most important pieces of language legislation enacted by successive Québec governments since 1969).

As McRoberts (1997: 110) argues, the adoption of Bill 22 by the Liberal government of Robert Bourassa in 1974 and of Bill 101 by the Parti Québécois under René Lévesque in 1977 demonstrated that "Québec francophones could support official bilingualism in Ottawa and recognition of French rights in other provinces yet also support the primacy of French in Québec." More importantly, Francophones in Québec appeared to prefer the relatively straightforward, hard-line approach of the Parti Québécois on the language question to the vacillation of the Liberals under Robert Bourassa, as manifested in the extremely unpopular—with Anglophones as well as Francophones—Bill 22 (see Table 10.2). Bill 101, The Charter of the French Language, enshrined three basic principles in law:

- French was declared the only language of the provincial state and all public institutions, as well as of commercial advertising;
- Only those students who had at least one parent educated in English *in Québec* had access to English-language schools;
- All firms in the province employing fifty or more workers were compelled to obtain a certificate of *francisation* from the Office de la langue française, attesting to an adequate use of French in internal communications, communications with clients and the public, in management, and on the shop floor.

Interestingly, in his *Memoirs*, René Lévesque remarks "with a certain astonishment that the language of advertisement didn't seem to us to be worth making a big fuss about" (1986: 266). Lévesque implies that if the Bourassa government had the political will to prohibit unilingual English signs in the province and to follow through on its stated intention in 1970 to allow bilingual

Table 10.2
A Chronology of Language Legislation in Québec

Year	Law	Particulars
1969	Bill 63	• Introduced by the Union Nationale government of J.-J. Bertrand. Guaranteed all parents the legal right to school their children in the official language of their choice. • Sparked riots and protests by Francophone nationalists in Montreal. In an attempt to appease the latter, the government had included provisions in the Bill requiring English-school graduates to demonstrate "competence" in French; it also established the Gendron Commission to investigate the state of the French language (it would report in 1972).
1974	Bill 22	• Made French the only "official" language of Québec, but French and English were still to have equal status in the National Assembly and the courts. • Created the *Régie de la langue française* to oversee *francisation* of the workplace: certificates of *francisation* were given to firms employing a "sufficient" number of Francophone managers and permitting the use of French on the workshop floor (though the *Régie* was given considerable latitude in determining whether the firm in question lived up to the standards of the law). These certificates were required by any firm wishing to do business with the provincial government or receive a state subsidy. • Required language proficiency tests for young people wishing to attend English schools. The latter provision was a public relations disaster, sparking Anglophones and Allophones to abandon the Liberal Party in the 1976 election and vote for a (briefly) resurgent Union Nationale—thereby contributing to the PQ victory.
1977	Bill 101	• The PQ's Charter of the French Language made French the only official language of the courts and legislature (eventually struck down by the Supreme Court in 1980). • Allowed access to English schools only to those students who had at least one parent educated in English *in Québec* (later superseded by the Charter of Rights and Freedoms). • Program of *francisation* initiated by Bill 22 continued, but made compulsory for all firms with more than fifty employees. The *visage français* of Québec was to be strengthened by banning the use of bilingual commercial signs (later declared unconstitutional by Supreme Court in 1988). • Created a new language bureaucracy: Office de la langue française, Conseil de la langue française, Commission de surveillance
1988	Bill 178	• Bourassa government's response to the Supreme Court decision in December striking down the sign provisions of the Charter of the French Language. Enacted using the *non obstante* (notwithstanding) provision of the Charter of Rights and Freedoms. Dubbed the "inside-outside" law, because it allowed for bilingual signs inside a commercial establishment, but French only on the outside. Some key Anglophone cabinet ministers (Richard French, Herbert Marx, Clifford Lincoln) resigned in protest; sparked a wave of anti-French sentiment in English Canada and contributed to the growth of neanderthal groups like the Alliance for the Protection of English Canada (APEC); contributing factor in the demise of Meech Lake Accord.
1993	Bill 86	• Relaxed sign law provisions, allowing bilingual commercial signs provided that French is predominant.

advertising, so long as French was predominant,[7] then the whole issue of the language of commercial signs might never have become the running sore in Québec political life that it now appears to be.

Only five years after Bill 101 was passed, the Trudeau government's Canadian Charter of Rights and Freedoms was entrenched in the Constitution. Section 23 of the Charter, governing minority-language rights, conflicted with Bill 101 in a number of key respects, and a series of court decisions in the 1980s and 1990s eroded the authority of the provincial legislation (see Table 10.2). Despite this fact, which has undeniably heightened tension between Ottawa and Québec nationalists, Bill 101 has had a profound impact on Québec's politics, economy, and social life. In the next section of this chapter, I examine the most important changes that the Charter of the French Language has wrought in Québec society.

THE IMPACT OF BILL 101 ON QUÉBEC SOCIETY

On September 7, 1995, Louise Beaudoin, the PQ minister of culture and communications, and the person responsible for the implementation of the Charte de la langue française, created the Comité interministériel sur la situation de la langue française au Québec (Québec, 1996).[8] In laying out the committee's terms of reference, the minister noted that "significant progress" had been made in the use and quality of French in the province since the adoption of Bill 101 in 1977. Nonetheless, she affirmed that the principal objective of Bill 101, to make French the normal and customary language in Québec, had not yet been attained in the workplace, in the school systems, or in the integration of immigrants into the dominant culture, especially in Montreal. Moreover, the minister noted, globalization and the new communications revolution were having a profound impact on the status of French as a language of work and leisure, and the implications of these trends needed to be studied (Québec, 1996: 3-4).

Perhaps surprisingly, the Comité interministériel's assessment of the state of the French language in Québec in the 1990s was highly positive. Despite the dire predictions of demographic doomsayers in the 1960s and 1970s, the report noted that Francophones had remained remarkably stable as a proportion of the total population in Québec between 1951 and 1991. This is true whether the indicator used is mother tongue (Table 10.3) or language spoken at home (Table 10.4). Table 10.3 shows that persons of French origin (mother tongue) constituted 82.2 percent of the total provincial population in 1991, as opposed to 82.5 percent in 1951. In metropolitan Montreal, Francophones increased from almost 65 percent in 1951 of the population to 68.5 percent in 1991. Only on the island of Montreal did Francophones decline as a percentage of the population. In all cases—in the province as a whole, in metropolitan Montreal, and on the Island of Montreal—those of English origin declined in numbers, in some cases quite markedly. In metropolitan Montreal, for instance, Anglophones constituted 26.5 percent of the population in 1951 but only 15.7 percent in 1991. Allophones, on the other hand, have increased as a proportion both of the provincial population (from 3.7 percent in 1951 to 8.1 percent in 1991) and of

Montreal's population. On the Island of Montreal, where the linguistic conflict
in the province is most acutely felt, and where nationalists have focused most of
their energy, allophones have increased from 15.1 percent of the population in
1951 to 22.6 percent in 1991.

Language spoken at home is a more accurate indicator of the vitality of a
language than mother tongue, and Table 10.4 confirms the trends highlighted in
Table 10.3. Francophones have increased as a proportion of the total population
in Québec and in metropolitan Montreal, although on the Island of Montreal,
they have declined between 1971 and 1991, from 61.2% of the population to
58.5%. Anglophones, meanwhile, have declined in number at all levels—
province-wide, in metropolitan Montreal, and on the island of Montreal—while
allophones have increased proportionately at all three levels.

Table 10.3
Mother Tongue in Québec (% of population) by Region, 1951-1991

Region	Mother Tongue	1951	1961	1971	1981	1991
All of Québec	French	82.5	81.2	80.7	82.4	82.2
	English	13.8	13.3	13.1	11.0	9.7
	Other	3.7	5.6	6.2	6.6	8.1
Metropolitan Montreal	French	64.9	64.8	66.3	68.5	68.5
	English	26.5	23.4	21.7	18.4	15.7
	Other	8.6	11.8	12.0	13.1	15.8
Island of Montreal	French			61.2	59.9	56.8
	English			23.7	22.3	20.6
	Other			15.1	17.7	22.6

Source: Québec, Ministère de la Culture et des Communications (1996), Table 1.1

In an article published in the early 1990s, Jacques Henripin concedes that
virtually all demographers in Québec in the 1970s were predicting "an eventual
decrease in the proportion of French-speaking people in the province. ... The
conclusion, although quite logical, was erroneous" (1993: 315). What Henripin
and other demographers had failed to consider was the massive exodus of
anglophones from Québec, beginning in the early 1970s and accelerating after
the PQ victory in 1976 and the implementation of Bill 101 in 1977. Henripin

Table 10.4
Language Spoken at Home (% of population) in Québec by Region, 1971-1991

Region	Mother Tongue	1971	1981	1991
All of Québec	French	80.8	82.5	83.0
	English	14.7	12.7	11.2
	Other	4.5	4.8	5.8
Metropolitan Montreal	French	66.3	68.6	69.4
	English	24.9	21.9	19.3
	Other	8.8	9.4	11.3
Island of Montreal	French	61.2	60.0	58.5
	English	27.4	27.0	25.7
	Other	11.4	13.1	15.9

Source: Québec, Ministère de la Culture et des Communications (1996), Table 1.2

notes that the marked decline in fertility among francophones in the 1960s and 70s has been "compensated for by an increase in the rate of emigration from Québec to the rest of Canada of members of the English-speaking community. No one realized this beforehand" (ibid.).

Table 10.5 indicates that the linguistic minorities in Québec have made an obvious effort to integrate into the majority culture. Levels of bilingualism have increased among all three language groups between 1971 and 1991. Among francophones, those able to conduct a conversation in both English and French increased from just under twenty six percent in 1971 to almost thirty two percent in 1991, the smallest increase in any of the linguistic groups in the province. Among anglophones, the figures were just under thirty seven percent in 1971 and almost sixty percent in 1991. Finally, among allophones, those possessing a knowledge of both English and French increased from thirty percent in 1971 to almost forty seven percent in 1991.

Table 10.5
Knowledge of French and English in Québec (% of language group)
by Mother Tongue, 1971-1991

Mother Tongue	Year	Knowledge of:			
		French Only	French & English	English Only	Neither French nor English
French	1971	74.3	25.7	–	–
	1981	71.2	28.7	–	–
	1991	68.4	31.5	–	–
English	1971	–	36.7	63.3	–
	1981	–	53.4	44.8	–
	1991	–	59.4	39.2	–
Other	1971	14.0	33.1	35.8	17.0
	1981	17.7	44.6	26.1	11.6
	1991	22.0	46.6	20.9	10.4

Source: Québec, Ministère de la Culture et des Communications (1996), Table 1.4

Another measure of the success of Bill 101 in forcing immigrants to integrate into the majority culture can be gleaned from the data in Table 10.6. In 1971-1972, a mere ten percent of allophones sent their children to French-language schools (including pre-school, primary and secondary levels). By 1994-1995, this figure was 78.5 percent. The Comité interministériel acknowledges in its report that these figures demonstrate a certain amount of "progress" in integrating allophones into the dominant culture. However, the report cautions that many immigrant students are enrolled in French-language schools where only a minority of the students are actually francophone. This tends to slow down the "rate of linguistic mobility"—that is, the tendency to adopt French as a home language, rather than one's mother tongue—among allophones (Québec, 1996: 138-139).

Table 10.6
Percentage of Students (Pre-School, Primary & Secondary Levels) in French Schools by Mother Tongue and Region, 1971-1995

Region	Year	Mother Tongue		
		French	English	Other
All of Québec	1971-72	97.9	9.5	14.6
	1981-82	98.6	15.5	43.4
	1991-92	98.9	17.2	77.5
	1994-95	98.7	17.3	79:4
Island of Montreal	1971-72	95.3	9.5	10.0
	1981-82	96.8	15.5	40.2
	1991-92	97.7	15.9	74.8
	1994-95	97.4	16.2	78.5

Source: Québec, Ministère de la Culture et des Communications (1996), Table 5.3

The Charte de la langue française has been spectacularly successful in opening up occupational space for Francophones in the private sector and in neutralizing the effects of income discrimination against francophone workers that had been a prominent feature of the provincial economy until the mid-1970s. As Figure 10.1 indicates, the proportion of francophones in management positions in the private sector has increased dramatically in the wake of the adoption of Bill 101. In 1959, only thirty one percent of corporate presidents, chief executive officers (CEOs), members of boards of directors, and so on, were Francophone. This proportion grew slowly to thirty eight percent in 1977 but increased rapidly to fifty eight percent in 1988. The increased economic presence of Francophones has come at the expense of Anglophone managers, who have seen their numbers tumble from sixty percent of all positions in 1959 to only twenty six percent in 1988. The number of allophones in management has been relatively stable since 1969, hovering between fifteen percent and seventeen percent.

While acknowledging the spectacular increase in the number and proportion of Francophone workers and managers in the provincial economy since the passage of Bill 101, the Comité interministériel nonetheless notes that the second economic objective of the Charte de la langue française, that of trans-

Figure 10.1
Percentage of Management Positions* in Québec Enterprises,
by Mother Tongue, 1959-1988

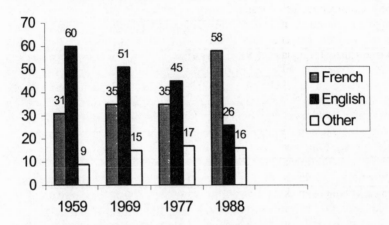

*   Includes: presidents of firms, chief executive officers, members of the board of directors, secretary, treasurers, comptrollers.

Source: Québec, Ministère de la Culture et des Communications (1996), Table 1.6

forming workplaces that historically had been dominated by English or had been "linguistically heterogeneous" into Francophone environments, had been more difficult, laborious, and complex in its implementation (Québec, 1996: 75-76). Nevertheless, even here, undeniable progress has been made since 1977. By 1995, eighty two percent of small and medium-size enterprises (those with 50 to 99 employees) had received certificates of *francisation* from the Office de la langue française, while seventy four percent of large firms (those with 100 or more employees) had received their certificates (80-81). The authors of the report worried, however, that the number of certifications had leveled off after the mid-1980s, and they speculated that there was both political and economic resistance to the efforts of the provincial government. Political resistance was prompted in part by the new legal environment that existed in Canada and in Québec after the entrenchment of the Canadian Charter of Rights and Freedoms in the Constitution, and in part by the business world's fear of what it perceived to be the heavy, bureaucratic process entailed in receiving a certificate of *francisation*. Economic resistance after 1982, according to the report, was the product of the two severe recessions of 1981-1982 and 1991-1993, which prompted firms to relegate the language question to the back burner (83).

The final impact of Bill 101 to be considered here is on the relationship between ethnicity and language, on the one hand, and income, on the other— precisely the issue that had been so explosive in the late 1960s, when the Royal Commission on Bilingualism and Biculturalism published its findings in Book III of its report, *The Work World*. This is perhaps the area in which the Charte de la langue française has had its greatest success. François Vaillancourt (1993:

413-417) has shown in a number of studies that the share of income accruing to Francophones in Québec has increased steadily since the late 1960s. The Comité interministériel also argues that "[l]e lien historique entre travailleur francophone et faible revenu n'a plus sa raison d'être aujourd'hui" (Québec, 1996: 68). Controlling for education, marital status, number of weeks worked, and years of experience, unilingual and bilingual Anglophones in 1970 earned on average sixteen percent more than unilingual Francophones, and eight percent more than bilingual Francophones. By 1980, the income gap between Anglophones (whether unilingual or bilingual) and bilingual Francophones had virtually disappeared. In 1990, bilingual Francophones had the highest average earnings in metropolitan Montreal, approximately four percent higher than unilingual and bilingual Anglophones. Research undertaken by François Vaillancourt indicates that French-speaking allophones in the province appear to suffer the greatest income discrimination; English-speaking allophones earn about the same as unilingual Francophones.[9]

In summary, in terms of the principal objectives of René Lévesque's government in 1977—making French the dominant, "normal" language of the workplace and the private sector, increasing the occupational space for Francophone managers, and compelling immigrants to integrate into the French-language school system—Bill 101 has been a resounding success. Even the Comité interministériel seems to acknowledge this in its discussion of Francophone culture:

> Le Québec, avec un bassin de population restreint, s'est donné le défi de vivre, de créer et de s'exprimer en français, dans une Amérique du Nord ou l'anglais règne en maître et dans un monde culturel et médiatique fortement dominé par la langue anglaise. La réalisation de ce dessein tient du miracle. À bon droit, on reste étonné de la vitalité de la langue française et de la culture québécoise d'expression française, qui s'épaulent l'une l'autre pour relever le défi. (Québec, 1996: 166).

If this is the case, then is Québec poised on the brink of an era of linguistic peace?

CONCLUSION: THE PROSPECTS FOR LINGUISTIC PEACE IN QUÉBEC

As I observed at the beginning of this chapter, there is a seeming paradox at the core of contemporary language politics in Québec. Although the principal demands articulated by nationalists in the 1960s have been met, in large part because of the implementation of the Charte de la langue française, tensions between the dominant and minority cultures in the province have not declined to the extent that one would have predicted. In part, this may simply be the unfortunate consequence of feckless political leadership and fumbled opportunities. Had Robert Bourassa acted on his party's promise to relax language laws in Québec when his Liberal Party defeated the PQ in the 1985 provincial election, at a time when public opinion among all the major linguistic groups appeared strongly in favour of greater liberalization of Bill 101 (especially on the issue of the language of signs), then perhaps the subsequent hardening and polarization of attitudes among Francophones, Anglophones and some allophones might not have occurred. But this is mere speculation, and perhaps attitudes would have hardened no matter what Bourassa had done.[10]

Three factors seem to have contributed to the persistence of linguistic conflict in Québec, despite the incontrovertible success of Bill 101 in ameliorating the status of the French language in the province. In the first place, extremists on both sides have captured media attention all too easily and thus played an unduly prominent role in the debate over language rights. For every Howard Galganov, the publicity-seeking and outrageous head of the Anglophone rights organization, the Québec Political Action Committee, there is a Guy Bouthillier, *pure laine* president of the Société St. Jean Baptiste. Moderates tend to get drowned out in the shouting between these two polar extremes.

Second, the issue of language is intimately tied up with the sovereignty project, and some *indépendantistes* (though not all, to be sure) seek to exploit linguistic tensions for tactical purposes. It does appear that support for sovereignty varies with the extent to which the French language is perceived as being threatened. The greater the threat to the status of French, the greater the support for sovereignty, ceteris paribus. This partly accounts for the inflammatory rhetoric of Yves Michaud, cited at the outset of this chapter, in which he warns of an impending linguistic "Munich" if any concessions are made to minority language groups in the province. Michaud's specific bugbear is the tendency of allophone students to enroll in English-language CEGEPs (the Collèges d'enseignement général et professionnel; an intermediate level of education between secondary school and university) in disproportionately high numbers: in 1983, 80.6 percent of allophones who completed their high school education in French enrolled in French-language CEGEPs. In 1994, only 63.9 percent of allophones did so (Québec, 1996: 297). For other militant *indépendantistes*, violations of the sign law provisions such as the existence of English-only trademarks—Second Cup and Future Shop, to name two— constitute an unacceptable breach of the Charte de la langue française. Still others point again to demographic projections (see Table 10.7), which show that Francophones will be a minority on the island of Montreal by the year 2011. All of these trends fuel the perception among some nationalists that, in spite of the progress that has been made since the enactment of Bill 101, the French language is still threatened in Québec.[11]

The third factor, and no doubt the most important, in keeping the language conflict in Québec alive today is the tendency for the politics of language to shade off into the politics of immigration. Many of the complaints of contemporary nationalists in Québec centre on what they perceive to be the too slow integration process of allophones into the dominant culture. To many allophones, it appears as though the nationalists have moved the goalposts, just when they were getting close to the end zone. It is no longer sufficient for allophones simply to learn and speak French or to send their children to French-

Table 10.7
Projected Population in Québec by Language Spoken at Home and by Region, 1996-2041

Region	Year	Language Spoken at Home			
		French	English	Other	Total (1000s)
All of Québec	1996	82.0	11.1	6.9	7,157
	2001	81.1	11.0	7.9	7,367
	2011	79.4	10.9	9.7	7,717
	2021	77.6	11.0	11.4	7,905
	2041	73.2	11.5	15.3	7,808
Metropolitan Montreal	1996	67.8	18.9	13.3	3,305
	2001	66.6	18.5	14.9	3,455
	2011	64.2	17.8	18.0	3,711
	2021	61.9	17.4	20.7	3,890
	2041	56.6	17.3	26.1	4,059
Island of Montreal	1996	54.6	25.9	19.5	1,801
	2001	52.4	25.6	22.0	1,835
	2011	48.8	24.9	26.3	1,911
	2021	45.8	24.3	29.9	1,976
	2041	40.4	23.7	35.9	2,078

Source: Québec, Ministère de la Culture et des Communications (1996), Table 1.6.

language primary and secondary schools, which they are doing in impressive numbers. Instead, allophones are expected to embrace the dominant culture, most importantly by speaking French in the home and using it as their normal language of public discourse. For a variety of reasons, immigrants in Québec have been slow to do this, although the data presented in this chapter and elsewhere suggest that they are indeed meeting these expectations in increasing numbers.

The central question of language politics in Québec today probably boils down to this: will allophones spurn English as they embrace the dominant culture? There are many reasons to believe that English will continue to exert an attraction to allophones living in Montreal, mainly because of Montreal's location in North America and its necessary connection to the world economy. A certain amount of cosmopolitanism, in the form of trilingualism (English,

French, and mother tongue), will inevitably provide economic and psychic payoffs to allophones in Québec. If a solution to Québec's linguistic conflicts is to be found, then, it will probably require nationalists to demonstrate a little more patience with, and tolerance of, the process of immigrant integration in Montreal.

Let me conclude with a personal anecdote and a question. I was in Montreal in May 2000 to attend the Parti Québécois' biennial convention as an observer. My hotel was near the Chinese district of downtown Montreal, just off the Rue St. Laurent. One night I went to a Chinese restaurant and was seated at a table next to three young women who were evidently from several different allophone communities. As I ate my dinner, I could not help but overhear their conversation, which consisted of a remarkable, uninhibited, three-way kaleidoscopic interchange in *both* French and English. I wondered at the time whether these three young women's use of both French and English as linguae francae would be viewed by moderate or so-called soft nationalists in Québec as a sign of the strength of cultural pluralism in the province or as a symptom of these allophones' refusal to integrate fully into the majority culture. The prospects for linguistic peace in Québec in the near future would seem to hinge on the answer to this question and others like it.

NOTES

1. Tremblay (1990: 140-141). All translations are mine.

2. According to Rioux and Dofny (1964), French Canadians, no matter what their class origins, tended to think of themselves as an ethnic collectivity; national identity, in this case, trumped class location. Francophones thus played a role in Canadian society analogous to the one played by a social class in a given society. This was a controversial thesis, and not all nationalists accepted it. For Bourque and Laurin-Frenette (1972: 186), the notion of an ethnic class was theoretically suspect and conducive to an "incoherent and opportunistic strategy": it "underlies all those political positions that favour joining the Parti Québécois and encourage tactical support for the bourgeoisie."

3. A similar pattern emerged when total income, combining investment with incomes and wages, was considered, though there were some slight changes in the rankings of individual groups.

4. For a remarkable and moving account of just how deeply some individuals have been affected by the Trudeauvian dream, see Catherine Annau's marvelous documentary film *Just Watch Me*.

5. La Commission d'enquête sur la situation de la langue française et sur les droits linguistiques au Québec, with Jean-Denis Gendron as the chairman, was created by the Union Nationale government of Jean-Jacques Bertrand in 1969 in part to appease nationalists in the province who were unhappy with the administration's decision to endorse freedom of choice in the language of schooling. See McRoberts (1997: 99).

6. This important point is made by Arnopoulos and Clift (1984: Chapter 10, "Rivalry over the Ethnic Minorities").

7. This was the principle that was eventually enshrined in Bill 86, adopted by the second Bourassa administration in 1993.

8. The chair of the committee from September 7, 1995, to October 4, 1995, was Marcel Masse of the Conseil de la langue française. He was succeeded by Nicole René of the Office de la langue française, who served as chair until the committee issued its report

in March 1996. Josée Legault, a well-known separatist intellectual in Québec, was the director of research for the committee.

9. Vaillancourt (1993: Table 23.10). The data are for 1985.

10. See Tanguay (1993: 186, 189-191) for a more detailed discussion of Bourassa's highly ineffective language policy from 1985 to 1988.

11. See Québec, (2000: "Présentation.") The notion of threat runs like a leitmotiv through this report, which almost seems designed to counterbalance the overly optimistic conclusions of the 1996 report of the Comité interministériel. This document was downloaded from the Web <http://www.mri.gouv.qc.ca/rapport_spl/>.

Appendix

Data. I interviewed 137 out of 200 top commission officials of A1 and A2 status between July 1995 and February 1997 and received from them 106 mail-back questionnaires with behavioral questions and thirty-two statements measuring orientations on political and social life (n = 106). I use 105 for data analysis here; one questionnaire was excluded because a comparison with corresponding interview excerpts raised doubts about the validity of some responses. A comparison between these *samples* on key characteristics (position, age, nationality, gender, education, prior career, seniority, commission cabinet experience, parachutage, nationality) reveals no bias. Testing sample bias with respect to the *population* is more difficult, as the commission does not publish sociodemographic data for its top officials. However, I test sample bias for nationality by using as a yardstick the common commission practice to seek a "geographical balance" in top appointments, that is, reflecting the distribution of seats in the Council of Ministers. French, British, and, to some extent, Italian and Dutch officials appear over-represented in my questionnaire sample, while nationals from the second (Greek, Portuguese, and Spanish) and third enlargement (Austrian, Finnish, and Swedish) are underrepresented. However, the chi-square statistic falls short of rejecting the null-hypothesis that distributions in sample and population are the same (alpha = 0.436).

Dependent Variable. Additive index of the two items in Table 4.1, divided by 2 (Cronbach's alpha of 0.63). Principal component factor analysis identifies a single dimension, with eigenvalue of 1.46 and 73.1 percent of variance explained.

Transnational Experience. Dummy takes on value of 1 if international education or work experience abroad (Source: biographical data from *The European Companion* [London: DPR, 1992, 1994]; interviews by author).

State Service. Dummy for national service. These concern positions in the executive branch of the state and hierarchically subordinate to central government: civil servants in line ministries, diplomats (excluding EU postings), and government ministers (but not national parliamentarians). For public officials with some autonomy from central authorities (courts, central bank, Parliament, public companies, local government) or in positions with a strong European component (European desks in foreign affairs or near the head of government), I allocate half of the time to state career (Source: biographical data).

Strong/ Weak Weberian. Two interaction dummies between state service and dummies for strong/weak Weberian bureaucratic tradition. I apply four categories for comparing bureaucracies developed by Page to classify traditions into strong/medium/weak Weberian bureaucratic tradition. I use country assessments by Page where possible. Strong cohesion: France, Ireland, United Kingdom. Autonomy of political control: much (Denmark, Ireland, Sweden, United Kingdom), some (France, Germany, the Netherlands, Portugal, Spain), little (others). Caste-character: France, Germany, United Kingdom. Non-permeability for outside interests: France, Ireland, Portugal, Spain, United Kingdom. So I divide national bureaucracies in three categories: strong Weberian (France, Ireland, Germany), medium Weberian (Denmark, Germany, Netherlands, Portugal, Spain, Sweden), weak Weberian (Austria, Belgium/Luxembourg, Finland, Greece, Italy) (Source: Page, 1995).

Length of (Commission) Service. Years in commission service (Source: biographical data).

Cabinet. A dummy, with value 1 for those with cabinet experience (Source: biographical data).

PowerDG. A composite index of formal and reputational measures. As formal indicators, Page measures three types of secondary legislative activity by the commission: regulations, directives, and decisions that require council approval; regulations, directives, and decisions that do not require council approval; initiation of European Court of Justice cases by the commission. The latter two indicate the extent to which the Commission has discretion to make rules or make others comply with EU rules and regulations. As there are no official statistics on legislative output per DG, Page and his collaborator White used keywords (author; form; year; subject) to scan the Justis CD-ROM for legislation over the period 1980-1994 (over 30,000 pieces) and allocated output to the DG considered to be the most plausible author. I did a manual recount for 1980-1994 for some policy areas and arrived at a comparable breakdown. Amendments to Page's data pertain to DGs created since 1994. Regulatory Commission output is measured in relative (percentage of total output: a value of 1 if below 30 percent, 2 for 30-59 percent, 3 for 60 percent or more) and absolute terms (a value of 0 if fewer than 500 pieces and 1 if 500 pieces or more). Autonomy in adjudication is based on the absolute number of Court cases initiated by a DG, with a value of 0 when no cases, 1 if fewer than fifty cases, and 2 if fifty or more cases (Sources: Page, 1997; European Commission, *Directory of EU Legislation in Force until Dec 1994*, n.d.). For the reputational indicator, I use a question posed to the 137 top officials in which they name the three or four most powerful DGs or services in the commission at the time of the interview. DGs with a high reputation (mentioned by 50 percent or more) obtain a value of 2, those with medium reputation (mentioned by 5–49 percent) 1, and the remainder 0. I then add scores for the four indicators to create PowerDG. Values range between 1 and 8.

Quality DG. A dummy taking a value of 1 for officials working in DG V, VIII, X, XI, XXII, XXIV (Source: biographical data; definition of quality of life based on Herbert Kitschelt, 1994).

Parachutage. A dummy taking a value of 1 for officials parachuted from outside the commission in A1 or A2 positions (Source: biographical data).

National Quota: The number of votes in the Council of Ministers for officials' country of origin, ranging between two and ten.

National Clubness. An index composed of assessments along three dimensions. Strong cultural cohesion is characteristic of the Austrian, Dutch, Irish, Portuguese and the three Scandinavian nationalities (Abélès, Bellier, and McDonald, 1993). Especially the Irish have a strong reputation in Brussels for social networking. The fact that Belgian officials live in their country rather than in an expatriate community may impede club formation. Second, the organizational and financial resources of the French, British, German, Spanish, and, to some extent, Italian communities outweigh those of any other nationality. Third, clubness may be forged by intentional policy. One indicator is direct national intervention, usually through the government; this is particularly outspoken for the French, British, German, and Spanish. French and British governments/civil services closely monitor personnel policy in the commission and consider postings in Brussels as an integral part of the training for their best and brightest (Christoph, 1993; Lequesne, 1993). For the French, this is part of a more general policy to organize French citizens scattered over European and international institutions. German officials do not feel so much the influence of their capital but of their national political parties, which in line with domestic practice divide senior German posts in Brussels among themselves. Partisanship is likely to emerge as an effective channel for Austrians and perhaps the Finnish as well. Spanish governments have a reputation for pushing their nationals hard in career matters, though this approach is sometimes weakened by sharp partisan conflicts. Proactive governmental or partisan lobbying sits uncomfortably with the strongly merit-based traditions of the Dutch, Scandinavians, and, to a lesser extent, the Portuguese. Finally, deliberate policy has traditionally been ineffective or unwanted by officials of the three remaining nationalities: no government tops the Greek government's reputation of ineffective performance in general and in personnel lobbying in particular; many Belgian and Italian officials have distanced themselves from their clientelistic home base (interviews). Another indicator of intentional policy to forge clubness is the extent to which commission cabinets give priority to the career concerns of their compatriots. For senior appointments commissioners of the involved nationality are usually consulted, but some take such consultation more seriously than others. To gauge the importance attached to personnel issues, I have coded number and rank of those responsible for personnel in each commissioner's cabinet under the Santer Commission. German, Swedish, and British cabinets devote most resources, followed by French, Italian, Irish, Portuguese, and Spanish cabinets; then by Belgian, Dutch, and Luxembourg cabinets; and finally by Austrian, Danish, Greek and Finnish cabinets (Source: American Chamber of Commerce in Belgium, 1997 *EUInfonnation Handbook* [Brussels:, 1997]). On the basis of these three streams of evidence, I divide the nationalities in three categories: weak clubness (Belgo-Luxembourgers, Greeks, Italians); medium clubness (Dutch, Scandinavians, Portuguese, Spanish); and strong clubness (Austrians, British, French, German, and Irish).

References

Abélès, Marc, Irène Bellier, and Maryon McDonald. (1993). *Approche anthropologique de la Commission européenne*. Brussels: European Commission.

Aberbach, Joel, Bert Rockman, and Robert Putnam, eds. (1981). *Bureaucrats and Politicians in Western Democracies*. Cambridge: Harvard University Press.

Almond, Gabriel A. (1956). "Comparative Political Systems." *The Journal of Politics* 18 (August): 391-409.

Almond, Gabriel. (1990). *A Discipline Divided: Schools and Sects in Political Science*. Newbury Park, CA: Sage.

Althusius, Johannes. (1964) *Politica methodice digesta*. Boston: Beacon Press.

Andeweg, Rudy B. (2000). "Consociational Democracy." Manuscript, Leiden University.

Andeweg, R., and G. Irwin (1993). *Dutch Government and Politics*. London: Macmillan Press.

Angell, Richard B. (1964). *Reasoning and Logic*. New York: Appleton-Century-Crofts.

Arnopoulos, Sheila McLeod, and Dominique Clift. (1984). *The English Fact in Québec*. 2nd ed. Kingston and Montreal: McGill-Queen's University Press.

Avio, Kenneth L. (1997). "Constitutional Contract and Discourse Ethics: The Agreement Theories of James Buchanan and Jürgen Habermas." *Journal of Theoretical Poltitics* 9(4): 533-553.

Aylward, Carol A. (1999). *Canadian Critical Race Theory: Racism and the Law*. Halifax: Fernwood Books.

Backhouse, Constance. (1999). *Colour-Coded: A Legal History of Racism in Canada, 1900-1950*. Toronto: Osgoode Society, University of Toronto Press.

Balibar, Etienne. (1991). "Race and Nationalism." In Etienne Balibar and Immanuel Wallerstein, *Race, Nation, Class: Ambiguous Identities*. London and New York: Verso, 37-67.

Balibar, Etienne, and Immanuel Wallerstein. (1991). *Race, Nation, Class: Ambiguous Identities*. London and New York: Verso.

Barry, Brian. (1975). "Review Article: Political Accommodation and Consociational Democracy. *British Journal of Political Science* 5: 477-505.

Baynes, Kenneth. (1995). "Democracy and the *Rechtsstaat*: Habermas's *Faktizität und Geltung*." In Stephen K. White, ed., *The Cambridge Companion to Habermas*. Cambridge: Cambridge University Press, 201-232.

Behiels, Michael. (1985). *Prelude to Québec's Quiet Revolution: Liberalism versus Neo-nationalism, 1945-1960*. Kingston and Montreal: McGill-Queen's University Press.

Bell, David, and Lorne Tepperman. (1991). *The Roots of Disunity: A Look at Canadian Political Culture*. Toronto: Oxford.

Bellier, Irène. (1995). "Une culture de la Commission européenne? De la rencontre des cultures et du multilinguisme des fonctionnaires." In Yves Mény, Pierre Muller, and J.-L. Quermonne, eds., *Politiques publiques en Europe*. Paris: L'Harmattan, 49-60.

Berton, Pierre. (1982). *Why We Act Like Canadians*. Toronto: McClelland and Stewart.

Blommaert, Jan, and Jef Verschueren. (1996). "European Concepts of Nation-Building." In Edwin N. Wilmsen and Patrick McAllister, eds., *The Politics of Difference: Ethnic Premises in a World of Power*. London: University of Chicago Press, 104-123.

Bohmann, James. (1996). *Public Deliberation: Pluralism, Complexity and Democracy*. Cambridge: MIT Press.

Bourque, Gilles, and Nicole Laurin-Frenette. (1972). "Social Classes and Nationalist Ideologies in Québec, 1760-1970." In Gary Teeple, ed., *Capitalism and the National Question in Canada*. Toronto: University of Toronto Press, 185-210.

Brown, Robert Craig, and Ramsay Cook. (1974). *Canada 1896-1921: A Nation Transformed*. Toronto: McClelland and Stewart.

Bumsted, J. M. (1986). *Understanding the Loyalists*. Sackville: Centre for Canadian Studies, Mount Allison University.

Canada. Royal Commission on Bilingualism and Biculturalism [RCBB]. (1967). Book I, Vol. 1: *The Official Languages*. Ottawa: Queen's Printer.

Canada. Royal Commission on Bilingualism and Biculturalism [RCBB]. (1969). Book III, Vol. 3A: *The Work World*. Ottawa: Queen's Printer.

Caporaso, James. (1996). "The European Union and Forms of State: Westphalian, Regulatory or Post-Modern?" *Journal of Common Market Studies* 34 (1): 29-52.

Careless, J.M.S. (1967). *The Union of the Canadas: The Growth of Canadian Institutions 1841-1857*. Toronto: McClelland and Stewart.

Chambers, Simone. (1995). "Discourse and Democratic Practices." In Stephen K. White, ed., *The Cambridge Companion to Habermas*. Cambridge: Cambridge University Press.

Chambers, Simone. (1996). *Reasonable Democracy: Jürgen Habermas and the Politics of Discourse*. Ithaca, NY: Cornell University Press.

Chambers, Simone. (1999). "Talking versus Voting: Legitimacy, Efficiency, and Deliberative Democracy." Manuscript, University of Colorado.

Chong, Dennis. (1996). "Rational Choice Theory's Mysterious Rivals." In Jeffrey Friedman, ed., *The Rational Choice Controversy: Economic Models of Politics Reconsidered*. New Haven, CT, and London: Yale University Press.

Christoph, J. B. (1993). "The Effects of Britons in Brussels: The European Community and the Culture of Whitehall." *Governance* 6(4): 518-537.

Chryssochou, Dimitris N. (1998). *Democracy in the European Union*. London: Tauris Academic Studies.

Chwe, Michael Suk-Young. (1999). "Minority Voting Rights Can Maximize Majority Welfare." *American Political Science Review* 93(1): 85-96.

Clarkson, Stephen, and Christina McCall. (1990). *Trudeau and Our Times*. Vol. 1: *The Magnificent Obsession*. Toronto: McClelland and Stewart.

Cohen, Joshua. (1989). "Deliberation and Democratic Legitimacy." In Alan Hamlin and Philip Pettit eds., *The Good Polity: Normative Analysis of the State*. Oxford and New York: Basil Blackwell.

Colomer, Josep M. (2001). *Political Institutions: Democracy and Social Choice*. Oxford: Oxford University Press.

Converse, Philip E. (1964). "The Nature of Belief Systems in Mass Publics." In David E. Apter, ed., *Ideology and Discontent*. New York: Free Press of Glencoe, 206-261.

Cook, Ramsay. (1995). *Canada, Québec and the Uses of Nationalism*. 2nd ed. Toronto: McClelland and Stewart.

Coombes, David. (1970). *Politics and Bureaucracy in the European Community*. London: George Allen and Unwin.

Cooper, Frederick, and Ann Laura Stoler, eds. (1997). *Tensions of Empire. Colonial Cultures in a Bourgeois World*. Berkeley: University of California Press.

Covell, M. (1993). "Political Conflict and Constitutional Engineering in Belgium." *The International Journal of the Sociology of Language*, no. 104: 65-86.

Cowlishaw, Gillian. (1997). "Where Is Racism?" In Gillian Cowlishaw and Barry Morris, eds., *Race Matters: Indigenous Australians and "Our" Society*. Canberra: Aboriginal Studies Press, 177-189.

Creighton, D. G. (1976). *The Forked Road: Canada 1939-1957*. Toronto: McClelland Stewart.

Crepaz, Markus M. L. (1998). "Political Institutions, Change, and Macro-economic Outcomes in Austria." Paper presented at the Conference on the Fate of Consociationalism. Center for European Studies, Harvard University, May 29-31.

Crepaz, Markus M. L. and Arend Lijphart. (1995). "Linking and Integrating Corporatism and Consensus Democracy: Theory, Concepts and Evidence." *British Journal of Political Science* 25 (2): 281-288.

Daalder, Hans. (1989). *Ancient and Modern Pluralism in the Netherlands*. Working Paper Series 22. Cambridge: Center for European Studies, Harvard University.

Day, David. (1996). *Claiming a Continent: A History of Australia*. Sydney: Angus and Robertson.

Day, Richard J. F. (2000). *Multiculturalism and the History of Canadian Diversity*. Toronto: University of Toronto Press.

Dehousse, Renaud. (1995). "Institutional Reform in the European Community: Are There Alternatives to the Majority Avenue?" *West European Politics* 18(3): 118-136.

Deschouwer, K. (1992). "Belgium." In R. Katz and P. Mair, *Party Organizations. A Data Handbook*. London: Sage, 121-198.

Deschouwer, K. (1994a). "The Decline of Consociationalism and the Reluctant Modernization of the Belgian Mass Parties." In R. Katz and P. Mair, *How Parties Organize: Adaptation and Change in Party Organizations in Western Democracies*. London: Sage, 80-108.

Deschouwer, K. (1994b). "The Termination of Coalitions in Belgium." *Res Publica*, 36(1): 43-55.

Deschouwer, K. (1996). "Waiting for the 'Big One.' The Uncertain Survival of the Belgian Parties and Party Systems." *Res Publica*, 38(2): 295-306.

Deschouwer, Kris. (1998). "Falling Apart Together: The Changing Nature of Belgium Consociationalism." Paper presented at the Conference on the Fate of Consociationalism. Center for European Studies, Harvard University, May 29-31.

Deschouwer, K. (1999). "From Consociation to Federation: How the Parties Won." In K. R. Luther and K. Deschouwer, *Party Elites in Divided Societies. Political Parties in Consociational Democracy*. London: Routledge, 74-107.

Döbert, Rainer. (1996). "§218 vor dem Bundesverfassungsgericht. Verfahrenstheoretische Überlegungen zur sozialen Integration." In Wolfgand van den Daele and Friedhelm Neidhardt, eds., *Kommunikation und Entscheidung*. Berlin: Sigma, 16-45.

Duchêne, François. (1994). *Jean Monnet: The First Statesman of Interdependence*. New York: Norton.

Duso, Giuseppe. (1998). "Una prima esposizione del pensiero politico di Althusius: la dottrina del patto e la costituzione del regno." Manuscript.

Edwards, John, ed. (1998). *Language in Canada*. Cambridge: Cambridge University Press.

Egeberg, Morten. (1995). "Organization and Nationality in the European Commission Services." Working Paper, Oslo.

Eichener, Volker. (1992). "Social Dumping or Innovative Regulation? Processes and Outcomes of European Decision-Making in the Sector of Health and Safety at Work Harmonization." European Union Information Working Paper.

Elkins, David. (1995). *Beyond Sovereignty: Territory and Political Economy in the Twenty-first Century*. Toronto: University of Toronto Press.

Elkins, David. (1997). "Thinking Global Governance and Enacting Local Cultures." Paper, University of British Columbia.

Erk, Can, and Alain-G. Gagnon. (2000). "Constitutional Ambiguity and Federal Trust: The Codification of Federalism in Belgium, Canada and Spain." *Regional and Federal Studies*, 10(1): 77-93.

Fields, Barbara. (1990). "Slavery, Race and Ideology in the United States of America." *New Left Review* 181, 342-393.

Flyvbjerg, Bent. (1998). "Habermas and Foucault: Thinkers of Civil Society?" *British Journal of Sociology* 49(2): 210-233.

Forsey, Eugene. (1974). *Freedom and Order*. The Carleton Library, No. 73. Toronto: McClelland and Stewart.

Freud, Sigmund. (1963). *The Complete Psychological Works of Sigmund Freud*. Vol. 18. New York: Washington Square Press.

Frye, Northrop. (1971). *The Bush Garden*. Toronto: Anansi.

Furnivall, J. S. (1939). *Netherlands India*. Cambridge: Cambridge University Press.

Gabel, Matt. (1998). "Research Note: The Endurance of Supranational Governance. A Consociational Interpretation of the European Union." *Comparative Politics* 30(3): 463-475.

Gellner, Ernest. (1995). "The Importance of Being Modular." In John A. Hall, ed., *Civil Society: Theory, History, Comparison*. Cambridge: Polity Press, 122-159.

Gerard, E. (1985). *De katholieke partij in crisis. Partijpolitiek leven in België (1918-1940)*. Leuven: Kritak.

Gerard, E. (1995). "Van katholieke partij naar CVP." In W. Dewachter et al., eds., *Tussen staat en maatschappij 1945-1995. Christen-Democratie in Belgie*. Tielt: Iannoo, 13-27.

Gerhards, Jürgen. (1997). "Diskursive versus liberale Öffentlichkeit. Eine empirische Auseinandersetzung mit Jürgen Habermas." *Kölner Zeitschrift für Psychologie und Sozialpsychologie* 49(1): 1-34.

Granatstein, J. L. (1986). *Canada 1957-1967: The Years of Uncertainty and Innovation*. Toronto: McClelland and Stewart.

Grande, Edgar. (1998). "Post-National Democracy in Europe: Problems, Premises and Perspectives." Paper presented at a conference on "Democracy Beyond National Limits?" University of Toronto, April.

Grant, Charles. (1994). *Inside the House that Jacques Built*. London: Nicholas Brealey.

Guindon, Hubert. (1964). "Social Unrest, Social Class and Québec's Bureaucratic Revolution." *Queen's Quarterly* 71(2): 150-62.

Gutman, Amy, and Dennis Thompson. (1990). "Moral Conflict and Political Consensus." *Ethics* 101: 64-88.

Gutman, Amy, and Dennis Thompson. (1996). *Democracy and Disagreement*. Cambridge: Belknap Harvard.

Gutman, Amy, and Dennis Thompson. (2000). "Why Deliberative Democracy Is Different." *Social Philosophy & Policy* 17: 161-180.

Haase, Martin. (1994). *Respekt: Die Grammatikalisierung von Höflichkeit*. München and Newcastle: Lincom Europa.

Habermas, Jürgen. (1972). *Theorie und Praxis*. Frankfurt: Suhrkamp.

Habermas, Jürgen. (1990). *Strukturwandel der Öffentlichkeit. Untersuchungen zu einer Kategorie der bürgerlichen Gesellschaft*. Frankfurt: Suhrkamp.

Habermas, Jürgen. (1991). *Erläuterungen zur Diskursethik*. Frankfurt: Suhrkamp.

Habermas, Jürgen. (1992). *Faktizität und Geltung: Beiträge zur Diskurstheorie des Rechts und des demokratischen Rechtsstaats*. Frankfurt: Suhrkamp.

Habermas, Jürgen. (1995). "Reconciliation through the Public Use of Reason: Remarks on John Rawls's Political Liberalism." *Journal of Philosophy* 92(3) (March), 99-132.

Habermas, Jürgen. (1996). *Die Einbeziehung des Andern: Studien zur politischen Theorie*. Frankfurt: Suhrkamp.

Hall, Peter A. (1986). *Governing the Economy: The Politics of State Intervention in Britain and France*. Cambridge: Polity Press.

Hall, Peter A., and Rosemary C. R. Taylor. (1996a). "Political Science and the Three New Institutionalisms." *Political Studies* 44: 936-957.

Hall, Peter, and Rosemary Taylor. (1996b). "Political Science and the Three New Institutionalisms." Paper presented at Max Planck Institut für Gesellschaftsforschung, Köln, June.

Halpern, Sue M. (1986). "The Disorderly Universe of Consociational Democracy." *West European Politics* 9: 181-197.

Heller, Hermann. (1964). *Staatslehre*. Leiden: A. W. Sijthoff.

Henripin, Jacques. (1993). "Population Trends and Policies in Québec." In Alain-G. Gagnon, ed., *Québec: State and Society*, 2nd ed. Scarborough, Ontario: Nelson Canada, 304-318.

Henry, Francis, et al. (1995). *The Colour of Democracy: Racism in Canadian Society*. Toronto: Harcourt, Brace.

Hindess, Barry. (2000). "Cosmopolitan Citizenship?" Paper presented at International Political Science Association World Congress, Québec, August 1-5.

Hirst, Paul. (1994). *Associative Democracy*. Amherst: University of Massachusetts Press.

Hirst, Paul, and Grahame Thompson. (1996). *Globalization in Question*. Cambridge: Polity Press.

Hix, Simon. (1994). "The Study of the European Community: The Challenge to Comparative Politics." *West European Politics* 17: 1-30.

Hobbes, Thomas. (1989). *Leviathan*. [1651]. Vol. 18. New York: Wadsworth Publishing Company.

Hoke, Rudolf. (1997). "Die antikaiserliche Reichspublizistik vor dem Westfälischen Frieden." Paper presented at annual meeting of the Johannes Althusius Society, Dresden, November 28-29.

Hooghe, Liesbet. (May 2000). "Euro-Socialists or Euro-Marketeers? Top Commission Officials on Capitalism." *Journal of Politics* 62: 82-103.

Hooghe, Liesbet. (2000). "Supranational Activists or Intergovernmental Agents? Explaining Political Orientations of Senior Commission Officials to European Integration," *Comparative Political Studies* 32(4): 435-463.

Hooghe, Liesbet, and Gary Marks. (1999). "The Making of a Polity: The Struggle over European Integration." In Herbert Kitschelt, Peter Lange, Gary Marks, and John Stephens, eds., *Continuity and Change in Contemporary Capitalism.* Cambridge: Cambridge University Press, 70-97.

Horowitz, Gad. (1978). "Notes on Conservatism, Liberalism and Socialism in Canada." *Canadian Journal of Political Science* 11: 73-102.

Hueglin, Thomas O. (1991). *Sozietaler Foederalismus.* Berlin: De Gruyter.

Huyse, Lucien. (1970). *Passiviteit, pacificatie en verzuiling in de Belgische politiek, een sociologische studie.* Antwerpen: Wetenschappelijke Uitgeverij.

Huyse, L. (1971). *Pacificatie, passiviteit en verzuiling in de Belgische politiek, Standaard Weten schappelijke.* Uitgeverij.

Ignatieff, Michael. (1993). *Blood and Belonging: Journeys into the New Nationalism.* Toronto: Viking.

James, G., and Johan P. Olson. (1989). *Rediscovering Institutions. The Organizational Basis of Politics.* New York: Free Press.

James, Roberta. (1997). "Rousseau's Knot: The Entanglement of Liberal Democracy and Racism." In Gillian Cowlishaw and Barry Morris, eds., *Race Matters: Indigenous Australians and "Our" Society.* Canberra: Aboriginal Studies Press, 53-75.

Joy, Richard J. (1992). *Canada's Official Languages: The Progress of Bilingualism.* Toronto: University of Toronto Press.

Kilbourn, William, ed. (1970). *"Red Tory" in Canada: A Guide to the Peaceable Kingdom.* New York: St. Martin's Press.

Kitschelt, Herbert. (1994). *The Transformation of European Social Democracy.* Cambridge: Cambridge University Press.

Knight, Jack, and James Johnson. (1994). "Aggregation and deliberation: On the Possibility of Democratic Legitimacy," *Political Theory* 22: 277-296.

Kriesi, Hanspeter. (1995). *Le système politique suisse.* Paris: Economica.

Kropotkin, Petr., (1902). *Mutual Aid.* London: Heinemann.

Kuper, Leo. (1997). "Plural Societies." In Montserrat Guibernau and John Rex, eds., *The Ethnicity Reader.* Cambridge: Polity Press, 220-228.

Lane, Jan-Erik, and Swante Ersson. (1997). "The Institutions of Konkordanz and Corporatism: How Closely Are They Connected?" *Swiss Political Science Review* 3(1): 5-30.

Larrimore, Mark. (1999). "Sublime Waste: Kant on the Destiny of the 'Races.'" *Canadian Journal of Philosophy,* supplementary Vol. 25: 99-125.

Lasswell, Harold D. (1936). *Politics: Who Gets What, When, How.* New York: McGraw-Hill.

Lehmbruch, Gerhard. (1967). *Proporzdemokratie: Politisches System und politische Kultur in der Schweiz und in Österreich.* Tübingen: J.C.B. Mohr.

Lehmbruch, Gerhard. (1993). "Consociational Democracy and Corporatism in Switzerland." *Publius* 23 (Spring): 43-60.

Lehmbruch, Gerhard. (1996). "Die korporative Verhandlungsdemokratie in Westmitteleuropa." *Schweizerische Zeitschrift für Politische Wissenschaft* 2(4): 19-41.

Lehmbruch, Gerhard. (1998). "Negotiated Democracy, Consociationalism and Corporatism in German Politics: The Legacy of the Westphalian Peace." Paper presented at the Conference on the Fate of Consociationalism. Center for European Studies, Harvard University, May 29-31.

Lequesne, Christian. (1993). *Paris-Bruxelles: Comment ce fait la politique européenne de la France.* Paris: Presses universitaires de la Fondation nationale des sciences politiques.

Lévesque, René. (1986). *Memoirs.* Trans. Philip Stratford. Toronto: McClelland and Stewart.

Lijphart, Arend. (1966). *The Politics of Accommodation: Pluralism and Democracy in the Netherlands.* Berkeley: University of California Press.

Lijphart, Arend. (1968a). *The Politics of Accommodation. Pluralistic Democracy in the Netherlands.* Berkeley: University of California Press.

Lijphart, Arend. (1968b). "Typologies of Democratic Systems." *Comparative Political Studies* 1: 3-44.

Lijphart, Arend. (1969). "Consociational Democracy." *World Politics,* 21: 207-225.

Lijphart, Arend. (1971). "Cultural Diversity and Theories of Political Integration." *Canadian Journal of Political Science* 4: 1-14.

Lijphart, Arend. (1977). *Democracy in Plural Societies: A Comparative Explanation.* New Havens, CT: Yale University Press.

Lijphart, Arend. (1989). "From the Politics of Accommodation to Adversial Politics in the Netherlands: A Reassessment." *West European Politics* 12(1): 139-153.

Lijphart, Arend. (1999). *Patterns of Democracy. Government Forms and Performance in Thirty-Six Countries.* New Haven, CT: Yale University Press.

Lijphart, Arend, ed. (1981). *Conflict and Coexistence in Belgium, The Dynamics of a Culturally Divided Society.* Berkley: University of California Press.

Lijphart, Arend, and Markus M. L. Crepaz. (1991). "Corporatism and Consensus Democracy in Eighteen Countries: Conceptual and Empirical Linkages." *British Journal of Political Science* 21(1): 235-246.

Linder, Wolf. (1994). *Swiss Democracy: Possible Solutions to Conflict in Multicultural Societies.* London: Macmillan.

Linder, Wolf. (1999a). "Politische Kultur." In Ulrich, Klöti, Peter Knöpfel, Hanspeter Kriesi, Wolf Linder, and Yannis Papadopoulus eds., *Handbuch der Schweizer Politik.* Zürich: Verlag Neue Zürcher Zeitung, 222-258.

Linder, Wolf. (1999b). *Schweizerische Demokratie: Institutionen, Prozesse, Perspektiven.* Bern, Stuttgart, and Wien: Haupt.

Linder, Wolf, Hans Riedwyl, and Jürg Steiner. (2000). "Konkordanztheorie und Abstimmungsdaten: eine explorative Aggregatsanalyse auf Bezirksebene." *Swiss Political Science Review* 6(2): 27-56.

Lipset S. M., and S. Rokkan. (1967). "Cleavage Structures, Party Systems and Voter Alignments" in S. M. Lipset and S. Rokkan eds., *Party Systems and Voter Alignments: Cross-National Perspectives.* New York: Free Press.

Lipset, Seymour Martin. (1990). *Continental Divide. The Values and Institutions of the United States and Canada.* New York: Routledge, London: Hogarth Press.

Lorwin, V. R. (1966). "Belgium: Religion, Class, and Language in National Politics." In R. D. Dahl, ed., *Political Oppositions in Western Democracies.* New Haven, CT: Yale University Press, 147-187.

Lustick, Ian. (1979). "The Control Model." *World Politics* 31(3): 325-344.

Lustick, Ian. (1997). "Lijphart, Lakatos, and Consociationalism." *World Politics* 50(3): 88-117.

Macedo, Stephen. (1999). "Introduction." In Stephen Macedo, ed., *Deliberative Politics: Essays on "Democracy and Disagreement."* New York, and Oxford: Oxford University Press, 59-77.

MacKinnon, Neil. (1986). *This Unfriendly Soil: The Loyalist Experience in Nova Scotia 1783-1791.* Kingston: McGill-Queen's University Press.

Majone, Giandomenico. (1996). *Regulating Europe.* London: Routledge.

Majone, Giandomenico. (1998). "Europe's 'Democratic Deficit': The Question of Standards." *European Law Journal* 4(1): 5-28.

Malmkjaer, Kirsten ed. (1991). *The Linguistics Encyclopedia.* London, and New York: Routledge.

Manin, Bernard. (1987). "On Legitimacy and Political Deliberation." *Political Theory* 15: 338-368.

March, James, and Johan Olsen. (1989). *Rediscovering Institutions. The Organizational Basis of Politics.* New York: Free Press.

Marks, Gary. (1992). "Structural Policy in the European Community." in Alberta Sbragia, ed. *Euro-Politics: Institutions and Policy Making in the "New" European Community.* Washington, DC: Brookings Institute, 191-224.

Marks, Gary, Liesbet Hooghe, and Kermit Blank. (1996). "European Integration since the 1980s. State-Centric versus Multi-Level Governance." *Journal of Common Market Studies* 34: 343-378.

Markus, Andrew. (1994). "The Idea of Race in Western Culture." In *Australian Race Relations, 1788-1993.* St. Leonards, NSW: Allen and Unwin, 1-17.

Marx, Anthony W. (1998). *Making Race and Nation: A Comparison of the United States, South Africa and Brazil.* New York: Cambridge University Press.

Mayntz, Renate and Fritz W Scharpf. (1995). "Der Ansatz des akteurzentrierten Institutionalismus" In Mayntz, Renate, and Fritz W. Scharpf eds., *Gesellschaftliche Selbstregelung und politische Steuerung.* Frankfurt and New York: Campus, 111-149.

McDonald, Maryon. (1997). "Identities in the European Commission." In Neill Nugent, ed., *At the Heart of the Union: Studies of the European Commission.* London: MacMillan, 27-48.

McKillop, A. B. (1999). "Who Killed Canadian History? A View from the Trenches." *The Canadian Historical Review,* 80: 269-299.

McRae, Kenneth D., (1975). "The Principle of Territoriality and the Principle of Personality in Multilingual States." *International Journal of the Sociology of Language,* 4: 33-54.

McRae, K. D. (1979). "The Plural Society and the Western Political Tradition." *Canadian Journal of Political Science,* 12: 675-688.

McRae, Kenneth D. (1986). *Conflict and Compromise in Multilingual Societies: Belgium.* Waterloo: Wilfrid Laurier University Press.

McRae, Kenneth. (1990). "Canada: Reflection on Two Conflicts." In Joseph V. Montville, ed., *Conflict and Peacemaking in Multiethnic Societies.* Lexington and Toronto: Lexington Books, 210.

McRae, Kenneth. (1992). "The Meech Lake Impasse in Theoretical Perspective." In A-G. Gagnon and B. Tanguay, eds., *Democracy with Justice: Essays in Honour of Khayyam Zev Paltiel.* Ottawa: Carleton University Press, 151.

McRae, Kenneth D., with the assistance of Mika Helander and Sari Luoma. (1999 [1997]). *Conflict and Compromise in Multilingual Societies: Finland.* Waterloo, ON, and Helsinki: Wilfrid Laurier University Press and Finnish

Academy of Science and Letters.

McRae, Kenneth D. (1998). *Conflict and Compromise in Multilingual Societies: Switzerland*. Waterloo: Wilfrid Laurier University Press.

McRae, Kenneth, ed. (1962). *Jean Bodin's "The Six Bookes of a Commonweale."* Cambridge: Harvard University Press.

McRae, Kenneth, ed. (1974). *Consociational Democracy: Political Accommodation in Segmented Societies*. Toronto: McClelland and Stewart.

McRae, Kenneth. (1974a). "Consociationalism and the Canadian Political System." In Kenneth McRae, ed., *Consociational Democracy. Political Accommodation in Segmented Societies*. Toronto: McClelland and Stewart.

McRae, Kenneth. (1974b). "Introduction." In Kenneth McRae, ed., *Consociational Democracy. Political Accommodation in Segmented Societies*. Toronto: McClelland and Stewart, 5-11.

McRae, Kenneth D. ed. (1978). *Jean Bodin: 1530-1596, The Six Bookes of a Commonweale*. New York: Arno Press.

McRoberts, Kenneth. (1988). *Québec: Social Change and Political Crisis*. 3rd ed. Toronto: McClelland and Stewart.

McRoberts, Kenneth. (1989). "Making Canada Bilingual: Illusions and Delusions of Federal Language Policy." In David P. Shugarman and Reg Whitaker, eds., *Federalism and Political Community: Essays in Honour of Donald Smiley*. Peterborough, ON: Broadview Press, 141-171.

McRoberts, Kenneth. (1997). *Misconceiving Canada*. Toronto: Oxford University Press.

Michaud, Yves. (2000). "Réflexions d'avant-congrès." *Le Devoir*, May 5.

Michelmann, Hans. (1978). *Organizational Effectiveness in a Multinational Bureaucracy: The Case of the Commission of the European Communities*. Westmead: Saxon.

Monnet, Jean. (1962). "A Ferment of Change," *Journal of Common Market Studies* 1(1): 203-211.

Montesquieu.Charles de Secon dat (1973). *De l'Esprit des Iois*, Paris: Barner.

Morrisroe, Darby A. (1998). "The State of 'State Offices' in Washington: A Critical Assessment." Paper presented at the annual meeting of the American Political Science Association, Boston.

Morton, Desmond. (1999). "Hyphenated Canadians: Is a Shared History Possible?" *National History*, special issue, 17.

Morton, W. L. (1964). *The Critical Years: The Union of British North America 1857-1863*. Toronto: McClelland and Stewart.

Mughan, Anthony, Janet Box-Steffensmeier, and Roger Scully. (1997). "Mapping Legislative Socialization" *European Journal of Political Research* 32: 93-106.

Müller, Jörg-Paul. (1993). *Demokratische Gerechtigkeit. Eine Studie zur Legitimität rechtlicher und politischer Ordnung*. München: dtv wissenschaft.

Murphy, A. (1995). "Belgium's Regional Divergence: Along the Road to Federation." In G. Smith, ed., *Federalism: The Multiethnic Challenge*. London: Longman, 12-39.

Murrin, John M. (1990). *Beneficiaries of Catastrophe: The English Colonies in America*. Washington, DC: American Historical Association.

Neidhart, Leonhard. (1970). *Plebiszit und pluralitäre Demokratie: eine Analyse der Funktion des schweizerischen Gesetzesreferendums*. Bern: Francke.

Nelson, William. (2000). "The Institutions of Deliberative Democracy." *Social Philosophy & Policy* 17: 181-202.

Nodia, Ghia. (1996). "Nationalism and the Crisis of Liberalism." In Richard Caplan and
    John Feffer, eds., *Europe's New Nationalisms: States and Minorities in
    Conflict*. Oxford: Oxford University Press, 13-39.
Nordlinger, Eric A. (1972a). "Conflict Regulation in Divided Societies." Occasional
    Papers in International Affairs. Center for International Affairs, Harvard
    University, January.
Nordlinger, Eric. (1972b). *Conflict Regulation in Divided Societies*. Cambridge: Center for
    International Affairs, Harvard University.
North, Douglass C. (1990). *Institutions, Institutional Change and Economic
    Performance*. Cambridge: Cambridge University Press.
Nugent, Neil. (1995). *The Government and Politics of the European Union*. London:
    MacMillan.
Olsen, Johan and Jones March. (1982). *Ambiguity and Choice in Organizations*.
    Bergen: Universiteoforlaget.
Ostrom, Elinor. (1990). *Governing the Commons*. Cambridge: Cambridge University
    Press.
Ostrom, Elinor. (1991). "Rational Choice Theory and Institutional Analysis." *American
    Political Science Review*. 85(1): 237-243.
Page, Edward. (1995). "Administering Europe." In Jack Hayward and Edward Page, eds.,
    Governing the New Europe. Durham, NC: Duke University Press, 257-285.
Page, Edward. (1997). *People Who Run Europe*. Oxford: Oxford University Press.
Pappalardo, Adriano. (1980). "La politica consociativa nella democrazia Italiana." *Rivista
    Italiana di Scienza Politica* 10(1): 73-123.
Paradis, Evelyne. (2000). "Citizenship and Racial Exclusion in Western European State."
    M. A. thesis, Carleton University, Political Science.
Parekh, Bhikhu. (1999). "Vico and Montesquieu: Limits of Pluralist Imagination."
    Canadian Journal of Philosophy, supplementary volume 25: 55-78.
Perczynski, Piotr. (2000). "Associo-Deliberative Democracy and Qualitative
    Participation". Unpublished manuscript. Leiden University.
Peterson, John. (1997). "The Santer Commission: Pillarized, Nationalized, or Just
    Normalized?" Paper presented at the biennial conference of the European
    Community Studies Association Centre, Seattle, May 29–June1.
Pierson, Paul. (1996). "The Path to European Integration: A Historical Institutionalist
    Analysis." *Comparative Political Studies* 29 (April): 123-163.
Pierson, Paul. (2000). "Increasing Returns, Path Dependence, and the Study of Politics."
    American Political Science Review 94(2): 251-267.
Potter, Janice. (1983). *The Liberty We Seek: Loyalist Ideology in New York and
    Massachusetts*. Cambridge: Harvard University Press.
Proudhon, Pierre-Joseph. (1863). *Du principe fédératif et de la necessité de reconstituer
    le parti de la revolution*. Paris: Librarie Internationale.
Putnam, Robert D. (1993). *Making Democracy Work: Civic Traditions in Modern Italy*.
    Princeton, NJ: Princeton University Press.
Québec, Ministère de la Culture et des Communications. (1996). *Le Français, langue
    commune: enjeu de la société québécoise*. Rapport du Comité interministériel
    sur la situation de la langue française.
Québec, Ministère des Relations internationales. (2000). *Les défis de la langue française
    à Montréal et au Québec au XXe siècle: constats et enjeux*. Rapport du Groupe
    de travail ministériel sur la langue française.
Rawls, John. (1971). *A Theory of Justice*. Cambridge: Harvard University Press.
Rawls, John. (1995). "Reply to Habermas." *Journal of Philosophy:* 92, 302-353.
Rawls, John. (1996 [1993]). *Political Liberalism*. New York: Columbia University Press.

Resnick, Philip. (1990). *The Masks of Proteus: Canadian Reflections on the State.* Montreal: McGill-Queen's University Press.

Rex, John. (1996). "National Identity in the Democratic Multi-Cultural State." *Sociological Research Online* 1(2): 87-132.

Rex, John. (1997). "The Concept of a Multicultural Society." In Montserrat Guibernau and John Rex, eds., *The Ethnicity Reader.* Cambridge: Polity Press, 205-219.

Reynebeau, M. (1995). *Het klauwen van de leeuw: de Vlaamse identiteit van de 12de tot de 21ste eeuw.* Leuven: Van Halewijck.

Rioux, Marcel, and Jacques Dofny. (1964). "Social Class in French Canada." In Marcel Rioux and Yves Martin, eds., *French-Canadian Society.* Toronto: McClelland and Stewart, 307-318.

Risse, Thomas. (1996). "Exploring the Nature of the Beast: International Relations Theory and Comparative Policy Analysis Meet the European Union." *Journal of Common Market Studies* 34(1): 53-80.

Risse, Thomas. (2000). "Let's Argue!: Communicative Action in World Politics." *International Organization* 54: 1-39.

Rohrschneider, Robert. (1994). "Report from the Laboratory: The Influence of Institutions on Political Elites' Democratic Values in Germany." *American Political Science Review* 88(4): 927-941.

Rohrschneider, Robert. (1996). "Cultural Transmission versus Perceptions of the Economy. The Sources of Political Elites' Economic Values in the United Germany." *Comparative Political Studies* 29(1): 78-104.

Ross, George. (1995). *Jacques Delors and European Integration.* Oxford: Oxford University Press.

Rothstein, Bo. (1998). *Just Institutions Matter. The Moral and Political Logic of the Universal Welfare State.* Cambridge: Cambridge University Press.

Rouillard, Jacques. (1989). *Histoire du syndicalisme au Québec.* Montreal: Boréal.

Rousseau, Jean-Jacques. (1762). *Du Contrat Social.*

Sanders, Lynn M. (1997). "Against Deliberation." *Political Theory* 25: 347-375.

Saul, John Ralston. (1992). *Voltaire's Bastards: The Dictatorship of Reason in the West.* Toronto: Penguin Press.

Saul, John Ralston. (1997). *Reflections on a Siamese Twin: Canada at the End of the Twentieth Century.* Toronto: Penguin Press.

Sbragia, Alberta. (1992). "Thinking about the European Future: The Uses of Comparison." In Alberta Sbragia, ed., *Euro-Politics: Institutions and Policy Making in the New European Community.* Washington, DC: Brookings Institute, 257-292.

Sbragia, Alberta. (1993). "The European Community: A Balancing Act." *Publius* 23: 23-38.

Sbragia, Alberta. (1996). "Environmental Policy: The 'Push-Pull' of Policy Making." In Helen Wallace and William Wallace, eds., *Policy Making in the European Union.* Oxford: Oxford University Press, 235-255.

Scharpf, Fritz W. (1994). *Optionen des Föderalismus in Deutschland und Europa.* Frankfurt and New York: Campus.

Scharpf, Fritz W. (1997). *Games Real Actors Play: Actor-Centered Institutionalism in Policy Research.* Boulder, CO: Westview Press.

Scharpf, Fritz. (1999). *Governing in Europe: Effective and Democratic?* Oxford: Oxford University Press.

Schauer, Frederick. (1999). "Talking as a Decision Procedure." In Stephen Macedo, ed., *Deliberative Politics: Essays on Democracy and Disagreement.* New York and Oxford: Oxford University Press, 9-34.

Schlesinger, Arthur, Jr. (1998). *The Disuniting of America: Reflections on a Multicultural Society*. New York: W. W. Norton.

Schmitter, Philippe. (1996). "Imagining the Future of the Euro-Polity with the Help of New Concepts." In Gary Marks, Fritz Scharpf, Philippe Schmitter, and Wolfgang Streeck, eds., *Governance in the European Union*. London: Sage, 121-150.

Schmitter, Philippe. (1999). "How to Democratize the European Union: Citizenship, Representation, Decision Making in the Emerging Euro-Polity." Manuscript.

Searing, Donald. (1969). "The Comparative Study of Elite Socialization." *Comparative Political Studies* 1: 471-500.

Searing, Donald. (1986). "A Theory of Political Socialization: Institutional Support and Deradicalization in Britain." *British Journal of Political Science*, 16(3): 341-376.

Searing, Donald. (1991). "Roles, Rules and Rationality in the New Institutionalism." *American Political Science Review* 32: 47-68.

Sebeok, Thomas A. gen. ed., (1986). *Encyclopedic Dictionary of Semiotics*. Berlin, New York, and Amsterdam: Mouton de Gruyter.

Senelle, Robert. (1996). "The Reform of the Belgian State." In Joachim J. Hesse and Vincent Wright eds., *Federalizing Europe?* Oxford: Oxford University Press, 266-324.

Shapiro, Ian. (1999). "Enough of Deliberation: Politics Is about Interests and Power." In Stephen Macedo, ed., *Deliberative Politics: Essays on Democracy and Disagreement*. New York, and Oxford: Oxford University Press, 77-101.

Sowell, Thomas. (1994). *Race and Culture: A World View*. New York: Basic Books.

Steiner, Jürg. (1970). *Gewaltlose Politik und kulturelle Vielfalt. Hypothesen entwickelt am Beispiel der Schweiz*. Bern: Paul Haupt.

Steiner, Jürg. (1974). *Amicable Agreement versus Majority Rule: Conflict Resolution in Switzerland*. Chapel Hill: University of North Carolina Press.

Steiner, Jürg. (1996). *Conscience in Politics: An Empirical Investigation of Swiss Decision Cases*. New York: Garland.

Steiner, Jürg. (1998). "The Consociational Theory and Switzerland—Revisited Thirty Years Later." Paper presented at the Conference on the Fate of Consociationalism. Center for European Studies, Harvard University, May 29-31.

Steinmo, Sven, and Kathleen Thelen. (1992). "Historical Institutionalism in Comparative Politics." In Steinmo, Sven and Kathleen Thelen. eds., *Structuring Politics. Historical Institutionalism in Comparative Analysis*. Cambridge: Cambridge University Press 13-52.

Steinmo, Sven, Kathleen Thelen, and Frank Longstreth, eds. (1991). *Structuring Politics: Historical Institutionalism in Comparative Analysis*. Cambridge: Cambridge University Press.

Strong-Boag, Veronica, and Anita Clair Fellman, eds. (1991). *Re-thinking Canada. The Promise of Women's History*. Toronto: Oxford University Press.

Sunstein, Cass. (1991). "Preferences and Politics." *Philosophy and Public Affairs* 20: 222-279.

Tanguay, A. Brian. (1993). "Québec's Political System in the 1990s: From Polarization to Convergence." In Alain-G. Gagnon, ed., *Québec: State and Society*, 2nd ed. Scarborough, ON: Nelson Canada, 174-198.

Taylor, Paul. (1991). "The European Community and the State: Assumptions, Theories and Propositions," *Review of International Studies*, 17: 109-25.

Taylor, Paul. (1997). *The European Union in the 1990s*. Oxford: Oxford University Press.

Tremblay, Michel. (1990). *Les vues animées*. Montreal: Leméac.

Tsebelis, George. (1990). "Elite Interaction and Constitution Building in Consociational Democracies." *Journal of Theoretical Politics* 2(1): 5-29.

Tullock, Gordon. (1990). "Letter to the Editor (Tullock on Steiner)." *PS: Political Science and Politics* (June): 136.

Underhill, Frank. (1966). "Foreword." In Peter Russell, ed., *Nationalism in Canada*. Toronto: McGraw-Hill, xix.

Vaillancourt, François. (1993). "The Economic Status of the French Language and Francophones in Québec." In Alain-G. Gagnon, ed., *Québec: State and Society*, 2nd ed. Scarborough, ON: Nelson Canada, 407-421.

Van Schendler, H.P.C.M. (1984). "Consociational, Pillarization, and Conflict Management in Low Countries." In special issue of *Acta Politica*, Vol. 19.

Van Waarden, Franz. (1998). "Consociationalism and Economic Performance: The Netherlands." Paper presented at the Conference on the Fate of Consociationalism. Center for European Studies, Harvard University, May 29-31.

Verba, Sidney. (1965). "Conclusion: Comparative Political Culture." In Lucian Pye and Sidney Verba, eds., *Political Culture and Political Development*. Princeton, NJ: Princeton University Press, 177-190.

Vickers, Jill. (1997). *Reinventing Political Science: A Feminist Approach*. Halifax: Fernwood Books.

Waite, Peter B. (1971). *Canada 1874-1896: Arduous Destiny*. Toronto: McClelland and Stewart.

Wallace, Helen, and William Wallace, eds. (2000). *Policy-Making in the European Union*. Oxford: Oxford University Press.

Wallerstein, Immanuel. (1991). "The Ideological Tensions of Capitalism: Universalism versus Racism and Sexism." In Etienne Baliba and Immanuel Wallerstein, *Race, Nation, Class: Ambiguous Identities*. London: Verso, 29-35.

Watts, Ronald L. (1997). *Comparative Federalism in the 1990s*. Kingston: Institute of Intergovernmental Relations.

West, Cornel. (1992). "The Postmodern Crisis of the Black Intellectuals." In Nelson Grossberg, and Treichler, eds., *Cultural Studies*. London: Routledge, 689-696.

"Who's Canadian?," Act IV in National Public Radio's *This American Life* series, produced by WBEZ Chicago and first broadcast May 30, 1997.

Williams, Garth. (1999). "Commentary: Past Lessons/Future Policy." *National History*, special issue: 103.

Wilson, V. Seymour. (1993). "The Tapestry Vision of Canadian Multiculturalism." *Canadian Journal of Political Science* 26(4): 645-669.

Wolin, Sheldon S. (1957). "Calvin and the Reformation, The Political Education of Protestantism." *American Political Science Review:* 435-453.

Zaslow, Morris. (1988). *The Northern Expansion of Canada 1914-1967*. Toronto: McClelland and Stewart.

Zolberg, A. (1974). "The making of Flemings and Walloons: Belgium 1830-1914." *The Journal of Interdisciplinary History* 5(2): 179-236.

Index

About the Contributors

ANDRÉ BÄCHTIGER is Research Assistant at the Institute of Political Science at the University of Berne, Switzerland. His research interests are political deliberation, international relations theory, and interdisciplinary research on political science and history.

STEPHEN BROOKS is Professor of Political Science at the University of Windsor and Visiting Professor of Political Science at the University of Michigan. His most recent books include *America through Foreign Eyes: Classic Interpretations of American Political Life* and *Canadian Democracy* (3rd ed.).

KRIS DESCHOUWER is Professor in the Department of Politics at the Vrije Universiteit Brussel and in the Department of Comparative Politics in Bergen. His main research topics are political parties and elections, federalism, and consociational democracy.

CAN ERK specializes in European integration, comparative federalism, and Canadian politics. He has been involved as a researcher with the Research Group on Multinational Societies based in the Québec Studies Programme at McGill University. His works have been published in *Regional and Federal Studies* and *The Cyprus Review*.

MILTON J. ESMAN is the John S. Knight Professor of International Studies, Emeritus, at Cornell University and former Director of Cornell's Center for International Studies. He is a long time student of ethnic politics and ethnic conflict. His book-length writings include *Ethnic Politics* (1994), *Ethnic Conflict in the Western World* (1977), and *Carrots, Sticks, and Ethnic Conflict: Rethinking Development Assistance* (with Ronald J. Herring, 2000).

ALAIN-G. GAGNON is Professor of Political Science and Director of the Québec Studies Programme at McGill University. He was the editor of *Politique et Sociétés* from 1995 to 2001 and is a founding member of the Research Group on Multinational Societies. Among his most recent publications are *Multinational Democracies* (coedited with James Tully 2001) and *The Canadian Social Union without Québec,* (coedited with Hugh Segal, 2000).

LIESBET HOOGHE is Associate Professor of Political Science at the University of North Carolina at Chapel Hill. Her principal area of interest is European integration, and she has also published on ethnic conflict, nationalism, and federalism. She is the editor of *Cohesion Policy and European Integration: Building Multilevel Governance* (1996); coauthor with Gary Marks of *Multi-Level Governance in the European Union* (2001); and the author of a book on the political preferences of top European Commission officials (forthcoming).

THOMAS O. HUEGLIN is Professor of Political Science at Wilfrid Laurier University. His main work is in comparative federalism and the history of political thought. His latest book is *Early Modern Concepts for a Late Modern World: Althusius on Community and Federalism.*

MARKUS SPÖRNDLI, is Research Assistant at the Institute of Political Science at the University of Berne, Switzerland. His research interests are deliberation in real-world politics, international political economy, and methods of comparative politics.

JÜRG STEINER is Professor of Political Science at the University of Berne and the University of North Carolina at Chapel Hill. Recent books are *Conscience in Politics* and *European Democracies.*

GORDON T. STEWART is Professor of History at Michigan State University. He is the author of several books and many articles on Canadian and British empire history, including *The Nova Scotia Yankees and the American Revolution, The Great Awakening in Nova Scotia 1760-1791, The Origins of Canadian Politics: A Comparative Approach, The American Response to Canada since 1776,* and *Jute and Empire: The Calcutta Jute Wallash and the Landscapes of Empire.*

A. BRIAN TANGUAY is Associate Professor of Political Science at Wilfrid Laurier University. He is the coeditor with Alain-G. Gagnon of *Canadian Parties in Transition* and has published (with Barry Kay) articles on the political activity of local interest groups for the Canadian Royal Commission on Electoral Reform and Party Financing and in the *International Journal of Canadian Studies.*

JILL VICKERS is Professor of Political Science at Carleton University. She was a student of both Michael Oakeshott and Kenneth McRae. She is the author of several books, including *The Scientific Mode of Enquiry in Political Science: Systems theory in the Works of Easton, Almond, Kaplan and Deutsch* and *Re-Inventing Political Science: A Feminist Approach.*

DATE DUE

APR 0 6 2004			
DEC 1 2 2004			
		AUG 1 3 2004	

Demco, Inc. 38-293

DEPAUL UNIVERSITY LIBRARY

3 0511 00839 7754